TERRIFYING MUSLIMS

TERRIFYING MUSLIMS

RACE AND LABOR IN

THE SOUTH ASIAN DIASPORA

Junaid Rana

Duke University Press   Durham & London   2011

© 2011 Duke University Press
All rights reserved
Printed in the United States
of America on acid-free paper ∞
Designed by Amy Ruth Buchanan
Typeset in Quadraat by
Keystone Typesetting, Inc.
Library of Congress Cataloging-in-
Publication Data appear on the last
printed page of this book.

CONTENTS

In any effort such as this book, there are many to thank. Although I am solely responsible for the research and content of this book, many took part in making it possible. In many ways, I have been lucky. In my intellectual journey, I had the pleasure to be part of a number of scholarly and political communities that have profoundly shaped my ideas and thinking. At the University of Texas, Austin, where this project found its inception as a dissertation, I was fortunate to have the guidance of Kamala Visweswaran, James Brow, Edmund T. Gordon, and Kamran Asdar Ali. All are models of intellectual responsibility and commitment. Kamala was an ideal adviser. She prodded but never told us where to go, and for that I am grateful. Her intellectual brilliance, along with a faculty committed to the issues of social justice through the study of diaspora and an activist approach, for me was the right debate on theory, scholarly research, and engaged participation.

I remain indebted to those who came together as an intellectual collective that experimented in putting ideas into practice during graduate school: Matt Archer, Whitney Battle, Maribel Garcia, Kora Maldonado, Shaka McGlotten, Esmail Nashif, Jemima Pierre, Gilbert Rosas, Guha Shankar Michael Trujillo, Linta Varghese, Steven Ward, and Vincent Woodard (rest in peace). I am grateful to the many great friends I made during this time through our collective efforts who later sustained me in our migration to New York, including Shomial Ahmad, Vivek Boray, Elisa Shzu, and Quincy Tran. I also thank Ayaz Ahmed, Rich Blint, Mubasshir Rizvi, and Manu Vimalassery in New York for sharing their time, friendship, and homes.

During graduate school, I was fortunate to come across a community of like-minded desi academics and activists working for social justice, many who came together in the New York area, including Shabano Aliani, Vivek Bald, Bhairavi Desai, Usman Hameed, Alia Hassan-Khan, Anjali Kamat, Sangeeta Kamat, Surabhi Kukke, Amitava Kumar, Sunaina Maira, Rekha Malhotra, Biju Mathew, Ali Mir, Raza Mir (who also graciously agreed to serve on my dissertation committee), Rupal Oza, Prachi Patankar, Vijay Prashad, Sekhar Ramakrishnan, Ashwini Rao, Sujani Reddy, Mubbashir Rizvi, Svati Shah, Shalini Shankar, and Saba Waheed. It was here that I discovered how commitment and responsibility should be fun and enjoyable as much as they are hard work.

Over the years, many scholars have provided important feedback, support, humor, and advice: Falu Bakrania, Moustafa Bayoumi, Tom Boellstorff, Rick Bonus, Miabi Chatterji, Faisal Devji, Vince Diaz, David Eng, Rod Ferguson, David Gilmartin, Ruthie Gilmore, Gayatri Gopinath, Inderpal Grewal, Marcia Hermansen, Susannah Heschel, Virender Kalra, Ali Khan, Fariha Khan, Satish Kolluri, Robert Ku, Scott Kurashige, Saba Mahmood, Sunaina Maira, Anouar Majid, Ali Mir, Minoo Moallem, Lourdes Gutierrez Najera, Balumurli Natrajan, Bob Nichols, Gary Okihiro, Vijay Prashad, Gautam Premnath, Chandan Reddy, Gayatri Reddy, Uzma Rizvi, Lisa Sanchez-Gonzalez, Nitasha Sharma, Ella Shohat, Andrea Smith, and Rajini Srikanth. In particular, I am grateful to have found the intellectual comradeship of Evelyn Alsultany, Vivek Bald, Anila Daulatzai, Sohail Daulatzai, and Nadine Naber, whose scholarship is a beacon to the future.

At the University of Illinois, Urbana-Champaign, I am grateful to my colleagues in Asian American Studies that made the task of scholarly work enjoyable through their friendship, insight, and mentorship. In particular, I thank Nancy Abelmann, Lisa Cacho, David Cayoca, Augusto Espiritu, Moon-Kie Jung, Esther Kim, Susan Koshy, Soo Ah Kwon, Martin Manalansan, Lisa Nakamura, Fiona Ngo, Mimi Nguyen, Kent Ono, Yoon Pak, Yutian Wong, and Caroline Yang. Of course, nothing gets done without the diligent efforts of Mary Ellerbe, Viveka Kudaligama, and Pia Sengsavanh. In addition, I have benefited from the intellectual strength and insight of many colleagues in other departments, including Aide Acosta, Constancio Arnaldo, Marilyn Booth, Antoinette Burton, J. B. Capino, Ken Cuno, Hadi Esfahani, Anna Gonzalez, Lauren Goodlad, Wael Hassan, Muhammad Khalil, Rajeshwari Pandharipande, Wanda Pillow, Richard T. Rodriguez, David Roediger, Siobhan Somerville, and Stan Thangaraj. I thank Shefali Chandra and Saadia Toor for sharing all and making light of any situation during our initial stay in Champaign.

The research and completion of this book was generously funded by the Fulbright Foundation, the American Institute of Pakistan Studies, and several research leaves at the University of Illinois sponsored by the Illinois Program for the Research in the Humanities, the Center for Democracy in a Multiracial Society, and the Research Board. I thank the generosity of my extended family for opening their homes to me in Pakistan over the years and putting up with my odd schedule. Thanks to my great friend Khaled Adham and his family for offering refuge in Cairo and for driving me around the United Arab Emirates. The organizing work and friendship of several individuals in Chicago have sustained me. Tuyet Le, Sonia Matthews, and Saket Soni are the bedrock to building a different world. My love and thanks to Mireya Loza for making Chicago a place of boundless humor and possibility.

I thank Ken Wissoker at Duke University Press for his patience and dedication to this project from the beginning. Leigh Barnwell, Mark Mastromarino, Susan Deeks, and Amy Ruth Buchanan, made the process of completing the book as smooth as possible. I also thank the anonymous readers of the manuscript whose comments and insight greatly enhanced the final product. Special thanks to Huma Bhabha and her gallery Salon 94 in New York. Alisa Friedman and Christian Dietkus opened their offices to me, making the choice of cover art easy and fluid.

A portion of chapter 1 was published as "The Story of Islamophobia," *Souls: A Critical Journal of Black Politics, Culture, and Society* 9, no. 2 (2007): 148–61. A version of chapter 5 appeared as "Controlling Diaspora: Illegality, 9/11, and Pakistani Labour Migration," *Pakistani Diasporas: Culture, Conflict, and Change*, ed. Virinder Kalra (Karachi: Oxford University Press, 2009).

Migrants in a Neoliberal World

The Tragedy of the Market

As war raged in Iraq in the summer of 2004, the headlines flashed the latest deadly tactic to emerge out of the conflict: Diplomats, politicians, aid workers, contract workers, and labor migrants had become targets of abduction and kidnapping. For the last groups—contract workers and labor migrants—this proved particularly harrowing. Drawn from the transnational working classes of India, Pakistan, Nepal, and Sri Lanka and attracted by wages that provide temporary financial relief in their home countries, these subcontracted workers found themselves at the center of a strategic battle between occupiers and occupied in a web of violence wrought by a war led by the United States.

Amjad Hafeez, the first Pakistani to be abducted, worked as a truck driver for an American food-service company. His capture, which was announced in a widely circulated video, highlighted the importance of visual media as a form of technological warfare in circulating the effects of this strategy. Major television and other news-media outlets throughout the Middle East and South Asia constantly updated the story. Out of the many targeted for kidnapping, some were more vulnerable than others. In particular, truck drivers who navigate public roads based on set routes that make them easy to follow and intercept with little protection or security. Pakistani workers, a prominent part of this workforce, were some of the first people abducted when convoys delivering goods, products, and equipment required by the American military were attacked.

The lives of foreign migrant workers hired by subcontractors to service the U.S. military occupation were thus endangered by a scheme to create instability in the occupying forces' infrastructure and, ultimately, to expose the imperial hubris of the United States. Evidence of this intention circulated in the video-tapes sent to media outlets, which were often shot in a simple documentary style. These videos, played relentlessly on Pakistani satellite news programs, captivated another object—a national audience—with increasing public disapproval of, and protests against, the U.S. military adventure in Iraq in major cities throughout Pakistan.

Hafeez was fortunate to be released after a week of captivity. Two other Pakistanis—Sajid Naeem and Raja Azad Khan, a truck driver and an air-conditioning technician, respectively—were abducted shortly after Hafeez was released and held hostage on the charge that they had collaborated with the American oppressors. Earlier, other victims of kidnapping who had agreed to stop working in occupied Iraq also had been released, but as the strategy unfolded, it became increasingly desperate and lethal. For Naeem and Azad Khan, the unfortunate and grisly end came in videotaped beheadings. Both hailed from the Rawalkot district of Azad Kashmir in Pakistan and had worked for years for the Al Tamimi Group, a Saudi Arabian company in Kuwait. That these Pakistani workers were the product of yet another displacement, brought about by war and conflict between India and Pakistan in the disputed Kashmir region, had little significance to their captors.

The shocking news of their deaths brought the dangers confronting labor migrants to the fore of the Iraq conflict. The brutal tragedy also mapped the linkages among South Asia, the Middle East, and the United States, along with the creation of a labor diaspora of civilian foreign workers by disparate governments, militaries, and multinational corporations. It also recalled the familiar national subject of the migrant in the Pakistani media. As so often happens, the incidents in Iraq provoked a public debate in Pakistan over the promise of pursuing professional careers overseas and the dangers that labor migrants face. With the debate came a growing sense of discomfort within the Pakistani middle class that, in the eyes of the world, all Pakistanis abroad were being stereotyped as labor migrants, an image connoting an uneducated, brutish, people prone to violence and crime. But like all stereotypes, this is far from a full picture.

As kidnappings and abductions—a strategy that increasingly involved armed attacks and assassinations—spread, fear also grew as the new interim government took power in Iraq. Along with Pakistanis, the abductees included Bulgarians, Egyptians, Filipinos, Indians, Jordanians, Kenyans, Kuwaitis, Lebanese, Nepalese, Somalis, Turks, and others. Truck drivers, technicians, construction workers, and cleaners remained the main targets. The abductions began to take on a surreal quality. In late July 2004, seven kidnapped truck drivers were shown on videotape, with one wearing an orange jumpsuit—presumably a reference to the U.S. military prisons at Abu Ghraib and Guantánamo Bay but simultaneously the standard uniform of service-economy workers throughout the Persian Gulf region. The kidnappings, coupled with the circulation of the videos, seemed to draw from a tradition of choreographed propaganda spectacle used to evoke both fear and sympathy. The videotapes had an undeniable pathos that stemmed not only from the obvious distress of the victims and the banal ways in which the militant groups presented them, but also from the conditions that had put the workers in a dangerous war zone in which taking sides meant life or death.

In this example, the relationship of these workers to processes of globalization are intimately tied to the ravages of war, a neoliberal capitalist system based on accumulation and dispossession, and the treacherous claims to empire. In the eyes of Iraqi militants, transnational workers are the pawns of U.S. empire; conversely, Iraq has become yet another site from which to obtain labor from workers who must travel far to make ends meet in their home countries. As Hafeeza Begum, the sister of the slain Raja Azad, noted, "We don't have any enmity with Iraqi people. . . . Why is his life in danger?"[1] Clearly, when she referred to "Iraqi people," she meant the militants who abducted her brother, yet she was also referring to the job that put his life in jeopardy. Accounts of the fate of foreign workers in Iraq are some of the most immediate descriptions of the recent circuits of neoliberal empire orchestrated by the U.S. in the global economy.[2]

That Pakistanis are just one national group among many working in U.S.-occupied Iraq points to the complexity of global migration and the social and economic hierarchies created by globalization. In the neoliberal system of global capitalism, the impermanence of transnational work stands in for the temporary labor reserves traditionally held by international migrants that potentially become permanent inhabitants.[3] In this process, the meaning of labor migration itself has changed, partly through the dynamics of the migration industry, but also through the meanings attached to migrant workers themselves across the globe.

In collaboration with the state, multinational corporations and labor-subcontracting agencies control the fate of transnational workers. In large part, such labor is subcontracted and based in wage work. In other words, it is made legitimate through labor contracts in which terms are set for the worker and the employer. The risks in this form of labor are quite high, with the stakes being set at the value of life. Contracted work often fails to provide safety guarantees for transnational migrants and often does not ensure their status as legal migrants. Further, as a number of independent humanitarian organizations note, work conditions across national boundaries and the accountability of sovereign states to their citizens are far from laudatory. As migrant laborers have become one of the foremost commodities traded in the global economy, wage work has become the domain not solely of domestic labor unions but also of workers without frontiers who cross the planet in search of employment.

The extreme dangers of transnational migration raise another important issue: the specter of Islamic militancy. From the viewpoint of the U.S. security state, the greatest threat to American national interests in the contemporary moment is radical Islam in the form of so-called Jihadist culture, an English neologism that obfuscates America's strategic interests by labeling Islamic militancy as "terrorism."[4] From this geopolitical position, the War on Terror is formulated as an opposing binary: democracy and freedom versus terrorist radicalism and militancy. The Iraqi militants who kidnapped the Pakistani labor migrants are deemed extremists and terrorists—purveyors of evil. But how should the connection of the workers to their militant co-religionists, both of whom are read as Muslim, be understood? And why must these Iraqi militants be read solely in terms of "evil" and "terror," which refute the possibility of their own sense of human freedom?

As Faisal Devji (2008) argues, this dichotomy results from competing notions of humanism in which "humanity," as a concept of aspirational possibility, is stripped from the Islamic militant and that, in the face of terror, distinguishes between lives that should be grieved and those that should not (Asad 2007; Butler 2003, 2009). The immediate argument is that the terrorist militant must be inhuman, without humanity, and subsequently requires eradication for the so-called common good. War in this sense is both political and racial as it emerges from the foundations of an imperial and colonial ideology.[5] This is racism not simply in the sense of systems of control and hierarchy but also in the sense of determining who lives and dies as a strategy to maintain and legitimize the authority of a colonizing force. For such a rationale, races are populations ascribed an identity as friend or enemy and, more important, are bound and contained by an ideological profile. Such racism as war demands that the technological innovations and improvisations of the military and the media both mask and justify racialization as part of the common good toward the promise of a democratic future.

The recent case of the U.S. war in Iraq is quite literal in following this theory. By exercising power through imperial strategies, the war machine sutured militants to their labor migrant captives. Under the rationale of imperial colonization, both militants and migrants are disposable: One is an active military threat; the other is expendable in the service of military conquest. Foreign workers are not only used as low-wage subcontract laborers but are part of an imperial economy in which their worth and value are calculated according to where they are from and who they are as a population. This is not an isolated logic but a historical relationship that connects Islam and Muslims to a conception of race both domestically in the U.S. and in what has been referred to as the global racial system (Mullings 2005; Winant 2001, 2004).

Race is tied to terror and migration precisely through the conjuring of an enemy. The foe is defined in relation not only to democracy and freedom but also to the moral precepts of the ideologically motivated formation of a Christian subject that argues for just war as an obligation of secularity and imperialism. That this enemy is crafted as a *religious* entity, albeit a radically militant one, does not obscure the *racial* nature of the construction. In the overlap of religious and racial identity, historical conflicts are bound to political and social identity. It is in this sense that the terrorist militant and the labor migrant become the racialized "Muslim" in contradistinction to the white European or American Christian. The figures of the terrorist and the migrant are woven together in the figure of "the Muslim" as a racial type; as such, they are historically, ethnologically, and contemporaneously bound to each other. Such a configuration takes many forms and certainly leads to many conclusions. Suffice it to say here that this is the work of what I discuss later as a global system of racializing the Muslim as migrant, criminal, and terrorist.

Imagining South Asian America

Although Pakistan's cultural, linguistic, and historical affinity is to the South Asian subcontinent, in the post–9/11 Age of Terror, it seems to have shifted geographically to become part of the Middle East. In fact, in the global War on Terror, the Muslim world is increasingly imagined as a single geopolitical mass. Without doubt, the complex overlap of regions including South Asia, Central Asia, the Arab Gulf, and the broader Middle East, has intensified through the connections created by mass migration, satellite technology, and complex financial, social, and cultural flows. As Thomas Blom Hansen (2001a, 2001b) notes in the context of Muslims in India, labor migration provides global horizons to workers who imagine alternative possibilities and social landscapes through travel to the Middle East, Southeast Asia, Europe, and

North America. Although this form of globalization may be laudable, a refiguring of structures of social hierachy and control is also emerging that distinguishes groups of people through categories of identity.

Accompanying the homogenization of such cultural geographies as the "Muslim world" is the impact of an American nationalism defined in relation to a transnational and global world. The tensions of the category "South Asian American" become apparent when it is used to describe immigrants from Pakistan. "South Asia" as a regional concept has long been dominated by a hegemonic India; in many ways, the terms "South Asia" and "India" are synonymous. In this geography, India is celebrated as a vital democracy and growth economy that is a global competitor, while Pakistan is thought of as a failed state with nuclear capabilities constantly on the brink of running amok. In short, India is Bollywood and technology; Pakistan is terror and trouble (Gopinath 2005a).

Pakistan is thus formulated as a feeder state that produces terrorism to be exported abroad and that stands at the front lines of the War on Terror. The idea of migrating terror is encapsulated in the set of rationales that underlies the policing of labor migration and of immigrant communities. The problem in defining communities in the U.S. in terms of their home countries, however, lies not only in the continuity of homogenized and disarticulated geographies that separate Pakistan from South Asia and that place it into a larger group of Muslim countries and regions but also in complex migrations, foreign policies, and geopolitical strategies of empire building.[6]

Added to these broad configurations of regional geography and political strategy is the influence of the U.S. in South Asia and the Middle East. Pakistan is particularly important to the U.S. as a partner in the global War on Terror through the two countries' longstanding patron–client relationship. The role of the U.S. in Pakistan is deeply attached to geostrategic security concerns, anti-terrorism and anti-drug campaigns, militarism, and sociocultural development in areas that range from education and infrastructure to the control of international travel and migration. What happens to migrant workers has an impact that reaches far and wide, not only to locations within the U.S., but to other places within the diaspora. The U.S. economy has a vast reach in determining trends within the global economy; thus, migrant workers' fate is affected by fiscal demands, economic restructuring, and military adventurism. At a global level, labor migrations are put into place as a result of collusion in neoliberal economic policies and the interests of American imperialism (Duggan 2003; Harvey 2003, 2005). At the contemporary juncture, this is manifest in America's global War on Terror, which is important not only to the role of Pakistanis in international migration, but the representation of Muslims across the planet.

Defeating terrorism in Pakistan and Afghanistan and controlling migration to U.S. soil have taken on the highest importance for the American security establishment. Indeed, U.S. aid has contributed to the centralization of the domestic military industry in Pakistan (Siddiqa 2007). During the War on Terror, the U.S. government is increasingly targeting Pakistani migrants, alongside Arabs and other Muslims and immigrants, for deportation and detention as potential threats to the security of the American people. As an apparatus of the U.S. security state that caters to the public's desire for an appearance of law and order through the purging of manufactured perils, immigrants become a disciplined workforce that embodies these fears. Perils and menaces, such as the "yellow peril" that targeted Asian Americans and the "red menace" of internal communism and socialism, have been constructed throughout U.S. history. The most recent articulation is the "Islamic peril."[7]

Following Inderpal Grewal's (2005) theorization of a transnational America, which argues for a conceptualization that supersedes the territorial boundaries of the U.S. nation-state, I draw on a complex mapping of sovereign nation-states not only at the geopolitical level but also in terms of crafting imaginaries of migration that facilitate increasingly transnational and global theorizations. In such imaginaries, the possibilities and boundaries of everyday migration and the impact of macro-level foreign policies become apparent. Through the 1990s and into the twenty-first century, for example, America was represented as a haven for information-technology workers seeking H-1B visas (non-immigrant visas that allow American employers to employ foreign workers temporarily in specialized occupations), and the consequent ability to move up the global economic ladder. This generated a great deal of interest in temporary migration and guest work among educated and professional people. However, the same narratives of possibility circulated widely among less advantaged and less affluent migrants. Simultaneously, patterns of chain and step migration and shifts in U.S. immigration laws allowed families to reunify, creating new and complex class and social formations in increasingly heterogeneous immigrant communities. Such patterns and structures of migration play an important role in creating the migration fantasy. While television talk shows in the U.S. highlight anti–Americanism in Pakistan and across the Muslim world, America continues to be seen as a land of endless possibility, no matter how tormented this dream has become. The work of imagination is vast when it comes to geography and migration, as I learned in my fieldwork. Take, for example, one migrant's statement: "When you ask [many Pakistanis] what they think of America, they will criticize everything, but if you gave free visas, all of them would line up to get one."

In this book, I look at transnational workers within the global economy to highlight the relationship between neoliberalism and empire and the formation of worldviews, subjectivities, and life chances. In Weberian terms, these are largely worlds of enchantment and disenchantment in which migrants' lives are crafted through possibility and regulation. Rhetorically, this project asks how Pakistani labor migrants are made sense of and how they make sense of their world in the global economy. But I launch this argument not only from within the confines of the economic sphere, I also engage with the anthropology of globalization to investigate issues of social and cultural formation that drive diasporas into particular relationships—specifically, those that structure and control the possibilities of migrants' lives (Inda and Rosaldo 2008; Ong 1999, 2006; Ong and Collier 2005; Tsing 2005). To explore the themes of globalization and migration, I also look to scholarship on the South Asian diaspora to guide many of my arguments about Pakistani transnational workers.[8] In addition, this work is indebted to the insight and theoretical approaches forged in the field of transnational cultural studies in the examination of feminism, racism, transnationalism, gender, sexuality, and other relations of power (Grewal 2005; Grewal and Kaplan 1994; Kaplan et al. 1999; Moallem 2005; Puar 2007).

Following recent critiques of South Asian migration (Barbora et al. 2008; Shukla 2001), I expand the notions of one-way and bidirectional migration in favor of models of diaspora that emphasize the multiplicity of movement. In particular, I look at how social formations are constructed in diaspora through chain, step, and seasonal migration based on economic, cultural, social, and political factors. Tracing migration to a source country allows the role of internal migration and the placement of migration hubs in the process of sending and receiving migrant workers to be magnified. The politics of regional migration also plays an important role in crafting migrants' pathways to labor acquisition. In mapping such a labor diaspora, I argue that the social formations produced in home countries and through regional migration are an important aspect of how Pakistani workers are understood through the terms of criminality and deviance that are then racialized in the global War on Terror.

Indeed, for ethnic and racial studies in the United States, the study of Muslim populations spans broad racial and ethnic categorizations. Muslims are found in African American, Asian American, Arab American, Latina/o, white, and multiracial communities. Despite this ambiguity, the racialized Muslim is mobilized as a unitary figure. To frame my analysis, I evoke "the Muslim" as a category that encompasses many nationalities, social and cultural practices, religious affiliations (from Muslim Sunni and Shia to Christian, Sikh, and Hindu), and social realities that, through the process of state and popular racialization, is generalized.[9] The system of policing that targets Arab, Muslim, and South Asian immigrants for detention and deportation, as exemplified by the placement of "the Muslim" in the U.S. racial formation under the Bush administration's War on Terror, is crafted through a broad logic of anti-immigrant racism. What is particularly telling is the disproportionately high number of Pakistanis deported either through forced or voluntary means in the sweeps that followed 9/11.[10] Not only does Pakistan as a country represent terror, danger, and Islamic militancy, but Pakistanis in the U.S. are cast as perilous racial figures of indeterminate standing.

Although I focus on Pakistani migrants in the global economy and on the racialized Muslim under American empire, this work maintains a comparative and interdisciplinary approach. When possible, I have attempted to construct and analyze the issues of my research in relation to other relevant populations and subject matter. Although the ethnographic method is at the core of much of the cultural and material analysis in this book, it is not a conventional ethnography. Instead, I draw on ethnographic fieldwork to weave approaches to political economy, visual and cultural analysis, history, and critical race studies into an interdisciplinary study of the complex issues I elaborate. Specifically, I argue that conceptions of globalized racism are based in the circulation of specific racialized regionalisms that imagine the Muslim world as connected and interdependent. This, in turn, is imagined as part of a geography that connects migratory networks of Muslim countries to the metropoles of Northern countries in the global economy. Relying on ethnographic fieldwork conducted both before and after 9/11, this approach expands the framework of studies of race and migration by placing Muslim migrants into racial formations in the U.S. and as a central part of the global racial system. Within the South Asian diaspora, migrants from Pakistan historically have had a different relationship to the U.S. that is shaped by their identification and racialization as Muslims. Based on ethnographic research with Pakistani migrants, I argue that the economic, cultural, and social effects of neoliberalism have produced the figure of "the Muslim" in the current global economy as racialized.

Racialization and Labor Migration

As theorists of globalization argue, the concepts of transnationalism, diaspora, and migration, often studied in terms of the formation of particular flows and subjectivities (Appadurai 1996), reveal the patterns and processes of the movement of people, things, and ideas as much as they reveal the complex formation of identities and everyday life (Lowe 1996). Throughout this book, I investigate the global service economy, which necessitates class formation in the broadest sense—not only of an economically based class system, but also in terms of the complex subjectivities, desires, and practices that are produced out of transnational migration. The racializing of regional migration on a global scale is based in a social and economic system that is constantly in flux and requires the fixing of certain attributes. In particular, Pakistani migrants working in the global service economy represent part of a larger transnational working class that is racialized in multiple locations.

Nonetheless, it is important to point out the contingent nature of this designation both in terms of the mobilization of class as an analytical category and in terms of the impact of racializing discourses. An important attribute of any working class, without doubt, is its connection to wage-based labor and its incorporation into a capitalist system. But such an analysis is limited in certain ways to a specific political economy. Although I do not preclude such an understanding in my framework, I wish to unsettle and disrupt it in favor of a complex intersectional approach that not only understands class in relation to other categories of analysis and is wary of the categories themselves, but that also can dynamically shift according to context and historical location. In the production of representations of the Pakistani Muslim migrant, the concept of race is deeply intertwined with particular ideas about class and gender that, throughout the labor diaspora, have contrasting, conflicting, and sometimes oppositional meanings. Simultaneously, this migrant subjectivity is imbued with the values and beliefs attached to the concepts of illegality, criminality, and terrorism.

The figure of the Muslim in contemporary global discourse is already saturated with racialized, sexualized, and gendered terms, including, but not limited to, "terrorism," "fundamentalism," "clash of civilizations," "panic," "peril," "hetero-patriarchy," "oppression of women," "Taliban," "violent masculinity," "queered," "homophobic," "warlike," "fanatical," "radical," and "barbaric." In Pakistan, the majority of labor migrants are male and working class.[11] Hence, a transnational masculinity is found in the dynamics of these populations that I specifically describe as a labor diaspora. This masculinity is complicated in the experience of migration, in which the family must be refigured to maintain a patriarchal order. The social effects of class, race, and religion are intimately connected to these newly configured patriarchies that have varied meanings throughout the diaspora; for this reason, specific migration circuits have particular effects on subject formation. Thus, the male transnational worker from Pakistan is understood as inhabiting a particular kind of racialized masculinity from the viewpoint of so-called liberal-democratic publics and a simultaneous transnational class formation from the viewpoint of neoliberal capitalism that requires a service economy. Although complex in their formation, race and class for these workers are often subsumed in the characterization of migrant illegality. As a trait of the global economy, such a construction is tied to the legal apparatuses mandated by states and by the realities of complex global markets that cannot be regulated.

These overlapping frames of racialization and class formation come together in particular notions of underground economies and migrant illegality in which people and commodities are smuggled and trafficked through extralegal and extra-state spaces that are often portrayed as the global economy's dark underbelly. Although these issues are linked to economic vulnerability and structures of dominance, the relationship of these concepts to poverty and processes of migration is particularly vexed and troubling (Shah 2007, 2008). Such a configuration often unifies structures of poverty with illegality by using metaphors of terrorism and criminality to describe alternative markets. Primary components of these underground markets include migrants, sex work, cash, goods, drugs, terror, and smuggling networks such that illegal and criminal activities are conflated into a totalizing system. Here descriptions and theories of underground economies are placed in a netherworld of abjection that renders individual agency impossible, and the migrant worker is reduced to classifications of illegality and criminality.

Yet global labor migration is fraught with all sorts of possibilities, desires, and unexpected outcomes that transcend reductive structural explanations. Transnational work, at the outset, is a clear economic necessity in the absence of opportunity in home countries. Such labor also represents desires for transnational class mobility, or what I have tried to complicate in terms of work in the global service economy. What is considered working-class labor in the global North may lead to middle-class stability, status, and values in the global South. Such systems of capital mobilization also rely on wide transnational social and kinship networks that create complex ideas of family units (Mathew 2005: 167–

75). In these circumstances, social networks are heightened in terms of fictive kin and intimate relations. Migration in certain ways disrupts the heteronormative order in what Nayan Shah (2001) has called queer domesticity, so that heterosexual migrants are queered as non-normative. For ethnographies of Muslims in the post–9/11 world, the study of gender and sexuality through the lens of racialized masculinity reveals a wide variety of important insights into the effects of stigmatization (Ewing 2008a, 2008b; Maira 2009; Naber 2006). Migration studies have often normalized heterosexuality without a proper framework to understand queer and non-normative desires, practices, and subjectivities (Gopinath 2005b; Manalansan 2006). The act of migration itself might be understood as a liberating practice of desire and pleasure that in important ways highlights not only erotic socialities, but also other forms of non-sexual imagining that are fraught with structural barriers and impossibilities. For some, migration is a near impossibility that must be scrutinized and planned, while for others, access to migration schemes can seem preordained.

Transnational Classes in the Labor Diaspora

The political economy of oil and the financial dominance of the dollar have shaped the multiple migrations from South Asia most immediately to the Middle Eastern countries of the Persian Gulf region (and now, notably, Iraq),[12] then to Europe and North America, as destinations to obtain income. The petro-dollar economy increased the flow of cash available to the Gulf countries to fund the massive construction projects on which many South Asian labor migrants have toiled since the 1970s.[13] As mega-city projects have spread, countries such as Kuwait, the United Arab Emirates, and Qatar have attracted so many migrant workers that their foreign populations are now larger than their domestic populations. Labor migration, in turn, is an enormous boon to the domestic economies of South Asian countries, which send workers to the Gulf, relieving unemployment at home, and receiving remittances from them. For the labor migrants themselves, access to travel, work, and wages, and the economic and cultural changes that stem from the dynamic process of migration, create new social relationships. Besides work experience, they gain social networks and economic resources to fund migration to other countries and regions of the world.

The development of working-class migration from Pakistan has a particular history that emerged out of the crisis of the Pakistani state in the 1970s.[14] Labor-union busting in Pakistan originated in the 1950s, influenced by economists from Harvard University who arrived in the country with plans to modernize its economy. By the late 1970s, during the regime of Zulfikar Ali Bhutto, organizing by domestic labor unions in Pakistan effectively had been crushed. The goals of these policies, in the words of one of the main architects, were based on "squeezing the peasant" to build an industrialist class through the "social utility of greed" (Papanek 1967). The policies set in motion a developmental model aimed at achieving industrialization that was put into practice across Asia, Africa, and Latin America. The model, subsequently, exacerbated class differences by decreasing the resources available for agriculture and increasing poverty, all the while generating data that perpetuated the dependence model for development aid. The social upheaval this kind of development brought about in Pakistan sustained the argument in favor of subsidies and loans from international donors and the gradual liberalization of the Pakistani economy that continued into the early 1990s (Zaidi 2005).

The failure of organized labor to gain adequate protection from domestic trade-union laws played an important role in the flight of the laboring classes to transnational locations. Indeed, in the 1970s, as domestic labor unions were weakened, unemployed and underemployed Pakistanis looked for opportunities outside their home country. In the 1980s and 1990s, the migrants were popularly dubbed the *Dubai chalo* working class in contrast to the "Amrikan" Pakistani, revealing a split class system of transnational migrants.[15] The multiplicity of diasporic destinations and experiences among migrants consistently challenges such assumed categories. Nonetheless, the imagined migratory hierarchy remains educated professionals working predominantly in the U.S. and Europe, contrasted with unskilled laborers who toil on construction sites in Dubai and elsewhere in the Gulf region. Labor migrants from Pakistan, however, find their way to places all over the globe in search of work, education, and opportunity.

Pakistani migration parallels that of other South Asian countries. Indeed, many who participate in working-class migrations find themselves in categories that essentialize their social identity when they are working abroad. This results partially from the process of framing "labor" and "worker" as class categories, but it also results from racialized and gendered discourses of identity. This is to say that class position in a society is based on the kind of work one does and on one's access to capital. In this sense, class can be analyzed comparatively in terms of societal conceptions of work and the value attributed to different types of labor. Class is also a cultural construct that must be understood through its intersections with other social categories of analysis.

Thus, transnational labor migration from Pakistan has its own history that must be placed in the larger framework of regional and global patterns of labor migration.

When I use the terms "transnational classes" and "labor diaspora," I am referring to the condition of certain groups structured and formed in relation to one another, as well as to E. P. Thompson's (1966) famous evocation of class as a relational category. Class, as a complicated assertion that is illustrated through the contingencies of location and historical context, can have multiple meanings and positions in a diasporic context. In Pakistan, a worker's migration abroad may allow for a middle-class existence at home, yet the worker's status, salary, and position in the global economy compels a reading of belonging to a temporary working class.[16] This form of casual labor is often referred to as a contingent class in relation to the kind of work that is performed, and the contingent class under neoliberal capitalism is an underclass that gets by with temporary work. Thus, the complex notion of a transnational class depends largely on location, position, and social identity.

Alongside this class theory is an economic order that is defined by social, cultural, and political relationships. Particular features such as ethnicity, kinship, and social networks, as well as access to capital and other resources, allow certain migrants to enter the global economy as workers while others are excluded. Converting such social and cultural capital into economic forms comes through a certain sense of the world—what Pnina Werbner (1999), in the context of Pakistani working-class migration, has called a cosmopolitan attitude. These ethnic worlds of migration are ways to re-create cultural forms and systems in new social circumstances in which competition is stiff and access to capital is limited. Such cosmopolitanism implies the possibility of assuming multiple positions in contradictory circumstances, a worldliness that shows how multiple life worlds are imagined and structured.

In terms of globalization, labor migration has become a central component of the capitalist system. The state plays a great role in shaping transnational migration by generating the demand for labor migrants through guest-worker systems and the building of temporary labor reserves. Such flows increasingly follow a pattern of multiple migration circuits in which transnational laborers find access to work and to the accumulation of forms of capital. This process is in large part mediated by the state and by state-like institutions. I argue that, although "the state" is a complex, contradictory, and multifaceted concept, it appears as a uniform entity. That is, the state is not an integral, absolute concept; it is fractured through multiple actors, intentions, and rationalities that, under the neoliberal model, promote the production of state-like effects by non-state institutions alongside those of the state. Thus, state-like effects can be found in multiple arenas without direct state intervention.[17] For example, in the case of the Pakistani state and labor migration, international financial institutions such as the World Bank and the International Monetary Fund mandate a template for market reform in which corporate actors in the private sphere are responsible for contracting transnational labor. This was once the domain of the state in the public sphere. The state seeks to balance these spheres of international and private interests while reproducing them as its own. The multiplicity of state effects mediates the process of transnational labor migration by controlling such populations and creating a system in which multiple migration circuits take place.

As shorthand for policies, structures, bureaucracies, political actors, internalized logics, rationales, subjectivities, positions, strategies, and tactics, the state more often than not is more than it claims—and more than is possible. As a character that takes on multiple forms, it is not easily defined and contained conceptually as a coherent set of practices, intentions, or governmentalities. Yet, the state seeks to control, regulate, discipline, police, and restrict labor migration through repertories and technologies of governance that give it a sense of omniscience. Following the important work that has denaturalized the state by examining it as contingent and contradictory and as containing multiple intentions (e.g., Abrams 1988 [1977]; Aretxaga 2003; Corrigan 1994, 2002; Corrigan and Sayer 1985; Ferguson and Gupta 2002; Mitchell 1991, 2002; Scott 1998; Trouillot 2001), I examine the relationship of the state to migration in multiple social and cultural arenas: as a major component of localized practices of everyday life and as a macro-political actor in broader political and social issues. As an abstracted cast member with many roles, the state takes on different identities and names: modern state, police state, racial state, colonial state, capitalist state, imperial state, neoliberal state, warfare state, failed state, postcolonial state, military state, ghost state, and on and on toward the maddening state.[18] "The state" is a pivotal concept on which much of this book is organized, and I examine it in relation to the formation of labor diaspora and the global racial system that is fully elaborated in chapter 4.

In the aftermath of the tragic attacks on the World Trade Center and elsewhere on September 11, 2001, Muslims and Islam came to the foreground of the national imagination in the U.S. as a threat and an enemy. This was followed by a backlash against Muslims and "terrorist-looking" populations in a reign of racial terror that restated the problem of race. This was not strictly an American phenomenon: An effort to define and identify Muslims as friend or foe took place on a global scale. Far from an isolated incident in the post–9/11 world, this resurgent racism is part of a complex and old conceptualization of Muslims and Islam. Global systems of racial formation for some time have categorized Muslims as a racial group. As I demonstrate in chapter 1, "the Muslim" as a figure was racialized in the early formation of the concept of race in the so-called Age of Conquest.

In the context of labor migration from the South Asian subcontinent, many of the historical threads that link race to South Asian labor date to social formations established in what historians call the imperial age of Indian Ocean migrations (Bose 2006; Metcalf 2007). Indians traveled the world, from Malaya to East Africa to the Caribbean, as laborers and soldiers. Defined as "martial races" based on a kind of racial thinking that relied on colonial ideas of religious and ethnic difference, South Asians were recruited to work and fight for the British Empire. For example, Punjabi Muslims and Sikhs often were thought of as dutiful, disciplined, and hardworking soldiers, but when conflicts with Muslim lands increased as the British Empire expanded, Muslims increasingly were deemed untrustworthy.

In an ironic twist of imperial substitution in the early twentieth century, the British preceded the U.S. in invading Iraq. During the First World War, the British sent Indian troops on a military campaign in what was then called Mesopotamia (largely modern-day Iraq) and attempted to oust its Turkish rulers. The goal was to maintain Indian trade routes and secure important oilfields and a pipeline that had been established in Persia (contemporary Iran), and, subsequently, to establish another colony for the empire. Even as Indian troops secured the British Empire's military aims, the harsh conditions drove some deserters to join the Ghadar Party in San Francisco, a revolutionary diasporic group that sought independence for India. At first, Indian laborers were unwilling to honor work contracts because they feared the violence in Iraq, but they were ultimately delivered via a system of confinement in military-camp depots on their way to labor sites. The use of restricted environments to recruit laborers and stop desertion evolved into the employment of prisoners from Indian jails, who were offered remission from their sentences in exchange for labor. Creating an Indian administration in occupied Iraq meant acquiring colonial knowledge, and developing the Indian colony there included introducing colonial legal codes and revenue surveys established by the British, as well as an initially Indian-led police force and government bureaucracy. The experiment in Mesopotamia lasted five years, allowing the British to turn India into a sub-center of the empire while also looking to other colonies, such as those in East Africa, for potential bureaucratic and legal structures to take to the new colony in Iraq. Indian soldiers and laborers were never to be permanent inhabitants of the new Iraq; they were used as a workforce to secure the gains of the British Empire (Metcalf 2007). However, this brief colonial encounter established a relationship to Indian laborers that persisted into the twenty-first century.

These patterns of imperial migration therefore established South Asia as a source of military and manual labor. Indeed, the imperial rationale behind categorizing Indians as a "martial race" perpetuated a racial system of classification that, in the present day, has become a complex and structurally amplified global racial system. Muslims and Sikhs were used in the military and police forces because of what the British claimed to be these groups' violent nature. Other groups were also believed to be predisposed to particular occupations—for example, tribals as indentured laborers and Gujaratis and Tamils as traders. Workers were often described as "coolies," a racial description that encompassed people from many different populations. Chinese workers notoriously were referred to as "coolies" (Jung 2006; Yun 2008), but so were Arabs and South Asians in the labor camps built by American oil interests in Saudi Arabia (Vitalis 2007).

The British imperial system in the Indian Ocean that was established roughly between 1830 and 1930 thus created many of the patterns and routes, as well as the knowledge, of South Asian labor migrants that continue to resonate in the global economy. This Indian Ocean model expanded globally so that transnational workers still face the same issues as those established under the British Empire. American imperial interests, significantly in Iraq and Afghanistan, rely on these old patterns while creating new ones. It is under this rationale that the global War on Terror identifies the Middle East and South Asia as trouble spots even as these regions have become globalized in the expanding imperial reach for labor migrants.

Book Summary

As this chapter's opening vignette demonstrated, the complex migration flows from South Asia to the Middle East and to the U.S. are articulated in complex registers that I examine in the confluence of history, media and film representation, and ethnographic evidence. The book takes as its organizing parameters the themes of history and context, process and structure, institutions, and the role of the body in material life. Following the elegant analysis in *Frames of War* (2009), in which Judith Butler untangles the implications of the U.S.-led War on Terror, this book is divided into two sections that frame the conceptual relationships of race and migration and of the state and migration. As an interdisciplinary study, this work addresses the use of the categories of race and racism on Muslim bodies as they circulate in the global economy through concepts, media images, popular culture, narratives of migration and diaspora, and the production of illegality, criminality, and terror. As ethnography, it explores the multiple ways these racial categories are produced to place Pakistani labor migrants in the historical formation of the global racial system.[19]

Part I, "Racializing Muslims," begins with a conceptual analysis and history of the idea of race in the global circulation and formation of the racialized Muslim. This is followed by chapters on racial events and ethnographic cinema since 9/11. Taken together, the chapters in part I frame the elaborate process of racialization that has figured Muslims and Pakistani immigrants working in the global service sector as threats in the War on Terror. Using an interdisciplinary approach that combines historical and ethnological argument, media analysis, and critique of visual culture, I argue that the internal logics of racialization figure Muslims as a broad population that encompasses multiple nationalities, ethnic groups, and cultural experiences but that also depends on the peculiarities of the global economy and neoliberal capitalism.

In part II, "Globalizing Labor," I advance these conceptual arguments by outlining how South Asian migration and labor diaspora historically have been part of the global racial system and by providing an ethnography of the migration industry that produces workers in formal and illicit systems of labor diaspora. For Pakistani migrant workers, "illegality" is constructed throughout the diaspora that is pivotal to their transnational experiences and labor struggles. The final chapter of part II examines the post–9/11 world of racial terror and violence as seen in the U.S. detention and deportation system and in the migration patterns that have resulted in massive returns to Pakistan and other parts of the diaspora from the United States.

In chapter 1, "Islam and Racism," I introduce the concepts of Islamophobia and anti–Muslim racism and contextualize them in terms of the place of the figure of the Muslim in the Euro-American imagination. I construct this argument by providing ethnological evidence obtained from historical, literary, legal, and cultural archives. The chapter examines the historical construction of the figure of the Muslim and the concepts of race and Islamophobia. The Muslim is constructed as a threat to white Christian supremacy and in relation to anti–Jewish racism by employing a racial logic that crosses the cultural categories of nation, religion, ethnicity, and sexuality. The development of a religiously based racism, or Islamophobia, is grounded in a history of racial ascription of bodily comportment, superimposition, and dissimulation. These are all components of a theory of Muslim racial formation in which I trace the figure of "the Muslim" in the ethnological archive to conceptualize the contemporary racialization of Muslim communities, particularly under the U.S. racial formation and global racial system. Further, I explain Islamophobia through the workings of the biopolitics of the racialized body that is essential to the rationale of the U.S. racial state. The argument in chapter 1 traces the conceptual apparatus for how Muslim immigrant communities are placed in the U.S. racial formation and in the global racial system.

Chapter 2, "Racial Panic, Islamic Peril, and Terror," explores the role panics and perils have played in creating a vocabulary of terror in the U.S. racial formation. From evidence gathered surrounding two events—one an instance of moral panic and the other, of peril—I argue that such racial constructions are instrumental in anti-immigrant narratives and in forming conceptions of illegality. It is through this logic that transnational migrants are located as both religious and racial subjects in the U.S. public sphere and through which Muslims, with their patterns of multiple migration, become state targets of fear and panic. Chapter 2 is based on ethnographic fieldwork conducted in New York and in Lahore, Pakistan, after 9/11. Its argument is based on an analysis of how race and religion are combined in a rhetorical strategy that draws on terror, as well as illegality and criminality, to police migrants and control immigration.

Chapter 3, "Imperial Targets," examines the logic of the U.S. racial formation that, in recent times, has collapsed identities through ideas of race, culture, and religion. The history of these categories of race making are particularly vexing in the case of U.S. populations of Middle Eastern and South Asian descent, who are broadly racialized as "Muslims." The media, scholars, and activists now use the unwieldy categories of "the Muslim," "the Arab," and "the South Asian" to describe groups targeted for racial discrimination, violent hate crimes, and state policing. I argue, however, that Pakistani immigrants in the U.S. are simultaneously understood as South Asian and Middle Eastern, a classification that combines national origin, religion, ethnicity, and culture into a unitary conception of race and racial formation. Based on a critical analysis of visual culture—specifically, ethnographic cinema—I show how the racial figure of the Muslim is collapsed into an amorphous category and examine how this rationale is used in the construction and policing of Pakistani and Muslim migrants.

Chapter 4, "Labor Diaspora and the Global Racial System," contains an extensive ethnography of how the migration industry produces migrants, and it explores the racial and class implications of labor flows in the global racial system. In chapter 4, I also compare contemporary labor migration with that of indentured labor of the nineteenth century and early twentieth century both to describe the processes of exploitation in these labor diasporas and to argue for an alternate conceptualization of the transnational labor market. Juxtaposing the historical moment of indentured labor with the contemporary migration industry provides insight into the role that labor contracts play in the formation of labor migrants and the subsequent meaning of informal labor practices and notions of illegality. Through an ethnography of the migration industry in Pakistan, I trace the development of these patterns and the inclusion of migrants within the global economy and as a central component of the global racial system.

In chapter 5, "Migration, Illegality, and the Security State," I trace the relationship of Pakistani migrants within the state systems of transnational migration between Pakistan, the Persian Gulf, and the United States. To do this, I rely on ethnographic research I conducted both before and after 2001. As I argue, the historical relationship of the state to migration in Pakistan and abroad is pivotal to the production of transnational workers as an economic and social class. This occurs in terms of their place within the domestic economy and within international and transregional economies and is most immediately visible in labor migration to countries of the Persian Gulf region. This relationship itself demarcates Pakistani workers within a larger labor diaspora. On the U.S. side, what has emerged since 9/11 is a pattern of governance in a domestic War on Terror that seeks to identify potential criminality through broad concepts of migrant illegality and deportability. The identification of criminality is itself constructed through broad historical practices of demonizing and racializing migrants. Chapter 5 argues for an ethnographic study of the state through the issue of subject formation and the concept of the production of legality and illegality. Negotiating the terms of the state system for labor migrants is therefore also an important aspect of how the labor of migrants is constructed. As legal subjects, labor migrants are placed within the fields of power of the state that constructs migrant subjectivities in a dynamic that oscillates between legality and illegality.

In chapter 6, "The Muslim Body," I examine how social processes are inscribed into, and disciplined on, the immigrant body through the detention and deportation regime and the process of return migration. In doing so, I trace how the Muslim body is constructed through fear and anxiety but also as a site of containment and control. In my ethnographic research, I tracked return migration from the United States to Pakistan as a component of the recent history of detentions and deportations of Muslim immigrants—largely Arab and South Asian—since 2001. I examine how migration creates a site of memory and embodiment of bodily comportment, as well as the role of the racialized affect of fear and anxiety on the construction and literal disappearance of the Muslim body in the global War on Terror. Indeed, terror is diffuse in these multiple entanglements of sovereignty and in the everyday life of what is also a war on immigration. In this sense, I ask not only how the body is imagined as a site of containment and control through the policing of immigration, but also how this social process reproduces sovereignty in spaces of self-governance and zones of autonomous state-sanctioned force such as detention.

The conclusion, "Racial Feelings in the Post–9/11 World," reflects on the comparative and intersectional implications for research on the effect of 9/11 on the U.S. racial formation, the theory of a global racial system, and the future of critical race studies. By examining a critical depiction of Muslim migrant workers, the book closes with the imagined future of labor diaspora.

PART ONE

Racializing Muslims

ONE

Islam and Racism

Today, racism has been largely—though not entirely, to be sure—detached from its per-petrators. In its most advanced forms, indeed, it has no perpetrators, it is a nearly invisible, taken-for-granted, "commonsense" feature of everyday life and global social structure.... [If] we define racism as *The routinized outcome of practices that create or reproduce hierarchical social structures based on essentialized racial categories*, then we can see better how it extends from the transnational to the national to the experiential and personal, from the global debt burden to racial profiling, from Negrophobia to Islamophobia.

—Howard Winant (2004, 126)

From Racial Existentialism to Racial Phenomenology

How did "Muslim" become a category of race? In this chapter, I tackle the thorny question of the racialization of the Muslim and the modern history of the race concept in relation to Islam. As a historical pattern and process, the racialization of the Muslim reveals important details in the expanding and flexible concept of race. Examining how the Muslim is racialized establishes a historical and analytical framework to situate the condition of the Pakistani migrant in the contemporary global racial system discussed throughout this book. The question of whether "Muslim" constitutes a racial category places the debate within the arena of what might be called racial existentialism, which struggles to identify categories of race and, in its extreme, to deny the power of modern racism by arguing that race as a concept is no longer important. Rather than simply entertain questions about whether the concept of race is valid and how it is used in forms of Islamophobia, I contend that anti–Muslim racism is better understood by examining the complex variations of the concept of race and the history of how and when "Muslim" became a category of race.

From the inception of the race concept, Islam has been at the center of creating, representing, and justifying a system of dominance and control that has shifted according to historical context and practice. In the contemporary theory of racializing Muslims into the global racial system, the boundaries of race lie between the body and performances that aim to restrict and subjugate. To frame this historical discussion, I discuss the Muslim body in relation to the race concept to suggest a materialist approach from which the racialized Muslim is understood through everyday codes and interpretations. The configuration of "Muslim" as a category of race overlaps with the political economies of migration and recent domains of spatial surveillance and policing of religious, national, and ethnic groups. Further, conceptions of globalized racism are based on imagining the Muslim world as connected and interdependent.

To trace this history, I begin by framing the Muslim body not in a transcendental or theologically metaphysical sense but as an object of visual interpellation and translation. Feminist philosophers of the body have taken a phenomenological approach to elaborate the idea of the racialized body (Ahmed 2000, 2004, 2006; Alcoff 2001, 2006). Following their insights, I elaborate a racial phenomenology in which the Muslim is understood not only as a totalized biological body but also as a cultural and social entity constructed within a number of discursive regimes, including those of terrorism, fundamentalism, patriarchy, sexism, and labor migration. By invoking this idea of racial phenomenology, I examine bodies that appear in the visual register as characteristics of race and as performances of characteristics that are read as racial.

The Muslim body as an important site of the racial imaginings of sovereign power has its own particular history of survival in the United States (Roediger 2008). To trace the place of Muslims in the U.S. racial scheme, I take as an epistemological starting point the theory of a global racial system. Following the influential theory of racial formation as a structural model for understanding power relations as driven by racial divides (Omi and Winant 1994), as well as discursive critiques of race and racism (Goldberg 1993, 2002, 2009; Silva 2007), several scholars have elaborated the global racial system as one that was formed in relation to struggles for decolonization and the march of global capitalism (Mullings 2005; Winant 2001, 2004). Thus, the global racial system pervades social systems that span numerous, dynamically related historical, sociological, and geographic scales. The figure of the racialized Muslim is a contemporary example of this system. Incorporated into the U.S. racial formation through the domestic and global War on Terror, it can be traced to multiple histories and conceptual frameworks.[1]

The concept of race is mired in historical antecedents that move discursively between religion and race, culture and biology, and that are directly pertinent to the discussion of anti–Muslim racism and the related phenomenon of Islamophobia.[2] The process of reframing Islam from a religious category into a racial category in the contemporary U.S. speaks to a wider historical discourse that emanates not only from racism and the maintenance of white Christian supremacy, but also from the historical pre-eminence of imperialism and the maintenance of empire. Specifically, the process of racializing Islam through social identifications takes place through a kind of translation of the body and its comportment via a combination of identifiers, such as dress, behavior, and phenotypic expression. Gender and sexuality are also key components in understanding the place of the Muslim in this historical logic of racialization. The processes of queering and feminizing are simultaneous to the racializing of Islam and Muslims through a historical precedent that imagines religious groups as enemies.[3]

My aim in providing a comparative ethnology is to argue for a complex history of race and racism based in a theory of the cultural that is not linear but multivalent. This chapter engages in a framework that brings together comparative race studies and intersectional analysis to define the coordinates of the figure of the Muslim in the War on Terror and in the global racial system.

Ethnology and the Muslim Question

The figure of the Muslim in the ethnological archive is complex and fluid. From Orientalist studies to contemporary studies of Muslim populations, historical contexts and interpretations have influenced scholars who examine the complex social, cultural, and political formations of Muslim societies. Recent scholarship, for example, elaborates on Karl Marx's writings on the Jewish question, asking what the Muslim's place is in relation to Enlightenment modernity and late capitalism (Majid 2004, 2009; Mufti 2007). I refer to this provocation as the "Muslim question" and advance the intellectual agenda by addressing conceptual linkages to modern forms of racialization. In particular, my interest in the Muslim question is to examine how Islam became a racialized conception in the contemporary U.S. as part of the maintenance of modern statecraft, the racial state, and twenty-first century notions of empire and imperial sovereignty. Similarly, others have tracked the Muslim question as a longstanding interaction between Europe and Islam that defines the terms of modernity, civilization, empire, and nationalism, as well as modes of violence and war (Majid 2009; Moallem 2005).

Relying on select ethnological, historical, and philosophical evidence, I argue that anti–Muslim racism and Islamophobia are central to the narrative of modern nations—and to modernity itself—because they emerged in the contact between the Old World and the New World. Although "Islamophobia" is a fairly recent neologism, it has long existed as a conceptual framework; as a kind of racism that developed in relation to the history of the concept of race. Even though my arguments ultimately are situated in the context of recent U.S.-based racial formations and the rubric of old and new racisms, I nonetheless argue that Islamophobia and anti–Muslim racism must be understood in a global historical context.

The history of the concept of race is intimately tied to Islamophobia in that the racializing of Islam took place as the foundation of the concept of race took root.[4] Islam and Muslims are a central part of the concepts of race and racism through histories that span European and American forms of Orientalism and the formation and maintenance of empire through war and conquest. The conceptual history of Islamophobia is based in a theory of racial ascription of bodily comportment, superimposition, and dissimulation—that is, the assorted ways to define "race" based on visual attributes such as skin color and phenotype, as well as customs and costumes. The process of racializing Muslims involves placing biological and cultural determinism in a contradictory logic purporting that race is immutable and essential but simultaneously mutable and fluid. Including Islam and Muslims in the U.S. racial formation, as well as in a global racial system (Mullings 2005; Silva 2007; Winant 2001, 2004), requires a historical conceptualization of old and new racisms in which a theory of race is socially constructed between the concepts of the cultural and the biological.[5]

The racialized Muslim developed as a geographically external other that was demonized not only through notions of the body, but also through the superimposition of cultural features onto Muslim and non–Muslim groups. Because this process was not based exclusively on phenotypic or physical difference (although this was often imputed), some have been able to use a strategy of dissimulation—that is, disguising or concealing religious difference—to keep themselves from being interpreted in racial terms. In the American context of racial formation, for instance, Islam represented a liberatory identification for African Americans; however, this presented a threat to white Christian supremacy that was then used to further racialize immigrant and black Muslims. Thus, the figure of the Muslim became racialized through social and cultural signifiers across national, racial, and ethnic boundaries.

Ethnology, long associated with the field of anthropology, has as one of its central preoccupations the taxonomic classification of cultural and racial difference (e.g., Hodgen 1964; Stocking 1987). The observations presented as ethnological analysis in early anthropological practice often examined moral elements, social structures, languages, and cultural practices to ascertain fundamental, or innate, differences among peoples. Much of this scholarship has been debunked as racialist thinking, but it persists in common historical and practical use. In this sense, a critical analysis of ethnology offers fruitful terrain for investigating the meanings attributed to the figure of the Muslim in the scholarly archive. Here I understand "the Muslim" as a unit of analysis that is central to the examination of Islamic societies, cultures, and communities.[6] The Muslim, in this sense, is a diverse figure that is differentiated by its national, transnational, sectarian, ethnic, racial, gendered, and classed meanings.[7] The Muslim is also a transmigratory, global figure that enters and exits multiple terrains; thus, we can speak of the Muslim in Europe, the Americas, Asia, Africa, and elsewhere. As part of the ethnological analysis, I argue that at least four essentialized tropes are important in understanding the racialization of the Muslim: the infidel savage, the slave/captive, the terrorist, and the immigrant.[8]

Islamophobia: The Life of a Concept

"Islamophobia," which emerged as a neologism in the 1970s, became popular among European antiracism activists in the 1980s and 1990s. Originally, the term grew out of a need to address the increasing animosity and violence that Muslim migrants faced in European countries, as well as to address the supposed logic of a divide between the Western world and the Islamic world.[9] A broad sense of Islamophobia rose throughout Europe and America, and its satellites, alongside conflicts in the Middle East tied to the legacy of Zionism and the Israeli occupation of Palestine; several wars in the Gulf region; the aftermath of 9/11; and the revitalization of American imperialism in Iraq and Afghanistan (events that Tariq Ali [2002] refers to as the Oil Wars). Indeed, in the second half of the twentieth century, large populations from Muslim countries migrated to Europe and North America in response to economic shifts that required large pools of new labor reserves.

Pnina Werbner (2005, 8) has argued that Islamophobia is a particular kind of racism that is grounded in the fear of social and economic deprivation which, in turn, is elicited in the complex relationship of Islam to the West, which includes Europe's history of sectarian wars, the Crusades, and the Inquisition, all of which were integral to the formation of Western capitalism and modernity. Thus, Werbner argues that Islamophobic racism is reflexive and relies on comparative histories of imperial conquest, subjection, and systematic forms of oppression that relate Muslims to other racialized groups. In this sense, one might argue that racism has always had a sort of reflexive impulse not only in its dynamic ability to modify how racists imagine their object, but also in how it operates as a relational process. In other words, Islamophobia is a gloss for the anti–Muslim racism that collapses numerous groups into the single category "Muslim."

As is evident in the word itself, "Islamophobia" refers to a fear or hatred of Islam and Muslims. In the argument over whether Islamophobia counts as racism, the first question that arises is whether religious hatred is necessarily racial.[10] That is, if religion is not innate, can it be socially constructed as embodied in phenotypic or biological expression? Many European scholars define discrimination in terms of xenophobia and prejudice, whereas scholars in the U.S. have long argued for the importance of talking about race and racism as valid concepts of systematic oppression.[11] Similarly, many scholars disarticulate "Islamophobia" from the concepts of race and racism, instead referring to it as a form of cultural prejudice and religiously based discrimination.[12] In many ways, the debate over Islamophobia as racism mirrors the discussions of the utility of the race concept in the historical, conceptual shift from biological racism to cultural racism.[13]

In the culture wars of the 1980s and 1990s, which were heavily influenced by a concessionary multiculturalism, culture and ethnicity replaced race and racism as the tools for analyzing difference and identity.[14] As the "post-race" argument has gained dominance, explanations for the displacement of the concept of race have themselves been essentialized according to culturalist reasoning. By this, I mean that the race concept often is operationalized as a debunked concept premised on a faulty biological notion of scientific racism; it then follows that Islamophobia cannot be racism, because religion is a social practice and is not biologically preordained (although this, of course, assumes a secular logic of religious belief and practice). Islam as religion, then, is translated as a cultural practice, and Islamophobia results from a belief in Islam's cultural or religious inferiority. So if anti–Muslim sentiments persist, on what basis can culture be recognized in groups of people? Is it enough to argue that culture is essentialized and made to seem natural in Islamophobia? And what about the non-secular interpretations that explain religious difference as a naturalized essence of people from various parts of the world? Such an untethered notion of culture is far from sufficient to answer these questions and to explain Islamophobia and its relationship to racism.[15] Culture is central to race and racism, and, in particular, Islam and religion are an important aspect of the genealogy of the race concept.

From the conquest of the New World to the transatlantic slave trade, Islam figured as an important component in the early U.S. racial formation. Resurrecting this genealogy complicates the history of the concept of race by revealing a complex, overlapping racialization of categories such as "black" and "brown" with religious categories such as "Islam" and "Muslim." The racialization of Islam emerged in the Old World, was transposed on indigenous peoples of the New World, and subsequently took on significance in relation to black America and the Muslim immigrants. Thus, "Muslim" in the U.S. is simultaneously a religious category and a category that encompasses a broad concept of race that connects a history of Native America to black America and immigrant America in the consolidation of anti–Muslim racism.

Race and Religion

The scholarship on the history of the concept of race is curiously silent about the place of religion. For example, Michael Omi's and Howard Winant's canonical *Racial Formation in the United States* (1994) scarcely refers to religion. In Omi's and Winant's usage, "race" is most commonly associated with culture. In what they refer to as the evolution of modern racial awareness, they argue:

> The emergence of a modern conception of race does not occur until the rise of Europe and the arrival of Europeans in the Americas. Even the hostility and suspicion with which Christian Europe viewed its two significant non–Christian "others"—the Muslims and the Jews—cannot be viewed as more than a rehearsal for racial formation, since these antagonisms, for all their bloodletting and chauvinism, were always and everywhere religiously interpreted. (Omi and Winant 1994, 61)

In a footnote, they cite evidence for the emergence of anti–Semitism as anti–Jewish racism in eighteenth-century Europe, excising the relationship of anti–Semitism to anti–Muslim racism. If, indeed, religious persecution against Jews and Muslims was not part of a racial formation before the modern period, as they argue, could it still have been racism or evidence of the formation of a proto-racism? Further, there is a clear demarcation here between what is conceptualized as religious and what is conceptualized as racial. The former seems to be a category in flux and related to culture; the latter seems to be a category that is static and based in biological notions of naturalized difference. Omi and Winant continue:

> It was only when European explorers reached the Western Hemisphere, when the oceanic seal separating the "old" and the "new" worlds was breached, that the distinctions and categorizations fundamental to a racialized social structure, and to a discourse of race, began to appear. . . . The Europeans also "discovered" people, people who looked and acted differently. These "natives" challenged their "discoverers'" pre-existing conceptions of the origins and possibilities of the human species. The representation and interpretation of the meaning of indigenous peoples' existence became a crucial matter, one which would affect the outcome of the enterprise of conquest. For the "discovery" raised disturbing questions as to whether all could be considered part of the same "family of man," and more practically, the extent to which native peoples could be exploited and enslaved. Thus religious debates flared over the attempt to reconcile the various Christian metaphysics with the existence of peoples who were more "different" than any whom Europe had previously known. (Omi and Winant 1994, 61–62)

In this passage, the religious clash between the Old World and the New World is represented as a clash between Christians and indigenous heathens, thus eliding the Old World religious difference between Christian, Jew, and Muslim. For the discoverers, it was precisely their understanding of the religious other and of religious difference that formed the lens through which to understand *racial* difference in the New World. In this moment, religion was defined not only in terms of broad ideologies of belief, but also as states of being in relation to cultural notions of civilization and barbarity—as the terms of inclusion and exclusion within the "family of man." These were clearly innate and natu-ralized categories in which religion was regarded not just as belief but as a level of human evolution. Religion was thought of as a universal category of natural being in a hierarchy of civilizations—hence, the fervor to convert non-believers.

In *Racism: A Short History* (2002), George Fredrickson discusses the explicit relationship of religion to race in the conflict between Catholic Spain and Jews and Muslims in the fifteenth century and sixteenth century. His argument, however, follows a common tendency to use the modern term "anti–Semitism" to describe attitudes toward Jews in that era while acknowledging similar, if not worse, treatment of Muslims. As Fredrickson (2002, 31) argues, "In the late fourteenth and early fifteenth centuries an intensification of the conflict with the Moors heightened religious zeal and engendered an increase in discrimination against Muslims and Jews." The clash between Catholicism and Islam clearly had ramifications as an imperial shift was taking place. But as empires were shifting, power was also being displaced via the ideological containment of both Jews and Muslims. Like other historians, Fredrickson argues that Jews, as a minority community under the protection of the Moors, faced ongoing intolerance and pogroms that, by the late fifteenth century, had been transferred to Muslims.

For historians of race, then, the story of the race concept emerged out of the religious exclusion practiced in the fourteenth century and fifteenth century. For historians such as Fredrickson, these exclusions can be attributed to the anti–Semitism practiced against Jews, displacing any discussion of anti–Muslim racism and Islamophobia. In his magisterial *The World Is a Ghetto* (2001), Winant argues that the early sources of racism derived from competing imperial projects based in religious ideology. For European capitalism to expand, a religious other had to be created in Islamic rivals: the Turks and the Moors. Alluding to the conquest of the Americas and the Atlantic slave trade, Winant (2001, 41) argues that such treatment of the Muslims and Jews served as the paradigmatic example of racial othering and internal and external ethnic cleansing. Echoing Fredrickson, Winant (2001, 42) writes:

> The Jews were the early "outsiders" of premodern Europe. In the Crusades Jews were as fiercely assaulted as Muslims, and a series of expulsions drove the survivors from most of the later imperial powers as they were consolidated as nation-states (in the fourteenth and fifteenth centuries), and as imperial ambition dawned. The Inquisition, founded in 1229, came by the sixteenth century to embody fairly racial anti-semitism with its renewal of persecutions against *conversos* or *novos cristoes*. Now it was no longer the Jew's beliefs, but his or her essence, . . . that was seen as unredeemable; thus even conversion was not acceptable: only expulsion or extirpation would generally suffice.

The coming of racist violence and racism is curiously marked as anti–Semitism in this passage, a term that, as noted, came into usage in the mid-twentieth century. Winant attributes the shift in persecution from religious beliefs to the "essence" of Jews and their outsider status, but he easily could have been speaking of Muslims. Conversion to Christianity or death for Jews and Muslims was itself an act of shifting religious conceptions into racial conceptions. For the explorers, it is important to note, Muslims and Jews constituted an early category of religious and racial other to transpose onto indigenous groups of the New World. This model of race, as Winant correctly notes, was part of a shifting conception of religion as it related to notions of race. Spanish Jews and Moors could be racially cleansed through conversion and testing for the purity of their blood. In the dissimulation of religious belief, racialization became an issue of religious passing—hence, the phenomenon of crypto–Muslims and crypto–Jews—in which acceptance as a Christian meant adopting different styles of dress, appearance, bodily comportment, and religious ritual.

In the eighteenth century and nineteenth century, the story of the race concept followed a path toward secularization through the emergence of scientific racism and, subsequently, eugenicist philosophy that was shored up in the ideology of white supremacy throughout Europe and the Americas. Racism in its modern, Enlightenment form privileged biological difference as natural difference without including religion, which was seen as a discrete form of prejudice and persecution. Hence, the modern form of racism displaced religion and, consequently, Islamophobia as racism. The lingering effects of this displacement evoke a connection between race and religion in which Islam endures as an important feature of the early development of the race concept, offering important insights into the incorporation of Muslims into modern forms of racism.

Old to New: Muslim, Jew, Indian, Negro

The genealogy of the race concept that I trace thus began in the newly formed empire of Catholic Spain in the fifteenth century and sixteenth century and imagined its civilizational others in relation to the Muslim Moor and the indigenous people of the New World. As Nabil Matar (1999) and Anouar Majid (2004, 2009) have persuasively argued, this early recognition of religious difference dominated Spanish, and European, identity and may have provided philosophical and intellectual antecedents to the Enlightenment and its humanistic approach. In early Enlightenment philosophical thought, Islam was at the border, and at the margin, of the European imagination of the human subject (Majid 2004). This prototypical racism, which imagined itself as the antithesis of Islam and Muslims, shifted conversations about modernity and its provincialisms; it also created an important framework for thinking through contemporary racism, as well as the basis and existence of anti–Muslim racism. As imperial renewal was taking place in the Reconquista (Reconquest), clear ideas of race were being formed.

As noted earlier, historians of race often locate the origin of the concept in

Europe roughly to fifteenth-century and sixteenth-century Spain as part of the process of discovery that led explorers to the New World and, inevitably, to contact with Native Americans. The conventional argument places the formation of *raza* (race) in terms of the religious opposition of Christianity to the so-called American Indian heathen. Here, religion becomes the central feature from which to understand the development of the notions of biological and cultural difference encapsulated in the race concept.

Complicating this history, though, Matar (1999) points to a complex triangle that emerged in the exchange between Christians, indigenous peoples, and Muslims. As the empire of Catholic Spain expanded, it undertook the benevolent role of sending missionaries to spread the work of the Christian God to heathens in the Americas. It was through this interaction that notions of race were consolidated through ideas about nation and religion. The Age of Discovery came on the heels of the defeat of the infidel Moor and the expulsion or conversion of the Moors, along with the Jews, in the Iberian Inquisition and Reconquista.[16] For *conversos* (converts to Christianity), tests of religious purity conflated ideas of genetic descent and biology with those of religious faith and cultural notions of kinship. The distinction between *pater* and *genitor*, as that between legal and biological, demonstrated the symbolic and material importance of the notion of bloodline.

For the converted, religiosity was theoretically a social construct, not essentialized in the blood, and thus could be shifted to allegiance to a sovereign power such as Catholic Spain (Prashad 2001, 15; Smedley 1999, 67–69). An obsession with blood purity, however, led the Catholic church to issue certificates of *limpieza de sangre* (blood purification), which marked out the social boundaries of belonging, heritage, and genealogy. The notion of blood purity reinscribed a social consciousness of *castas* (castes) in which hierarchies of status placed those with "pure" Hispanic and Catholic genealogies above those with mixed, or "tainted," heritage. Mixed heritage was often, but not always or exclusively, associated with skin color and physical characteristics and with religious difference (L. P. Harvey 1990, 2005). Hierarchy, religious difference, and bounded notions of kinship often have been regarded as cultural differences rather than as racial ones. Nonetheless, they are important predecessors to the modern notion of race that solidified in the eighteenth century and nineteenth century.

In Catholic Spain from 1492 until 1614, when the official expulsion of the Moors ended, the production of biopolitical difference was not just based in the body; it also, importantly, classified a distinction between groups that otherwise could pass phenotypically for one another. From the perspective of a suspicious Catholic Spain, the Moorish body—or the Jewish body, for that matter—demanded cultural cleansing. By converting to Christianity, the argument went, Muslims and Jews could achieve religious cleansing. But Catholic Spaniards were still suspicious of the mind—that is, of covert practices by crypto–Moors and crypto–Jews—and the term "Moro" came to be associated with those who had darker skin color, even though most historical evidence does not support the idea that racial differences were visible between so-called Moors and Spanish Catholics (L. P. Harvey 2005, 3–10). Simultaneously, Catholic theologians increasingly articulated an anti-black racism that identified Islam partly with the complex Muslim populations in North Africa and West Africa (Gomez 2005; Majid 2009).

During the Inquisition, the term "raza" meant "blemishes" or "defects"— for example, in the phrase "sin raza de judios/moros (with no Jewish/Moorish blemish on their pedigree)" used in blood-purification certificates in the 1500s (L. P. Harvey 2005, 7, fn. 4). Throughout the Inquisition, when this racial logic of blackness was propagated to give meaning to suspicions not easily confirmed by visible characteristics, the issue of religious "passing" was of utmost concern. Religious passing came to be identified racially through the logic of darkening in which Moors were associated with darker skin color despite their actual appearance, and by relying on other kinds of available evidence, such as occupation, location of residence, dress, class and rank, and, for men during Inquisition examinations and "religious" riots, the foreskin.

Most scholars of race argue that the "animalization" of Jews and Moors as irredeemably evil; the creation of "monstrous races" in the margins of the known world; and the shift to viewing ethnocide as desirable mark the specific formulation of race in the medieval period and that exclusion was a precursor to practices of extermination and genocide (e.g., Fredrickson 2002; Majid 2004). In this moment of early racial thinking, evidence of "race" visible in bodily comportment, clothing, language, and cultural practices signaled supposedly inherent differences located in a Cartesian split between the body and the mind—that is, the body might represent one thing, but the mind could represent something else. This is an important point in the development of the race concept. Phenotype was never really everything; rather, it represented a number of discursive logics that connected culture to appearance, skin color, and all of the features that normally were presumed to stand in for race.

In addition, scholars often argue that Muslims were expelled from Spain in the context of war, but Jews were expelled as the result of longstanding anti–Semitism. Such historiography needs clarification. War and reconquest to consolidate Catholic Spain required that Muslims be recast as a racial other. Thus, anti–Semitism as an exclusive racial concept for Jews is a narrow interpretation. The use of conversion, although a messy business, points to the simultaneity of Jewish and Muslim religious otherness.[17] In other words, Catholic Spain constructed its enemy in Muslims and Jews as infidels, or heathens, and as non-believers in relation to Christianity. As Michael A. Gomez (2005, 5) argues:

> The Portuguese and the Spanish became well acquainted with Muslims, a diverse assembly of differentiated unequals that included Arabs, Berbers, Arabo-Berbers, and West Africans. Together, they comprised the unwieldy and heterogeneic category referred to as "Moors" by Europeans. Spanish use of the term *Moor* in the sixteenth century, therefore, was not necessarily a reference to race as it is currently understood. Indeed, Berbers and Arabs had had such extensive "contact with Negroes" that they had "absorbed a considerable amount of color." Rather, *Moor*, referred to a *casta* (as opposed to *nación*), a designation that "did not intend to imply a racial factor but rather a cultural characteristic—Islam."

This is not the modern concept of race. It is, instead, a concept of race that disregards the understanding of Islam as "cultural." Cultural characteristics, however, were an important aspect of the racialization of a heterogeneous group that could be classified only partially through phenotype and appearance.

Where physiognomy did not prove sufficient as a distinguishing factor, culture became a stand-in for racial difference. Muslims groups began to be defined via racial mixture and notions of blackness. It is here that the racial antecedents of the Semitic–Hamitic hypothesis are evident. Under this hypothesis, "Semites" as an ethnological category comprise Arabs and Jews, while "Hamites" (named for the biblical Ham) were those of the African-descended Negroids. These categories of identity were associated with a notion of Muslimness and of racial classifications based on ethnological difference. Further, fear of mixing bloodlines provided a pretext for classifying people according to the notion of "blackness" or "darkness," although it still did not provide a viable definition for groups that could blend easily into Spanish society. As noted, determining who was a crypto–Muslim or crypto–Jew after conversion was one of the central preoccupations of Catholic Spain, and the anxiety it produced created tremendous animosity against Muslims and Jews and against former practitioners of these faiths. That fear was an important feature in the transition from religious conceptualizations to racial ones.

On the other side of the Atlantic, Catholic Spain found other heathens who supported its belief in its own dominance.[18] In Christians' demonizing of Islam and Muslims, which prefigured colonial racism in the Americas, race gradually replaced religion as a way to distinguish among people, although in particular contexts race and religion remained interchangeable (Shohat 2006, 209–11). Thus, a triangle emerged that consisted of the heathen Indian, the Christian, and the infidel Muslim, and, as scholarship on the encounter between the Old World and the New World has shown, Native Americans were made sense of via stereotypes of Muslims. As Matar (1999, 98) explains:

> The Spaniards had partly defined their national identity through the encounter with the Moor and then the American natives. Because they had been well informed about the Muslims and their history, if only because they had been fighting them for centuries, once they began the conquest of America they applied their constructions of Muslim Otherness on the American Indians.

Contact with the Spanish led to a configuration of Indians as Muslims. Throughout the sixteenth century, and into the seventeenth century and eighteenth century, ideas about racial difference were encapsulated through religious difference and, in the case of Native Americans and Muslims, also through sexual difference. Muslims and Native Americans were classified as racially other—that is, barbaric, depraved, immoral, and sexually deviant. The stereotype of the Muslim, as presented in literary and theological documents, imagined the "Turk" as "cruel, tyrannical, deviant, and deceiving" and the "Moor" as "sexually overdriven and emotionally uncontrollable, vengeful, and religiously superstitious" (Matar 1999, 13). This creation of the figure of the Muslim as the Christian other became part of the ideological justification of holy war and imperial expansion.

The British imagination, by contrast, perceived Islam and Muslims through Spanish ethnologies of American Indians, which led to the configuration of Muslims as Indians (Matar 1999). That is, the British described American Indians as descended from North African Muslims and perceived them as having similar cultural practices and values, ranging from religious beliefs and rituals to marriage practices, kinship, and sexuality (Matar 1999, 101). Through Christian eyes, both Muslims and American Indians were seen as sodomites who engaged in widespread homosexuality. After the Moors were denounced by the

Spanish and other Europeans for engaging in perverse sexual behavior in North Africa and post–Conquest Iberia, such commentary was used in reports about Native Americans. As Matar (1999, 109) makes clear: "Nothing was more convenient to the *conquistadores* than to see the pervert as the Moor or the Indian. In America the homosexuality of the natives conveniently rendered them immoral in the eyes of the conquerors, thereby legitimizing their destruction, conversion, or domination—whichever best served the conquerors." Hence, drawing comparisons between American Indians and the Muslims of North Africa and Turkey implied perversity and lasciviousness. This inference, moreover, was based not only on sexual practices that were deemed immoral but also on the construction of forms of masculinity that were considered unsuitable to a patriarchal Catholicism. That is, the comparison of American Indians and Moors connected an othering practice with imperial desire: The ideological enemy created of the Moor in Christian Europe served the purpose of racializing Native Americans.[19]

As Islam and Muslims were eclipsed in European politics in the scramble of competing imperialisms, slavery took over the space they left open. Early on, black Africans were placed into a logic that paired them with Moors, Indians, and Jews. In the context of the American colonies, and then of the formation of the United States, religion was not far from the construction of the logic of nation and race. Racialized ideas about Muslims were transferred to African slaves to justify enslavement via claims of benevolent domination (e.g., the Hamitic hypothesis, which re-emerged in nineteenth-century and twentieth-century narratives of black Muslims in the U.S.) and, indeed, the forced migration of African Muslims to the Americas.

Infidel to Terrorist, Slave to Immigrant

The history of Islam in the Americas elaborates the religion's complex relationship to the race concept. Indeed, from conquest to slavery and the legacies they produced, Islam played an important role in constructing alternative ideas of self-identity to dominant modes of whiteness and Christianity. Throughout the early period of the U.S. racial formation, the genealogy of Islam in America remained mostly submerged. The incorporation of Muslims into American racial conceptions is undoubtedly complex, but in black America and immigrant America, Islam has played a significant role in shaping racialized identities in the context of what is perceived as a Christian nation.

Islam came to the New World with Columbus; converts, both crypto–

Muslims and crypto-Jews, arrived as sailors on explorers' ships. In addition, throughout the fifteenth century and sixteenth century, enslaved Muslim Africans continued to practice their religion in the New World; indeed, they launched the first series of slave revolts in Brazil that culminated in a major rebellion in 1835 (Diouf 1998, 153–63; Gomez 2005; Reis 1993). As can be seen from this remarkable history, which still requires much recovery, Islam remained a vital part of the history of the black diaspora (Curtis 2009). In the racial hierarchy that emerged among enslaved Africans, one axis of status was religion. Early on, Muslim slaves were identified using such racial terms as "overly tanned" and "Moor," giving an Arab valence to their Africanness (Turner 2003, 44). Such was the migration of racial and religious beliefs that European conceptions of the Muslim/Arab enemy persisted in the Americas.

The imperial struggle between European Christians and North African Muslims that ended in Spain's removal of its Muslims and Jews provided powerful ethnological knowledge to describe the foes of Christianity. The notion of the infidel Muslim as a menacing figure was transferred into the Americas as part of the reigning "common sense." Many enslaved Muslims were literate—both a sign of civilization and a potential danger to the white enslavers, who assumed they held a monopoly on knowledge and feared that enslaved people could harness their education in social and political organization. The awareness of Muslims' difference was further racialized by coupling phenotypic descriptions of Africans with ethnic classifications such as Mande, Fula, or Wolof (Gomez 2005). African identity thus was translated into racial categories in America in which religion and notions of culture remained central.

The history of enslaved Muslim Africans took a different path in the early twentieth century, when, seeking to displace notions of biological race, Noble Drew Ali and his followers founded the Moorish Science Temple. In doing so, they sought to identify not with enslaved Africans but with a different category—that of "Moorish American," or descendants of people from Morocco. The term "Moor," a common appellation for Muslims and Arabs in U.S. popular culture in the nineteenth century, was in direct contradistinction to the notion of "slave." (Take, for example, the case of Abdur Rahman, the so-called Prince among Slaves, who was defined racially as "Moorish" rather than as "black" once his royal lineage was revealed [Curtis 2009].)[20] For Ali's followers, claiming a Moorish background represented a shift from racial identification to ethnic and religious identification that, they hoped, would shield them from discrimination and prejudice. They even produced Moorish American identity cards as an alternative to being perceived as black Americans. But their blackness remained a visible fact in an America that defined proper citizenship and nationality through whiteness. Nonetheless, this early turn toward Islam and Afro-Asiatic solidarity is noteworthy because of its construction of a complex genealogical relationship to African Islam.

During the 1920s, this history of overlap took on greater significance in the multiracial interactions and alliances formed by the Ahmadiyya Muslim movement in the U.S. Richard Brent Turner notes that the Ahmadiyya movement, one of the first multiracial models of American Islam, provided an important link between immigrant Muslims and African Americans. The Ahmadis, who came from what was then an undivided India, disseminated information on Islam and converted white and black Americans; the movement's followers included Arabs, Persians, Africans, Tartars, Turks, Albanians, and Yugoslavs (Turner 2003, 110). In the U.S., the Ahmadis provided an important link between South Asian Muslims and the Nation of Islam and the Moorish Science Temple in forging pan–Islamic unity. The mission of the Ahmadi Muslims in large part was to overcome racial and ethnic separation that existed not only within the Muslim community, but in the U.S. and around the world. For many who followed the Ahmadiyya movement in the U.S., converting to Islam reiterated a belief in the possibility of the de-racialized Islam of Noble Drew Ali, a position maintained within the Nation of Islam.

As Robert Dannin (2002, 25) argues, economic displacement during the Great Migration and Great Depression, and the structural obstacles to gaining access to resources presented by organizations such as the Christian (read, white) church and labor unions, formed the context for the success of Islam among African Americans in the 1930s. For many in the black community, identifying with Islam seemed to offer a way around "race," as well as possible entitlement to full citizenship rights as Americans. Religion, it was believed, superseded race, an idea that Elijah Muhammad of the Nation of Islam also took up when he stated, "The very nature of the black man is a Muslim" (Gomez 2005, 315)—another attempt to subvert biological determinism via notions of religion and culture. Yet both the Ahmadiyya movement and the Nation of Islam remained trapped in the early-twentieth-century logic of race, which would not allow them to transpose their blackness.

For African Americans, identifying with Islam did not prevent racial classification. Indeed, this position miscalculated Christian America's longstanding antagonism toward Islam. Scholars of American Orientalism have argued that, throughout cultural, popular, and diplomatic history, Islam and Muslims have been part of the American imagination (Little 2002; Marr 2006). As Fuad

Shaban (1991, 2005) argues, the Puritan roots of American religious and political culture historically have positioned the U.S. in opposition to, and as suspicious of, the Muslim world. What he calls "Christian Zionism" is indebted to the legacy of racism and its emphasis on the religious difference that has pitted Muslims against Christians. The particular construction of American Orientalism posits a divine order in which religious and racial difference are part and parcel of imperial conquest, whether through the logic of Manifest Destiny or in the missionary zeal of Christian evangelism. Thus, identifying with an alternative religion to Christianity has represented a threat to the idea of American exceptionalism, and Islam, specifically, has threatened the maintenance of a U.S. racial and religious order based on the idea of white Christian supremacy. Further, claiming Muslim identity interfered with the established formation that saw race not as a continuum but as a polarity between black and white, even as immigrant Muslims of all kinds were beginning to enter the U.S.

The Syrian and the Hindu in America

As African American Islam gained ground in the early twentieth century, Arabs and Asians were being framed within established racial ideas in the U.S. In the history of the U.S. racial scheme, Arabic and Asian regions were often conflated in the racialized figures of the "Syrian" and the "Hindu." The so-called Syrian hailed from the late Ottoman provinces of geographical Syria that include present-day Lebanon, Syria, Palestine, and Jordan. In the late nineteenth century, many immigrants from these lands were also categorized as "Turks from Asia," including those who claimed Assyrian and Armenian descent (Moore 1995, 47). "Hindu" was a catchall term in late-nineteenth-century America for those from the Indian subcontinent, primarily immigrants from what today are the nations of Bangladesh, India, Pakistan, and Sri Lanka. The term "Hindu" did not differentiate between those who practiced the Sikh, Hindu, Muslim, and Christian religions—or, for that matter, subcontinental atheists.[21] "Hindus," as a proxy for South Asians, also overlapped with "Mohammedans" (Muslim and Christian Arabs, as well as South Asians). In the U.S. racial formation, this conflation of religious and racial difference extended into legal constructions of the foreigner as a threat and an enemy. U.S. legal history therefore provides a genealogy of legal-juridical containment of threats and perils imagined through racial figures. This logic is instrumental in explaining the history of exclusion that immigrants have faced (Hing 1993; Ngai 2004). The genealogy of the abject immigrant combines the notion of the foreigner with the idea of the enemy of the nation.

As David Cole (2003) demonstrates, detentions and deportations that have been carried out since 9/11 have been based on such precedent as the Alien and Sedition Acts of 1798, the Chinese Exclusion Act of 1882, the internment of Japanese Americans during the Second World War, and the postwar persecution of supposed communists based on political ideology. The Alien and Sedition Acts, authorized by President John Adams during a time of war, sought to detain, deport, and limit the rights of foreigners in order to protect the rights of American citizens. The Chinese Exclusion Act continued this pattern by providing a plenary-power doctrine of selective enforcement that also was later implemented in the internment of Japanese Americans. Selective enforcement is grounded in suspicion of designated populations that are defined through the articulation of race and nationality. In this scheme, individual culpability is replaced by group-based presumptions of potential threat, a feature that intensified after 9/11, particularly in the U.S. government's Special Registration system (Bayoumi 2006).

From the late nineteenth century to the mid-twentieth century, the racial threat posed by "Asians" was disarticulated from this broad category into specific nationalities, such as Chinese and Japanese. Nationality was also disarticulated in the case of the imagined threats of communism and anarchism; in targeting "radical aliens," the Palmer Raids of 1919–21 defined a foreign threat as a non–American ideology rather than as a particular non–American national group. The red scare is analogous to the amorphous War on Terror, in which Al-Qaeda represents a non-state actor. The U.S. Patriot Act follows these logics by pinpointing nationally based and ideologically based groups as the focus for pre-empting potential terrorism and by prosecuting immigration and criminal violations through a system of detention and deportation. By specifically targeting Muslims from Arab American and South Asian American communities based on national origin and the potential to adhere to an Islamic militant agenda, the U.S. government has followed a precedent of restricted liberties and suspect constitutionality (Chang 2002; Cole and Dempsey 2002).

A parallel legal logic has been expressed through the U.S. judiciary. Arguments in cases regarding access to citizenship rights for Syrians in the early twentieth century depended on racial classification and ethnology to define religious difference based on an opposition between Muslim foreigners and white Christian citizens. The racial label "Muslim," for example, was assigned to Arab Christians who, paradoxically, were racialized as the religious other of white European Christianity. In *Ex Parte Shahid* (1913), Faras Shahid, an Arab Christian, was cast as polygamous, conflating Arab practice with Islamic practice and thus denying him the right to naturalization. In *re Dow* (1914) took the relationship between race and geography further. Dow, a Syrian, claimed to be of the Semitic race (thereby distancing himself from Islam), and thus "white," based on a precedent that included European Jews in that category. The court, however, ruled that Dow did not appear to be Caucasian or of the Semitic race because "Caucasian" translated as having a European origin, and Syrian was defined, in an ethnological and geographic sense, as "Asiatic," "whether [a person was] Chinese, Japanese, Hindoo, Parsee, Persian, Mongol, Malay, or Syrian" (Moore 1995, 53). Thus, Syrians, who were regarded as a racial group from West Asia, were properly "Asiatic" and excluded from naturalization. This decision was reversed on appeal (*Dow v. United States* [1915]). Although the case ultimately established so-called Syrians' claim to whiteness, and thus their right to naturalization, the courts continued to view Arabs and Muslims ambiguously through the 1930s and 1940s (Gualtieri 2001, 2009; Naber 2000).

Concurrent with these decisions was *U.S. v. Baghat Singh Thind*, an oft-cited case in Asian American legal studies arguing that "Hindus"—that is, all South Asians, whether Sikh, Hindu, or Muslim—were ineligible for naturalization because the right to citizenship was based on popular notions of the white race. The court acknowledged that Thind was Caucasian based on an argument purporting North Indians' link to an Aryan race, even though common people on the street would not have viewed him as a white person (Haney López 1996; Moore 1995). The logic of popular racial consensus became the guiding precedent for cases that involved Afghans, Arabs, Persians, Syrians, and Turks—national groups that were categorized as racially other through their association with Islam. In this way, Syrians and Hindus, in their broad sense of identification, were connected through a logic of racial exclusion based on a definition of the U.S. citizen as white and Christian.[22] Through ethnological and popular understandings of racial difference, "Arab American" and "South Asian American" thus were perceived as similar categories.

The peculiar relationship of racial ethnology and popular racism, and their prevalence, are summarized in two unusual cases. The first, *United States v. Ali* (1925), centered on ethnological and lay distinctions between religion, ethnic, and racial difference. In the case, John Mohammad Ali claimed that, because he was an Arab Muslim, he was eligible for citizenship even though he had been born in Punjab Province in India. At issue was whether Ali was "Hindu" or

"Arabian," because the U.S. Supreme Court had already deemed Hindus ineligible for naturalized citizenship in U.S. v. Baghat Singh Thind. Ali said that he was not a Hindu but of Arab descent, a claim made by certain Muslim groups from the Indian subcontinent. The court, however, referred back to the decision in Thind to state that descent was not enough to determine whether one was Caucasian. Based on Ali's dark skin, the judge decided that he could not possibly be white (Moore 1995, 60). In a second case, In re Feroz Din (1928), the court again rejected arguments based on ethnological evidence of racial difference in favor of common understandings of race, denying citizenship to Din because his "typical Afghani" appearance made him more "Hindu" than Caucasian (Moore 1995, 60–61).

Thus, in a racial formation that defined difference in terms of whiteness and blackness, Arab and South Asian immigrants were complexly located between the poles. Histories of genocide, conquest, enslavement, and exploitation set the terms from which to racialize Muslims. Black Muslims, already racialized through ideas about skin color and slavery, became an exceptional threat through their association with a racialized Islam. Indeed, Arab Americans and South Asian Americans are linked to African Americans through this shared racialization of Islam. Thus, it is to blackness that Muslims are racially assigned, yet it is to whiteness that immigrants generally aspire for citizenship rights and class mobility. These precedents are important predecessors of the legal exclusion of immigrants and the making of enemies that has been mobilized in popular visual representations since 9/11. Yet these multiple figures of racialized Islam, from African to Arab and Asian, are differentiated through cultural ideas of nation, ethnicity, language, and other identifiers. To understand how this multiracial figure of the Muslim has been racialized, I briefly expand on the incorporation of religion into modern racism through biopolitics.

Homo Muselmann and Modern Racism

Michel Foucault (2003) argues that the rise of the biopolitical—that is, control over who lives and dies—comes with the presence of order, discipline, science, and the rise of modernity. In terms of the race concept, it was in the seventeenth century that religious difference was "biologized" into the kind of scientific racism that justifies racial difference according to hierarchies of social evolution and the binary of civilization and "barbarity" (a term used in the historical register to describe the regions of North Africa in which Arab Muslims live). Under scientific racism, religious meanings were evacuated in favor of identifying differences of a secular kind such that the difference between racial and religious became axiomatic. Scientific or biological racism was also reinterpreted through the frame of a secularized racism that disarticulated religion from phenotypic conceptions of difference. But this did not mean that religion was no longer a key component of the race concept and the practice of racism in the modern era.

The philosopher Giorgio Agamben discusses the use of the term "Muselmann" to describe the physical appearance of Jews at the Nazi death camp at Auschwitz.[23] Citing several passages from the works of Primo Levi, Agamben explains how the term was applied to people dying from malnutrition who, when seen from afar, were said to resemble "Arab Muslims" praying in a "swaying motion" (Agamben 1999, 41, 86). The origin of the derogation most likely lies in the meaning of "Muslim" itself—that is, one who submits unconditionally to the will of God. Quoting the *Encyclopedia Judaica*, Agamben (1999, 45) also notes that "Muselmann," as used at Auschwitz, "appears to derive from the typical attitude of certain deportees, that is, staying crouched on the ground, legs bent in Oriental fashion, faces rigid as masks." This description both signals an overlapping racial history of Jews and Muslims and attempts to undo their entanglement in a shared racialization by calling Muslims "Orientals" and describing them as supplicants with rigid dispositions, itself an old description of Muslims that relies on European stereotypes of the Turk and Moor based on bodily comportment. Hence, this particular conflation of the Jew as Muslim projects a racialized mutability as a condition and not only a religious practice that somehow becomes an essential character of the figure of the Muslim as represented in bodily comportment and practice.

On the surface, this example outlines how the racial state developed containment as a system of population control through notions of racial assignment, mutability, and comportment (Goldberg 2002). It is no accident that Muslims and Jews were tied together through language in the Nazi death camps. Indeed, as I have argued, this is a manifestation of European historical conceptions that understood Muslims and Jews as the racial and religious other of the Christian. In an important sense, the Jew was the internal enemy, and the Muslim, the external enemy.[24] Jews were seen as existing within the European nation, whereas Muslims were a competing nation. The logic that places Muslims outside of the modern nation-state remains a complex racial economy of inclusion and exclusion of religious groups within the contemporary national imaginary of Euro-American states.

The articulation of the Jew as Muslim at Auschwitz is part of a system of knowledge that differentiates religious difference as racial. Prevalent racial theories offered the Semitic hypothesis as an ethnological explanation based on religious and cultural similarity and classifications of related language families. These approaches were based in polygenist theories of racial division that explained the creation of separate racial groups through descent. These differences were important in classifying the moral capacity of particular social groups and, ultimately, a hierarchical classification of superiority and inferiority. Thus, scholars grounded their ethnological and linguistic explanations in a biblical anthropology that viewed Jews and Arabs as derived from the same racial stock. Indeed, many Christian theologians saw Islam as a heretical version of Christianity and as a corrupt extension of the Judeo-Christian tradition (Hodgen 1964, 303). In Nazi Germany, Semites were understood in opposition to elite Aryans under the theory of racial supremacy. Semites, for someone like the Comte de Gobineau, were a white hybrid race that had suffered from mixture with blacks (Arendt 1968, 174, fn. 39). As Mahmood Mamdani (2001) has argued, the related Hamitic hypothesis has been employed throughout the experience of colonial domination, manifesting most recently in the case of Rwanda.

In ethnological parlance, the Semitic and Hamitic races were classified as a family of people who spoke Afro-Asian languages. Yet between the cracks of this ethnological explanation also lurks a relationship to Islam. This is evident in explanations that emerged in the nineteenth century. In the case of the Semitic race, Arabs and Jews began to be disarticulated so that by the twentieth century, "anti–Semitism" referred specifically to anti–Jewish racism and excluded racism directed toward Arab Christians and Muslims. Under the Hamitic hypothesis, a wide range of cultural groups were placed within that racial classification, thus effacing religious differences (Sanders 1969). It was the idea of racial inferiority of Hamitic peoples that, for example, rationalized the enslavement of black Africans in the Atlantic slave trade based on biblical notions of scientific knowledge.

Both the Semitic and the Hamitic hypotheses began to unravel when decolonization began and nationalist projects that no longer relied on such notions of racial ethnology proliferated. Yet this mixing of racial ethnology and popular racism that connected Muslim to Jew was an important part of the process of historical racialization of diverse populations of Muslims, from Arabs and Asians to Africans in this conception, into one racial group.

Conclusion

The argument set out in this chapter recuperates Islam and the figure of the Muslim in the history of the race concept. In doing so, it places the history of the concepts of race and racism at the heart of the shared and overlapping relationship between Muslims and Jews in opposition to white Christian supremacy. Through my evidence, I develop a theory of the racial ethnology of the Muslim that is based on a racial ascription of bodily comportment. In other words, the racialized Muslim developed as a geographically external other through physiognomic interpellation, cultural representation, and social practice. The racialized Muslim, further, developed through the superimposition of cultural features onto non–Muslim groups.

To return to Islamophobia, religion is central to the history of the race concept. The "raceing" of Islam has taken place not in a vacuum but within the context of specific historical relationships. In the current racial formation, Islam and Muslims have taken on a familiar, yet strange, meaning that is often evoked in terms such as "war," "conquest," "terror," "fear," and "the new crusades." The racial figure of the Muslim ranges far and wide to include populations that hail not only from the Middle East, but Africa, South Asia, and elsewhere.

A pervasive logic connects the tropes of religion and race. The contemporary racialization of Muslims in the United States reconnects these histories. Indeed, this process ranged quite widely, cutting across notions of national origin, ethnicity, gender, and color. The contemporary Muslim in the U.S. is, first, what Nadine Naber (2000, 2006) has referred to as the "Arab–Middle Eastern Muslim," a conflation of Arab Americans with Muslims but also, significantly, with South Asian Americans and others, as is evident in so-called terrorism-related arrests in the U.S. of whites, Latinos, and African Americans. For the latter two groups, race and racialized religion present a double threat. Media analyses of the arrests of Latino and African American Muslims suspected of terrorist activities inevitably draw connections to ghettoes, gangs, and hip-hop music, all of which are also characterized as threats (Aidi 2002). Indeed, as Mahmood Mamdani (2004) argues, in the context of the Cold War and the subsequent War on Terror, religious identities are often cast as political identities that mobilize religious idioms. But it is equally appropriate to ask when such political identities become racialized in the engagement with modern forms of power. Here a broader view of modern racism as biologically and culturally based is required.

In the U.S. War on Terror, the Muslim is being incorporated into a racial formation that is already adamantly anti-immigrant. Certainly, anti–Muslim racism has much in common with anti-immigrant racism premised on social characteristics associated with "foreignness." As Vijay Prashad (2001, 120–25) has suggested, perhaps "immigrant" itself is a racial category in which xenophobia is expressed in perpetual scapegoating. Within the U.S. racial scheme, anti-immigrant racism and Islamophobia collapse people from several disparate social and cultural groups—Arabs, blacks, Latino/as, South Asians, and even whites—into the singular, threatening "Muslim" (Salaita 2006a). As American empire and exceptionalism expand in the domestic and global War on Terror, historic processes of disenfranchising communities of color through policing and state and popular violence persist by combining "the immigrant" with "the Muslim" in a reinvigorated racism that goes beyond the black-versus-white U.S. racial formation (Rana and Rosas 2006). This racism is also exported globally by states, in popular culture, and in pervasive political discourses and ideologies.

TWO

Racial Panic, Islamic Peril, and Terror

"Sand nigger," I'm called,
and the name fits: I am
the light-skinned nigger
with black eyes and the look
difficult to figure—a look
of indifference, a look to kill.
—Lawrence Joseph (1988), 27.

Outside the Law

Since September 11, 2001, a number of scholars have used the concept of moral panic to analyze the growth of anti–Muslim racism and Islamophobia (Ewing 2008b; Maira 2007; Razack 2008; Werbner 2005). The rapid escalation of racial violence that followed 9/11 normalized an atmosphere of racial terror whose logic was later demonstrated through the explicit use of gender-based violence and sexual humiliation in the torture abuse scandal at Abu Ghraib prison (Puar 2007; Razack 2008). This early moment of post–9/11 racial terror made visible a target enemy through which to enforce an emerging racial order through state policies, media, and popular culture. The moral panic that followed was instrumental in conceptualizing a coherent racialized figure to place within the U.S. racial scheme.

In this chapter, I offer a theoretical framework that connects moral panics to the concept of Islamic peril and the formation of a global racial system that incorporates the "dangerous Muslim" as a racial category. By focusing on two events—one an instance of moral panic; the other an instance of peril—I argue that racial constructions of potential terrorists are instrumental to anti-immigrant narratives that rely on ideas of illegality and criminality. Considered a watershed moment, 9/11 shifted the configuration of a number of groups that had long been considered racially ambiguous but had been racialized nonetheless; the events of that day altered the terms of dominance and subordination from which subjectivity is materialized, particularly for those caught in the middle of the emerging racial formation. What I here call "terror events" are instances of racial events that vary in meaning and influence as parts of historical and cultural memory. As a number of critical scholars of race have outlined, racial events—from race riots to regimes of racial terror and violence—are significant in solidifying the ideological grip of racism and the formation of racial categories (Gilroy 1987, 32, 154; Omi and Winant 1994; Silva 2007; Winant 2001). Imbued with meaning and historicized as part of a public imagination, the racial event works to unify moments that in fact have multiple meanings in experience and interpretation (Badiou 2005).

In the aftermath of 9/11, a moral panic set in that resulted in violent attacks and assaults across the United States. Muslims were not the only targets in these attacks; indeed, racial profiling was also done of those who appeared to be Muslim, including members of other faiths such as Sikhs, Hindus, and Christians, as well as Latinos and others with brown skin and "Muslim-like" features (Grewal 2005). In the eight weeks that followed 9/11, more than a thousand incidents of racial violence were reported, including the murders of at least nineteen people; attacks on places of worship, work, and living; and countless acts of personal intimidation and harassment (Ahmad 2004, 1266). Because of the racial logic that underlies profiling policies and domestic policing, legal scholars have argued the U.S. government was complicit in these vigilante and extralegal attacks (Ahmad 2004; Hing 2006; Volpp 2002).

The concept of moral panic is a useful framework for describing specific policies and practices of the U.S. government designed to contain Muslim immigrants who are identified as a racial threat.[1] As other scholars have noted, the regulatory policing of race through gender and sexuality intensified in a variety of ethnographic and spatial registers after 9/11 to include, among others, gay men of color in New York City, Arab American youth in San Francisco, and sex workers in Mumbai (Manalansan 2005; Naber 2006; Shah 2006). Although each of these groups has its own particular sociocultural context and historical nuances, the connections point to a widespread shift and widened reach of state policies, procedures, and practices.

Racial violence targeting Arabs, South Asians, and Muslims in the U.S. escalated throughout the twentieth century. In the first half of the century, the lynching of Nola Romey and the shooting of his wife in Lake City, Florida, and the bombing of a Syrian family in Marietta, Georgia, in 1929 were defining events that racialized Arabs in the Jim Crow South (Gualtieri 2009). The division of Palestine since the Balfour Declaration in 1917 and the oil politics of the Middle East in the mid-twentieth century consistently have been tied to anti–Arab racism and systematic repression that, in the second half of the century, would culminate in an escalation in hate crimes, assaults, and targeted destruction of property (Abraham 2004).

The early twentieth century was also a tumultuous period for South Asians in the U.S. Many South Asian immigrants came to the U.S. to work in agriculture in California and the timber industry in the Pacific Northwest. In 1907, South Asians were rioted against by white workers in Bellingham, Washington (Prashad 2000, 72). This "tide of turbans," as South Asian immigrants came to be called, became a racial wedge in the labor struggles taking place across the nation. This early wave of South Asian laborers was followed by larger populations of immigrants that arrived after 1965 as technical workers from the Indian subcontinent who, in the 1990s, would be incorporated into the U.S. racial scheme under the "model minority" myth, even as the population of working-class South Asians in the U.S. also grew dramatically. In the post–9/11 era, all of these demographic groups became suspect, racialized under a rationale that imagined them as part of a geographic and cultural continuum even though they were divided by nationality, religion, ethnic region, language, and socio-economic status.

As part of this racial thinking, the violence that immediately followed 9/11 most resembled a moral panic surging in waves through the U.S. population. In that moment, though, the moral panic was more like a racial panic,[2] the kind often compared to the fear generated throughout the U.S. after the attack on Pearl Harbor that led to the internment of Japanese Americans in the Second World War (Bayoumi 2008). Racial panics in American history are intimately related to sex panics, red scares, and other forms of acting out against social, cultural, and political difference that express modes of moral reform and regulation (Duggan 1995; Rubin 1984). Violence and persecution often follow these moments, as demonization and scapegoating become part of an exclusionary logic of purging problems and threats. Deviance then becomes the measure by which to reiterate the dominance of a heteronormative social structure and upward mobility through dispossessing others of their resources and rights (Duggan 2003).

The goal of such moral reform, therefore, is to maintain forms of inequality present in society and to sanction racial, sexual, and gendered regulation, particularly through the control of migration (Luibheid 2002). The concept of the moral panic thus receives its specificity through the contextual practices of national fear at the local, everyday, level that are then expanded through the creation of specific demonized figures. The role of the racial panic is to intensify the categories of racialization within the racial formation.

The comparative aspects of such racialization as they cross the axes of gender and sexuality rely on a reductive equation in which the Muslim is racialized not only in relation to terror, but also in relation to ideas of illegality and criminality that historically have been associated with racialized populations in the U.S. In other words, diverse groups of immigrants are imagined to possess related characteristics that connect them to suspicious activity. The conceptual linkage of connection and comparison relies on a logic of fungibility in which a number of objects, things, and ideas are conflated into a particular racial figure. The fungibility of comparative racialization imagines the racialized Muslim as a potential terrorist threat connected, for example, to border crossing by Latinos and militancy among African Americans (Ahmad 2004, 1278).

Comparative racialization operates not only at the level of different populations, but also at the level of different processes, such as migration, labor, and informal economies. The act of migration, then, becomes a suspect activity in which particular kinds of labor are deemed part of underground and illicit activities. In the case of the migration of women, for example, sex work and migration have been inextricably connected to poverty and trafficking, rather than to an implicit political economy of structural neoliberalism and economic survival (Shah 2007, 2008). Similarly, the post–9/11 Muslim migrant is suffused with the potential of terror through the rhetoric of illegality and criminality and the broad danger of an Islamic peril that has sociological, political, and cultural overtones that do not address issues of structural inequality in the global economy.

The violence that followed 9/11 profoundly connected normalized constructions of gender to racialization. Muneer Ahmad (2004), for example, has eloquently argued that the legal explanation of post–9/11 racial violence as "crimes of passion" is based on patriarchal and heterosexual constructions of men's humiliation. The archetypal logic of the crime of passion is based on the case of a husband killing his wife's paramour upon discovering their adultery. In this argument, hate killings after 9/11 are understood as crimes of passion committed in a context of love in which the feminized nation and the restoration of men's patriotic honor, with the "paramour" standing in as the illicit social relation of Muslim-looking racialization, are sexualized through homophobia and misogyny (Ahmad 2004, 1309). Thus, the crime of passion argument treats such crimes as morally understandable, although still illegal. In this gendered and sexualized rendering of post–9/11 racial violence, then, moral regulation through the law is explained through an affective response that constitutes social and political norms that designate sanctioned forms of violence, and the law produces ideologies of profiling that foment homophobia, misogyny, and racism that target Muslims and those who look like Muslims (Ahmad 2004, 1323–25).

Through the logic and language of terror, the construction of transnational migrants in the U.S. public sphere locates Muslims as both religious and racial subjects. In this case, multiple diasporas overlap in meaning and time as certain migrant profiles are collapsed with the illegal and criminalized activities of terrorism. "Terror," "fear," "panic," and "peril" are the rhetorical terms that organize these religious subjects as racial subjects and through patterns of multiple migrations. Migration, in turn, is imagined as part of a shadowy global underground economy of trafficking and illicit activity in which laborers become commodities, like drugs, arms, and other contraband. At the center of this construction are the logic, tactics, and strategies of a national security state that targets the racialized Muslim as an enemy in the global War on Terror. It is the articulation of this fear through a homogeneous racial discourse that allows the racial state to comprehend Muslims as a terrorist threat. Hence, false terror threats and the moral panics surrounding Muslims emerge out of a climate that forebodes the possibility of terrorism. To delineate the terms of the crisis, the Muslim folk devil is defined using adjectives such as "radical," "militant," and "fundamentalist," which permits the state to take certain kinds of action aimed at social control instead of protecting civil liberties and human rights. Social anxieties that rely on a racist logic, then, become permissible to achieve more effective social control.

Profiling the racialized Muslim means imagining levels of terror potential in which race, religion, and nationality are intertwined as fields of visible identity. The state is not merely an abstraction; nor is it a unified entity. As an ideological project, the state is constantly re-creating itself in a barrage of mythology to legitimate the illegitimate (Abrams 1988 [1977]; Corrigan 1994, 2002). The multiple faces of the state serve to rule and regulate populations and bodies cast as dangerous and threatening through moral, political, social, and historical subjection. Hence, the racial state, the national security state, the war state, the imperial state, and the postcolonial state represent the uneven application of power by the institution of the state to officially regulate informal sectors of the global economy, such as economic, social, and political migration.

For the fields of U.S. comparative ethnic studies and race studies, these racial techniques force a geographic reconsideration of Muslims from West Asia, South Asia, and Southeast Asia as part of their political project. This model of the Islamic world requires a rethinking of nation-based studies that, rather than dismantling the idea of nationality, must pay closer attention to historical and sociological models of comparative study and pan-ethnicity and pan-racialism (Espiritu 1992). Indeed, the example of the so-called yellow peril in Asian American history informs the construction of a Muslim or Islamic peril (Karim 2000) within the bounds of the U.S. and beyond. Simultaneously, Muslim Americans must be considered within a comparative framework, given that Arab Americans and other Muslim groups are part of ambiguous racial categories in the U.S. that are often categorized as Asian American, African American, and white (Gualtieri 2009). This challenge to the study of race and racism raises important historical questions in terms not only of the racial techniques of the state but also of the constitution of U.S. ethnic studies and racial studies (Maira and Shihade 2006). Beyond these fields of study, the racialization of the Muslim is now transnational and must be considered in terms of its global effects. Indeed, the work of panics and perils must be examined in the context of the role of the state in a system that enacts biopolitical difference in terms of race, gender, sexuality, religion, and civilization and the relationship to violence and terror that proceeds at a global level (Puar 2007).

"Terror" has become a keyword of the twenty-first century, even as some argue that its antecedents go back as far as the first century C.E. (Laqueur 2001, 7). In its simplest sense, terror is about manufacturing fear. The War on Terror seeks to manage this fear by making the categories of friend and enemy coherent (Anidjar 2004). Throughout the 1980s, U.S. foreign policy established terrorism as acts by organized groups against particular kinds of democratic states. The term "terrorism" was instrumental to the Reagan–Bush mandate to construct terrorism as an enemy of the state and the dominant paradigm of foreign-policy intervention (Collins 2002). Defining terrorism in this way made it advantageous to eliminate political and social opposition, most often in the effort to quash leftist movements. Using the language of counterinsurgency inherited from colonial military strategies, terrorism was easily interchangeable with low-intensity conflict and counterterrorism to propagate rationales for warfare and build consensual support among the U.S. public. With the advent of the global War on Terror, this strategy has spread to nation-states throughout the Middle East, South Asia, and Latin America that seek to eliminate domestic opposition groups.

In a useful definition of "terrorism," Eqbal Ahmad (2001, 17) calls it "violence that is used illegally, extra-constitutionally, to coerce." In Ahmad's definition, both the state and the law are potential instruments of terror, an argument that runs counter to postulations of terrorism as violence against the state. Talal Asad (2007), in an important analysis of suicide bombing, argues that the difference between state terror thrust on civilians and that inflicted by militants is one of scale. The modern state is able to destroy life on a much grander scale than militant terror can, yet it is state-sanctioned violence that is permissible, thus foreclosing the possibility of grieving victims of state terror though the affective responses of revering life or destroying it. As Judith Butler (2009) argues, this political subjectivity values human "life" as a modern telos in which those who disregard this life require destruction to maintain the properly living. Such rationales preclude the possibility of feeling horror, outrage, indignation, and grief over certain political atrocities, while others deemed morally reprehensible entail a vehement reaction. Terror, then, is an issue of proportion and of an affective distribution of unequal political responses.

This is not to say that the state has a single rationale when it comes to constructing terror threats. Rather, the mobilization and practice of multiple tactics, strategies, and ideologies have the effect of reinforcing popular discourses, particularly through racialization. As I argue, the rhetoric of terror in the domestic and global War on Terror is instrumental to constructions of racialized Muslims within the U.S. racial formation and a much broader global racial system. Terror enables the fiction of an enemy that goes beyond an action and continues to have an effect through waves of meaning (Zulaika and Douglass 1996). It is in this way that the use of panics and perils as techniques of racial formation are a fictionalizing process of risk, fear, and potential, but also serve the purpose of fictionalizing the racialized nation. This process has developed a vocabulary in the post–9/11 landscape that describes the terrorist, the criminal, and the immigrant in the racial figure of the Muslim.

The state as the arbiter of racial violence proliferates its exertions of power through widespread racial panics that resonate not only in the law, but also through the news media, in popular culture, and in social ideologies. In the midst of examples of racial profiling and the illegalization and criminalization of Muslims is a logic and history of a population considered a threat. Moral panics as a symptom of social control are also an expression of manufactured fear and racial formation. The anxiety over assumed threats is the result of a racist common sense that couples racial profiling with racial violence. By exploring the creation of racial panics and the constitution of an Islamic peril through the language of terrorism throughout this chapter, I map the shifting terrain of race and racism in which anti-terror is equated to anti-immigrant leading to the construction of a seemingly transparent racialized Muslim. Further, I explore how these techniques of fiction making maintain their effects through the biopolitics of racism. To describe this racial reasoning in the post–9/11 era, I recount the racial techniques in the state's use of the rhetoric of terror through panics and perils, through newspaper accounts, reports, and insights from ethnographic fieldwork. These examples lay bare how the state's logic of anti-terror becomes a form of anti-immigrant racism through moral regulation, policing, and immigration control.

Terror Event 1: Panic

On December 29, 2002, the Federal Bureau of Investigation (FBI), in collaboration with the Department of Homeland Security, released an alert identifying five individuals who were believed to have entered the United States illegally and to present a potential, and immediate, terrorist threat. News-media outlets quickly distributed this information across the U.S. and globally as a high-level terror alert, warning of a plot designed to disrupt the New Year's holiday. Pictures of the men, along with their names and possible dates of birth, were copied from the original FBI press release and prominently displayed in the electronic and print media. The FBI's press release stated:

> The Federal Bureau of Investigation is seeking the public's assistance in determining the whereabouts of the following individuals:
>
> ABID NORAIZ ALI, D.O.B. AUGUST 15, 1977
> IFTIKHAR KHOZMAI ALI, D.O.B. SEPTEMBER 20, 1981
> MUSTAFA KHAN OWASI, D.O.B. DECEMBER 11, 1969
> ADIL PERVEZ, D.O.B. DECEMBER 27, 1983
> AKBAR JAMAL, D.O.B. NOVEMBER 1, 1974
>
> The above identified individuals, whose names and dates of birth may be fictitious, are believed to have entered the United States illegally on or about December 24, 2002. Although the FBI has no specific information that these individuals are connected to any potential terrorist activities, based upon information devel-

oped in the course of on-going investigations, the FBI would like to locate and question these persons.

The FBI has been working with Homeland Security agencies (U.S. Customs, INS [Immigration and Naturalization Service], TSA [Transportation Security Administration]) to locate these individuals. The above information has also been disseminated to the appropriate law enforcement agencies around the United States and throughout the world.

Anyone with any information pertaining to these individuals is asked to contact their nearest FBI office. Photographs of the [sic] these individuals can be found on the FBI's website at www.FBI.gov.[3]

Although the FBI admitted that these "names and dates of birth [might] be fictitious," this did not cause the media to question the reliability of the information; rather, it served to heighten the risk of impending terror. Based on the release, as well as information provided during a press conference, the *New York Times* reported, "An administration official said it was unclear if the men were simply illegal immigrants or if they were involved in something connected to terrorist activities."[4] Instead of questioning the lack of specific information in the FBI alert and the plausibility of any "threat," the news media propelled the alert into a story about a heightened security threat and the need for vigilance. The rush to invoke a threat to security, and the panic that ensued, depended on connecting illegal immigration to terrorism. "In New York City, the police increased their counterterrorist efforts as a result of the warning," the *Times* continued. "The names of the five men listed in the alert have been sent to all police department commands." Hence, the FBI press release unmasked a number of uncertainties within the security and intelligence community that translated a call for questioning into a national security panic.

In this example, the ambiguous FBI alert contained a system of signs and symbols that were readily interpreted into a racialized figure, conjuring notions of illegal border crossing and terrorist radicalism. Such profiling is often interpreted as a cautionary measure that requires the definition of threats and dangers to national security. In other words, deterring terror requires outlining target profiles. In a caption, the FBI release stated that the men were of Middle Eastern descent and had entered the United States around the Christmas holiday. Here, "Middle Eastern" is an obvious stand-in for "Arab" and "Muslim." And marking the Christian holiday season amplifies stereotypical notions of Islamic radicals' desire to disrupt American capitalism's most important shop-

FBI terror ring, New Year's Eve, 2002. Courtesy Getty Images.

ping season. Because of the incoherence of the information, fear and anxiety spread rapidly. A faulty syllogistic logic unraveled in which the terms "illegal immigrants *may have* terrorist intentions" changed into the imagined "Middle Eastern illegal immigrants *have* terrorist intentions."

By January 2, 2003, the national panic over the terror alert had slightly subsided. Nothing had happened, despite the widespread warnings. The *New York Times* ran a follow-up article explaining the situation. It turned out to be a case of mistaken identity—or, rather, stolen identity. One of the five terror suspects, the individual identified as Mustafa Khan Owasi, was in fact Muhammad Ashgar, a jeweler from Lahore, Pakistan. Ashgar claimed he had never set foot in the United States but had attempted to travel to Britain two months earlier using forged documents. He was stopped at the airport in Dubai, where his false documents were detected, and was immediately deported to Pakistan. The *Times* article ended by stating:

> FBI agents investigating falsified identity papers are expanding their dragnet for a growing list of foreign-born men they believe may have entered the United

States illegally from Canada. Officials caution they have no specific evidence the men are involved in any terrorism plot, but said they may have connections to a fake-ID and smuggling ring that involves people with terrorist connections.[5]

This drew an even closer connection than the vague FBI alert between illegal migration, underground smuggling networks, and terrorist activity. Also, the misidentification of the Pakistani Ashgar as "Middle Eastern" in origin articulated how the terms of race, religion, and geography solidified during this panic. The circulation of the alert unwittingly revealed a system predicated on the social construction of threats to match terrorist profiles, the targets of which are not ambiguous but, for the purposes of public consumption, may be presented as such. This example demonstrates how the Islamic world and Muslims are homogenized as a single group to fit the needs of the U.S. security apparatus. Muslims, as embodied in the religious practice of Islam, are figured as ideological opponents to the United States. Such a representation serves to translate religious difference not only into cultural difference but also into innate and essential differences between the United States and Islam. Going against the logic of the U.S. racial formation that generally assigns race according to phenotypic characteristics, the War on Terror broadly defines racial phenotype in terms of Islam as a religion that is naturalized and biologized into Muslims' bodies. As a version of cultural racism this alternative geography defines terror as emanating from the Middle East, and from Islamic countries, as regions that are riddled with terrorists. Pakistan, generally considered part of South Asia, is part of a flawed geographic continuum that constructs terrorist threats out of global Islamic trouble spots, equating Muslim men with Arabic-sounding names, and purports the Middle East has a greater propensity for terrorist activity.

In this racial panic, the attribute of illegality connects migration to terrorism through the object relations of fungibility and dissimulation. Illegality itself is constructed as a global system that conflates the criminality of smuggling and trafficking with terrorism. The final statement by the *New York Times* confirms this by connecting immigration with terrorism in a logic that defines illegality as a set of practices and networks brought together through a causal link. Illegal immigration, terrorism, and trafficking go to together in this schema of interchangeable objects that ultimately work to control and regulate immigration through the rhetoric of anti-terrorism. In other words, uncontrolled border crossing brings not only dangerous people but also dangerous objects, ideas, and practices. In this sense, undocumented migrants represent potential terrorist activity. The body is itself racialized as a container of dangerous ideas and uses. Thus, in the range of post–9/11 regulatory policing, illegal immigrants, at most, represent the potential of terrorist violence and, at least, the manipulation of systems of migration and the violation of legal sovereignty. A second anxiety that appears in this construction of illegality is the apparent duplicity of the immigrants themselves. Using fake, stolen, and mistaken identities confounds systems of surveillance that cannot clearly differentiate bodies that might bear a close resemblance. As a frame of visual dissimulation, such interchangeable identities point to the threat of concealment that depends on the discernment of racialized biological difference.

Almost a week after the incident, and on the other side of the globe, the Pakistani press began to report the details of the increasingly absurd case. In an article dated January 8, 2003, the *News* (Lahore) reported that the FBI had been given fabricated evidence by a smuggler named Michael John Hamdani, who had been arrested in Canada in October 2002 on human-trafficking charges. His smuggling racket brought people from Pakistan to the United States via Canada and Britain. Hamdani, a Pakistan-born Canadian, voluntarily submitted to extradition to the United States, where he named the five men the FBI originally thought might pose a terrorist threat. Muhammad Ashgar, when interviewed, admitted that he knew Hamdani, but he also stated that his picture and false identity may have been used by another smuggler.[6] On January 12, 2003, another article appeared in the *News* based on an extensive interview with Ashgar, in which he stated: "Initially, I tried to dismiss it as a mistake our newspapers make daily but when I went home in the evening, every television channel was broadcasting the photograph with ominous warnings by American authorities. . . . I was horrified."[7] The FBI's mistakes were thus compounded by the panic that was generated by this assumed threat.

Ashgar worked as a jeweler and goldsmith in the lower-middle-class neighborhood of Krishan Nagar in Lahore. Developed as a colonial neighborhood in the early 1920s, Krishan Nagar had been known for its high number of Hindu jewelers and gold traders (Glover 2008, 149). After partition, however, most of the Hindu residents fled to India, and the neighborhood transitioned mainly into a residential area (renamed Islampura), although it continued to maintain a reputation for jewelry making. As an older neighborhood, it is removed from the newer commercial areas of Lahore where many of the lucrative jewelry shops are located. Many goldsmiths in Krishan Nagar service the wealthier jewelry shops that open in the city's new commercial developments. Thus, an elaborate and highly tiered system has been created, both geographically and economically, in which relatively low-wage jewelry makers operate in Krishan Nagar while wealthier shop owners and jewelry sellers operate in the elite developments.

It was in this context that Ashgar worked as a jewelry maker, and dreamt of owning his own shop. Married with three children, he wanted a better life for his family. To accumulate the capital needed to achieve his goals, he planned to travel abroad and take positions selling jewelry overseas whenever the opportunity arose. Relying on his social networks, he traveled to Dubai several times, building contacts and attempting to establish a history of business travel that, he hoped, eventually would allow him to travel to destinations that offered greater opportunity.[8] Eventually, Ashgar went to Hong Kong, where he sometimes sold costume jewelry and counterfeit merchandise. By his own admission, he had hoped to obtain a business visa to the U.S. or the U.K. It was in Hong Kong that he came into contact with Hamdani, who promised to help him travel to the U.S. Hamdani sold Ashgar the false documents that he later used in his negotiations with the U.S. authorities. A few days before the FBI terrorist alert was released, Ashgar had been deported by authorities in the United Arab Emirates and released to the Federal Investigation Agency in Pakistan.[9] He was held in Islamabad for seven days, where interrogators questioned him about his fake identity documents and his work abroad, and about the social networks that had aided him in obtaining these things. The intensity of the extended interrogation and incarceration terrified Ashgar; it is likely that he was investigated in connection to illegal smuggling and to Hamdani, who was already under observation by international intelligence agencies.[10]

The tragedy of this incident is that it relied on a system of racial formation that turns migrants who are simply seeking opportunity into villains. Migrants in these circumstances are easy targets for those who want to manufacture racial panics and emphasize the importance of moral reform, regulation, and social control. This racial panic solidified a connection between illegality, terrorism, and migration. It also constructed an enemy profile of "dangerous Muslims" that expanded the notion of "Middle Eastern" to all those with Arabic-sounding names; a geography that conflated Arab countries and Pakistan; and an image of illegal border crossing as a potential terrorist activity. The barriers to migration are now compounded by state controls that work not only to physically bar such movement, but to create an ideological terrain in which such migration of certain groups of people—namely, Muslims—is tied to larger threats of terrorist activity.

The process of conjuring Muslims as a racial composite is ultimately about how culture is translated into race to manage and configure fear, risk, and potential terrorism (Bayoumi 2006). Thus, the central factor in the racial containment of Muslims within the U.S. racial formation is the potential of a terrorist threat. This logic has a long history in the modern Euro-American conception of Islam and, more recently, in Euro-America's geopolitical relationship to the Middle East and Muslim countries (Little 2002; Marr 2005; McAlister 2005). The figure of the Muslim and the terrorist are expressed in moral panics that have continued to influence public opinion and awareness throughout the United States and Europe since September 11.

Mapping American Orientalism and Islamic Peril

In the early twentieth century, the terms "Near East," "Middle East," and "Far East" became strategic classifications of important geographic regions. The "East" spanned the area from Turkey to India and Japan, with Europe understood as the center. This was a way to divide up an area that had already become a subject of much fascination—the Orient—a mythic land in which the colonial imagination began to construct images and representations of diverse and heterogeneous groups of people. In the groundbreaking *Orientalism* (1978), Edward Said established a framework that many scholars have taken further. Primarily discussing French and British Orientalism in the Muslim world— what, for the most part, is considered the Near East and the Middle East—Said argues the Orient and the East became a homogenized whole through the discursive practices and processes of colonial scholarship and forms of knowledge production. The Orient, it was assumed, could be understood and categorized in relation to European civilization, and the civilizing mission of imperial Europe was to colonize the Orient and re-create it in its image.

As Lisa Lowe (1991) reminds us in her work on British and French Orientalism, this was a process of homogenization that was both constantly dividing and enumerated through scientific and rationalist discourses. Orientalism simultaneously homogenizes and divides; it represents a discursive formation that organizes race, class, and gender into a historical project. The difference in forms of Orientalism was also apparent in the geographic division of European and American interests. While European Orientalism concentrated on the Middle East, India, and China, American contact with the Orient focused on creating influence and ties in East Asia and Southeast Asia. American Orientalists nonetheless constructed representations of this entire region based on their domestic experience of Asian migrants to the U.S. and through the political and economic relations of the U.S. and Asia. Importantly, European and American strands of Orientalism articulate with one another to form a similar position in relation to Asia and Asians. Orientalism organizes racial difference according to understandings of class, gender, and sexuality. The significance of this lies in the range of discourses deployed to construct this difference. In this approach, it is not so much that Orientalism is one homogenous discourse but that it is one of the technologies through which discourse is produced.

American Orientalism also significantly combined these effects in reference to the "Other Asians," as Kathleen Moore (1995) puts it, to construct an "Oriental" world of Muslims and Arabs in America (Little 2002; Marr 2005; Schueller 1998; Shaban 1991). This is significant to the shaping of Asian America, a disciplinary and popular conception that for the most part has taken for granted that "Asia" refers to East Asia and, more recently, to the Pacific Islands, South Asia, and Southeast Asia. Muslims and Arabs are incorporated into this all-encompassing world of the exotic Orient and, importantly, contribute to the dissent against the legal discourse of American citizenship in the nineteenth century and early twentieth century. As John Tchen (1999, xvi) argues, American Orientalist thinking combined the geographic regions of China, India, and the Arab world as once glorious civilizations that had passed their prime. The next great civilization was that of American empire forged out of the pursuit of a manifest destiny that propelled it westward.

Orientalism placed Asians arriving in America in unusual categories. The first Asian immigrants in the U.S.—those from China and Japan—for instance, were commonly referred to as "Oriental." Legal, political, and popular discourse of the late nineteenth century and early twentieth century also employed the misnomer "Hindoo" for those who had come from the Indian subcontinent. "Hindoo" was a homogenizing category that referred to South Asian immigrants mainly from Punjab Province; it encompassed not only Hindus, but also practitioners of the Sikh and Muslim religious (Jensen 1988). The racializing narrative of the Hindoo as a religious category is also found in the history of the West's encounter with the "Mohammedans" of North Africa, West Asia, and South Asia (Shaban 1991).

The concept of "Oriental" solidified in movements hostile toward Asian immigrants. Local agitators eventually succeeded getting in state and federal legislation passed to slow the immigration of Asians and to exclude them from citizenship. This organized fear, cast as a "yellow peril," resulted in the Chinese Exclusion Act of 1882 and culminated in passing of legislation by Congress in 1917 to bar immigration of anyone from the so-called Asiatic Barred Zone. The zone itself was constructed using Orientalist practices of racializing geographical regions. This law mandated that any immigrant whose ancestry could be traced to the Asian continent or to the Pacific Islands would be denied entry as a so-called Oriental.[11] In 1952, this racial geography would again come into play when limited immigration was extended to the Asian–Pacific Triangle of East Asia and South Asia. This was an important policy in the U.S. government's postwar program of racial exclusion and containment.

The idea of the yellow peril placed Asians within a national and international context.[12] While containing the space of Asians as racialized immigrants, this fear was defined in relation to a notion of white supremacy. This was important domestically in terms of understanding Asians in the white imagination, and also in terms of a geopolitics that pitted the United States in competition with Asia. This construction of perils in U.S. history culminates in the Cold War era with the threat of various domestic menaces. As Robert Lee (1999, 146) writes:

> Three specters haunted Cold War America in the 1950s: the red menace of communism, the black menace of race mixing, and the white menace of homosexuality. On the international front, the narrative of ethnic assimilation sent a message to the Third World, especially to Asia where the United States was engaged in increasingly fierce struggles with nationalist and communist insurgencies, that the United States was a liberal democratic state where people of color could enjoy equal rights and upward mobility. On the home front, it sent a message to "Negroes and other minorities" that accommodation would be rewarded while militancy would be contained or crushed.

With the demise of communism and rise of international competition in the global order, Islam has emerged as the new menace, and the U.S. is focused on solving the problem via the War on Terror. Islamic peril is grounded in the history of American Orientalism that has placed the Muslim world in opposition to U.S. nationalism. Political diplomacy, popular culture, and the media construct the threats and dangers of Muslims in relation to other prominent constructed perils and menaces of the U.S. (Little 2002; McAlister 2005).

Terror Event 2: Peril

False alarms are symptomatic of the national security panics that take place in the United States. In the aftermath of 9/11, it appeared as if the U.S. racial formation had changed in a fundamental way. Arguments circulated widely that Muslim Americans had become the new suspect racial category. I argue, instead, that the process of racialization simply incorporated new forms of racial demonization and policing based in older histories of racism. In this moment, "the Muslim" emerged as a category of race that was policed through narratives of migration, diaspora, criminality, and terror. Arabs from Saudi Arabia and Yemen were suddenly linked to people from Pakistan and Afghanistan through a broadly defined notion of the Middle East; these same people were tied to Filipinos, Indonesians, and others who encompass the larger Muslim world. All of them are centrally linked to Palestinians and their struggle for liberation. In the New Year's terrorist threat fiasco of 2002, the connection of terrorism to illegal migration revealed some of the new logic on race and racial formation—first, that terror must be associated with illegal activity, an idea that presupposes that anything linked to terrorism, or its possibility, must be illegal. Because of their ties to the underworld of forged documents and smuggling, illegal immigrants therefore might be connected to the underworld of terrorist activity. It is in this sense that the possibility of terror is the new language of pre-emption, social control, and racial boundary making.

The place that Muslims as a category are filling in the U.S. racial formation is associated with the discourse on immigration, Islamic fundamentalism and radicalism, and terrorism. Further, the racial mapping of Muslims is increasingly transnational, linked to a geography of diaspora. For example, in mapping terror threats facing the United States and Europe, the *New York Times* charted what it called a "Terror Diaspora" of Al-Qaeda operatives targeting American and European interests. The *Times* described this challenge thus:

> It is a frustratingly uncertain business, hunting terrorism. The impulse is to want to connect the dots, so that a recognizable picture of the enemy will emerge. But the very nature of the quarry—secretive, multi-headed, loosely structured and passionate about staying so—keeps the picture blurry and incomplete.[13]

Hence the so-called Terror Diaspora demonstrates a shift in enemy for U.S. foreign policy that is linked not only to 9/11 but also to the end of the Cold War, a period marked by the transition from enmities between nation-states—that is, communist Russia and democratic America—to the isolation of rogue "terrorist" states, reconfigured as the "Axis of Evil," as well as those of drug cartels, arms traffickers, and the illegal underworlds of transnational criminal activity. For the intelligence industry, this kind of mapping is centrally about a clash of civilizations in which the impulse is to connect the "dots" to identify a uniform threat—that is, in one way or another, the notion of Islamic peril. This is informed by a racist logic that disregards causal links—and, for that matter, guilt and innocence—to find the "enemy."[14] In this logic, moral panics are necessary to the production of a larger peril that constructs a racial object of vilification. As a technology of terror prevention, racial panic manufactures an enemy for the state to mobilize against in the name of security.

The language of diaspora connecting Islam and terror was used after 9/11 by op-ed writers such as Thomas Friedman of the *New York Times*, who used assimilationist and culturalist arguments to explain terrorism and its appeal to Muslim immigrants. Rather than explore how racism historically has operated in collusion with the power to dominate, Friedman argued that Muslim diasporas must change their culture.[15] Muslim societies, he argued, are invested in a culture of terror (which somehow is an inherent trait) that explains the violent history of the Muslim world. This is a reified sense of culture that can be changed through "civilizational" growth and the adoption of market capitalism. Friedman's appeal to neoliberal economic strategy thinly hides a cultural racism that places the blame on Muslims by relying on a frozen idea of culture without regard for how power operates. The thrust of arguments like Friedman's, which channel the "clash of civilizations" arguments of Samuel Huntington and Bernard Lewis, is that it is up to Muslim moderates to change their society. Following this neoliberal idea of self-care and market reform, therefore, after 9/11 Muslims must become compliant subjects of the economic hegemony of the U.S. and the global North (Duggan 2003). Just as this kind of thinking homogenizes Muslims throughout the world, it arbitrarily places blame on an abstraction called "the culture of terror." But terror is a much messier business than this, particularly in terms of the role U.S. foreign policy has played in training, producing, and controlling forces of counterinsurgency (Gill 2004).

What is remarkable about the language of such arguments is that they fail to see any connection with the botched racial profiling, panics, and perils evident in, for example, the mistaken FBI press release discussed earlier. Constructions of Muslims as a racial group are drawn from a historical genealogy that comprehends Islam as the antithesis of Western modernity and that further perceives Islam as a threat to modernity and democracy and the freedom that they bring. These are not new ideas; they are, in fact, echoes of the historical confrontation of the Islamic world and the Western world. Both in Europe and in the U.S., this construction of a new racism has led to the rise of moral panics that places Islam as an enemy and a threat. Moral panics in this instance serve to consolidate fear by racializing conceptions of criminality in which criminality itself shifts from petty crime to terror and crimes against humanity. This thinking fits into the streams of anti-immigrant sentiment that have fed racist backlashes on both sides of the Atlantic.

An example of the kind of peril manufactured through these moral panics can be found in the capture of Khalid Sheikh Mohammed in March 2003. "KSM," as he is called in security and intelligence circles, has been described as a "paradigmatic" terrorist entrepreneur.[16] An outline of his personal traits in connection with the attacks on the World Trade Center and the Pentagon in 2001 describe him as

> highly educated and equally comfortable in a government office or a terrorist safehouse, KSM applied his imagination, technical aptitude, and managerial skills to hatching and planning an extraordinary array of terrorist schemes. These ideas included conventional car bombing, political assassination, aircraft bombing, hijacking, reservoir poisoning, and, ultimately, the use of aircraft as missiles guided by suicide operatives. (National Commission on Terrorist Attacks upon the United States 2004, 145)

Khalid Sheikh Mohammed—regarded as Al-Qaeda's third in command, after Osama bin Laden and Ayman al-Zawahiri—was captured in Rawalpindi, outside the Pakistani capital, Islamabad. The photograph released to the media depicted him as an ogre-like, slouching man stripped down to his undershirt and appearing to be in a stupor. He was arrested by Pakistan's elite police forces in collaboration with the FBI; during interrogations by U.S. officials, he admitted to plotting the 9/11 attacks, as well as to the bombing of U.S. embassies in Tanzania and Kenya, the murder of Daniel Pearl, and a total of some thirty-one plots.[17] Ramzi Youssef, who was found guilty of bombing the World Trade Center in 1993 and was also captured in Pakistan, is a cousin of Mohammed's through marriage. Following Mohammed's arrest, a number of stories appeared in the print media that followed a "making of a terrorist mind" narrative. Many of these stories, more often than not, contained migration narratives, as well as pondered the role of race, religion, ethnicity, and nationality to terror.

Mohammed was born in Kuwait to Pakistani immigrants from Balochistan Province, on the Iranian border. His parents had gone to Kuwait in the 1950s to work in the oilfields. Kuwait's stringent citizenship laws make it nearly impossible for foreign nationals to become citizens. More than 1 million of Kuwait's inhabitants, or about one-third of the country's current estimated population of 3 million to 4 million, are non-citizen labor migrants. Mohammed's father,

Ali Mohammed al-Jazmi, worked as a merchant; little is known about his mother, Halema, who it is believed to have worked cleaning women's bodies for burial. Mohammed was born in 1965 in Ahmadi, an immigrant town with a large population of foreign workers, many of whom are Egyptian, Palestinian, or Pakistani. This context forms the basis for journalistic explanations of why Muslim youth living in foreign working-class neighborhoods are discontent and alienated; it also provides an imagined geography that connects Muslim workers in the Middle East to South Asia.[18]

In the 1980s, Mohammed left Kuwait to study engineering in the United States.[19] It is assumed he became radicalized when he went to Afghanistan to fight against the Soviet Union and, later, became involved with the Taliban, with whom the Central Intelligence Agency (CIA) was directly involved in training (Rashid 2001). As a Pakistani national fluent in Arabic and English, Mohammed played an important role as a mediator not only for Arabs, Pakistanis, and Afghans, but presumably also for the CIA. Ironically, his linguistic capabilities and diasporic life story have led some reporters mistakenly to call him an "Afghan Arab," a term used to describe the many Arabs who stayed in Afghanistan and Pakistan after they were recruited to fight for the Taliban.

The case of Khalid Sheikh Mohammed is emblematic of an overwhelming trend to understand terrorism and the rationalization of it through the terms of Islam, migration, and alienation. For Mohammed, and for others with stories like his, the peril is not only one of terror but also one of migration. For example, the life stories of John Walker Lindh, Jose Padilla, Richard Reid, and other numerous Britons who joined the Taliban or Al Qaeda—and, more recently, the cases of Malik Nadal Hassan and David Headley (also known as Daood Gilani)—were reconstructed by the media mainly through the lens of pathological behavior, expounding psychological and social issues that created these figures and ultimately drew them to the terrorism of radical Islam and so-called jihadist culture.[20]

The real and imagined terror encompassed in the notion of Islamic peril envisions a network of sleeper cells connected by illicit transactions of money, goods, and people across borders. This kind of peril is nothing new: like the perils represented by Asian America, this kind of peril centers on ideas of immigration and cultural contestation of white supremacy. Here, in a modified form, the threat of Islam is placed against a larger global order, not only because of the potential of terror, but also because of the expanding notion of the U.S. racial formation brought on by the need to racially categorize Muslims as part of profiling and state security. The intelligence apparatus of the U.S.

Khalid Shaikh Mohammed

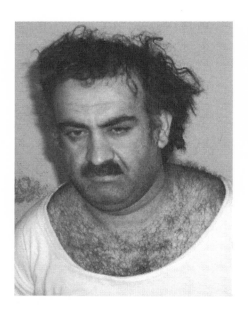

Images of Khalid Sheikh
Mohammed circulated by the U.S.
State Department and CIA (above):
in a suit as a potential sleeper
agent; and in traditional Arab
dress (courtesy Getty Images)
and (left) as a captured terrorist
(courtesy Associated Press).

government, alongside media and popular culture, map the formation of such threats onto a racialized geography of the world.

The visual representations of Khalid Sheikh Mohammed that have appeared in the press—at home in Arab dress, in Western-style professional clothing, and, more pervaseively, as a disheveled and disoriented captive—depicted a "model terrorist" that is mutable and can shift in comportment. The multiplicity of images of Mohammed reinforces what are believed to be other hallmarks of terrorists, who are trained not only to act in a chameleon-like way in sleeper-cell environments, but also to maintain multiple aliases and forged documents in order to confuse law enforcement.[21] One can argue that Mohammed, as a so-called terrorist mastermind, used the protocols of international migration to his advantage. But his profile is also undoubtedly paradigmatic of a narrative that the ideological War on Terror has used more generally to police transnational migrants.

Conclusion

In these examples, the biopolitical grammar of racism also challenges notions of kinship, sexuality, and the body. The pattern of understanding heteronormative modes of kinship is an idea central to assigning the logic of terrorist cell structure to notions of migrant patterns of kinship and gender. That the profile of the suspected terrorist is overwhelmingly male goes without saying, but this male subject is feminized in a heterosexual framework in which figures of the immigrant, the terrorist, and the Muslim are deemed to have abnormal sexualities, deviant gendered relationships, and failed domestic lives. As Chandan Reddy (2005) has argued in the context of framing the "gay Pakistani immigrant" in the struggle over immigrant rights in the U.S., notions of family and enforced heterosexuality within U.S. immigration law regulates a policed boundary that excludes queer subjects through assumptions about masculinity, heterosexuality, race, and terror.[22] This exclusion of migrants through sexuality makes certain figures within the South Asian diaspora (Gopinath 2005b; Puar 2007)—and in the case under discussion, the everyday life of the Pakistani transnational migrant—invisible.

Framing Muslim bodies through race, gender, and sexuality has naturalized the idea of the male body as a terrorist and, indeed, a migrant. The process of exclusion has eliminated women and families from this narrative in favor of ideas of cell structures as the language of kinship and family structure—thus eclipsing the notion of a transnational family structure. With the idea of clandestine sleeper agents ready to awaken out of terror cells, migrant workers are similarly framed through the invisibility and concealment of an underclass. Further, queer immigrants who do not fit the narrative of the heteronormative immigrant are in yet another bind through regulations that use the language of family to restrict sexuality-based rights.

The broader argument in relationship to migrants is that there is a logic of race and gender that depends on notions of kinship and cultural ideas of how social relationships are arranged for the racialized Muslim migrant. This logic depends on a racial and sexual economy to define the ideological values associated with migration that is then overlapped in a logic about the War on Terror. Suspects of terror plots in the current global War on Terror are more often than not immigrant men, whom the media read outside the context of family and social relationships. When they are read in terms of kinship, they are read in terms of male relationships, most prominently patrilineal and consanguineous terms of father–son and the metaphors associated with this relationship. The imagination of familial linkages works to further imagine the *biological* and social terms of the relationship. This can be seen as a rudimentary analysis of the most basic relationships of terror plots in which this relationship becomes a metaphoric one through the notion of fictive kin. Leaders of terror cells become like fathers, as do the benefactors of migrants who enter into paternalistic relationships in their transnational social networks. The reliance on modes of kinship to analyze terrorism and migration serves to analogize these two issues in the formation of narratives of race and racialization.

For some time, scholars of race have argued that the modern form of Western racism emerged out of the fifteenth century fear of Islam and Judaism. This did much to consolidate European ideas of Christian civilization against the peoples of North Africa, the Middle East, and South Asia. Race and racism have shifted a great deal since that time, yet the genealogy remains an important source of historical reference. As geographies of racism shifted from religion to race, Europe went from Christian to white, and the so-called Mohammedan went from Muslim to brown. With groups of people migrating throughout the modern world, racial geographies have broken down, only to be re-created in new ways. The historical shifts do not deny the meanings attributed to them as a possible rearticulation of racism. Hence, moral panics surrounding notions of an Islamic threat collapse the terms of the Muslim, the terrorist, brownness, illegality, and criminality into one rubric.

In the two events discussed in this chapter, the racial formation of a Muslim subject is made apparent in the use of the discourse of terror, racial panic, and

Islamic peril. Narratives of migration, illegality, and criminality are central to the explanatory frameworks that attempt to comprehend terrorism and thus to police transnational migration. The complex global system based on the concept of race; labor migration; neoliberalism; and imperial, colonial, and capitalist systems of exploitation are masked in this process of representing terror, race, and migration. The terms that connect terror to migration are based on establishing the figure of the Muslim as a racialized subject both in the U.S. racial formation and in the broader global racial system. This system of race making depends on the history of colonial labor migration discussed in chapter 4 that established state control of this movement and that, in the post-colonial era, depends on the apparatus of state security and the functions of a global economy that work through the strategies of neoliberalism, empire, and capitalism elaborated in chapter 5.

THREE

Imperial Targets

"What is it like for Muslims in the U.S. these days?" I was asked this question often when I returned to Pakistan after 2001. It was not hard to understand why: Several years had passed since 9/11, and the economic situation in Pakistan was becoming bleaker by the day. Many who asked were eager to find out how to get to the U.S. for the first time; others wanted information to plan an eventual return. An older man elaborated: "When I was in the U.S. twenty years ago, Muslims were doing really well, getting lots of jobs and making lots of money, but now it seems like it is hard to practice Islam. Is it true that Muslims are treated as badly as the blacks [in the U.S.]?" I asked him what he meant. "When we watch American movies here in Pakistan, the blacks are the ones that are treated badly," he said. "For example, . . . they were slaves, and now they live in terrible places and commit lots of crimes. The same thing with the Native Americans in all of the cowboy movies, where they get killed off. Is that what it's like for Muslims now?"

After pausing to confirm that I understood what he was saying, I continued the conversation by describing how the history of U.S. race relations made each group he had described into separate entities, marking their experiences as different and unique. Even though I offered historical context and was careful to provide a complex explanation, in the end it was just a long-winded way to affirm his suspicions. Although he did not use the formal terms of theories of race, his analysis probed a world of hierarchy in which racial formation is tied to structures of migration that often become part of migrants' calculations.[1]

Desi, Arab, Muslim

Newspapers and other media, popular-culture productions, and personal stories and experiences play a central role in the forming of global interpretations —in this case, of the Muslim condition in the U.S. after 9/11. In my conversation, the idea of the "Muslim condition" was itself a complicated one: It simultaneously referred to a broad, pan-ethnic, multiracial community of believers and evoked terms of possibility for labor migration. These comparisons point to the complex place of Pakistani migrants in the global racial system and their configuration through visual culture and ethnographic cinema. Cinematic representation in the post–9/11 world relies on using old imagery to conflate racial categories to offer seemingly realistic explanations of historical conflict. The blurring of fiction and nonfiction creates and perpetuates explanatory frameworks that depend on racial categories. The history of these categories of race making are particularly vexing in the case of U.S. populations of Middle Eastern and South Asian descent who are broadly racialized as "Muslims," because media, academics, and activists use the categories "Muslim," "Arab," and "South Asian" to describe groups targeted for racial discrimination, violent hate crimes, and state policing.[2] Although awareness of the differences among these categories is increasing, the process of merging them into the racialized figure of "the Muslim" is far more prevalent.

Pakistanis in the U.S., like many immigrants of the post–1965 wave, are a transnational population with a particular history and socioeconomic makeup.[3] Although the Pakistani immigrant population is generally understood as originating in South Asia, from the perspective of religious and social identity, Pakistan is considered part of the Muslim world that is collapsed into the term "Middle East." In the North American vernacular, the Middle East spans from North Africa to West Asia but, at the same time, most often refers to countries identified as ethnically Arab.[4] The Middle East, in turn, is constructed as a conflicted region marked by the struggle for Palestinian self-determination on one end,[5] and, at the other, the oil-rich and gas-rich former Soviet republics of Central Asia, leading to the porous border shared by Afghanistan and Pakistan —the front line in the global War on Terror.[6] The part of South Asia in which Pakistan is located has been fraught with conflict and war since the subcontinent was partitioned into India and Pakistan in 1947. The secession of Bangladesh in 1971 increased rivalry and enmity within the region that continues into the twenty-first century.

"Desi" is a crosscutting term used to refer to people of South Asian origin in the diaspora (Maira 2002; Prashad 2000; Shankar 2008). It has the most resonance for people from Pakistan and parts of central, western, and northern India and less meaning for Bangladeshis and Sri Lankans. As an overlapping category, it presents the possibility of a far-reaching identity that unsettles the divisions created by partition that are inherent in the category "South Asian," which came into widespread use in the 1990s. "Desi," nonetheless, is similar to "Arab" and "Muslim" because of its usage as a pan-ethnic category.[7]

"Desi," "Arab," and "Muslim" are important terms in constituting the racial formation that makes Muslims indistinguishable from one another in U.S. popular culture. Although these terms have their own histories and particular valences, the populations they refer to are often conflated to connote terrorism and immigration—rationales that are placed within the context of post–9/11 explanations of global conflict and violence. One version of the fictionalized, racialized narrative that flourishes in Hollywood productions and across the globe posits a structural explanation in which the global economy and historical circumstances have victimized working-class labor migrants into anti–American terrorism; more disturbing portrayals blame terror and violence on multiculturalism, upward mobility, and the access to resources for immigrants.[8] Such popular narratives are based on assumptions about the U.S. empire and its claims to benevolent imperialism. For example, in the context of the War on Terror, Muslim women are cast as burqa-clad, isolated, and suffering under the violent patriarchy of Islam and thus reliant on colonial narratives of rescue (Razack 2008). These narratives are rearticulated in terms of the colonial "white man's burden," imposing a sexual economy that claims white men must save Muslim women from Muslim men.[9] Incorporating the figure of "the Muslim" into the U.S. racial scheme thus involves translating these hierarchies and assumptions about domestic racial orders to global and transnational formations. To imagine this multiracial figure of "the Muslim," the concept of race— and its cloaked relation to Islam—is invoked in terms of the racial legacy of U.S. statecraft, at whose heart are subjugation and conquest. The expansion of this kind of racial logic to Muslim populations presents distinct challenges to theories of race and racism that include articulating anti–Muslim racism at the nexus of culture, religion, and race; the role of imperial racism; and the expansion of the global racial system

Race, Imperial Geography, and American Exceptionalism

Racial domination in the U.S. is not isolated to the domestic sphere; rather, it relies on a complex relationship to migration, transnationalism, and globalization that is more formally a global racial system. In its system of violent subjugation, older forms of racism that rely on mass extermination and genocide are integrated with late-twentieth-century forms of political racism based in foreign policies of abandonment and dispossession, as well as in the kind of cultural racism that views inherent "essences" as an explanation for broad social and cultural differences. What unites this social formation is the placement of the Muslim into the broad framework of an American empire that, via its chameleon-like characteristics, is able to hide elements of its domination in plain sight. In William A. Williams's (1980, 162) well-known argument, the strategy of American empire from the Civil War onward has been "annihilation unto unconditional surrender." This approach, which became U.S. foreign policy after the Second World War, extended the reach of American capitalism through surrogates such as multinational corporations and international banking reform. By creating a global marketplace, America dictated the terms of economic reform while maintaining "imperialism without colonies" (Magdoff 1969, 2003). In this configuration, branches of the U.S. military and intelligence services have been used to support state-sponsored violence (Gill 2004) while causing minimal disruption to domestic life and security.

The American empire also has taken a systematic approach to accumulation through dispossession by imposing an economic framework that relies on the violent means of permanent war and the politics of spectacle (Harvey 2003; Retort 2005). Imperial spectacles, as a way to gain popular consent for these policies, have involved the construction of a shared enemy by making that enemy visible while concealing covert forms of state power in the name of national security (Rogin 1993). By creating a racial demonology and domesticating it as foreign policy, these forms of spectacle and secrecy ultimately serve state-sanctioned domination (Kaplan 2002). In the twenty-first century, the return of overt domination through military means has made such imperial spectacles all the more apparent.

An example of such racial semiotics in imperial warfare can be found in the recent invocation of the term "Indian Country"—racial symbolism drawn from the colonial settlement of the U.S. West in the nineteenth century—by U.S. military personnel in the war in Iraq. Originally, "Indian Country" had multiple meanings. From Native American perspectives, it denoted indigenous territory and ancestral landscapes; to the U.S. military, it meant hostile enemy territory and active war zones (Silliman 2008, 237). In the current racial encounter, the Middle East as a social imaginary thus has come to stand in for the American empire's most recent colonial war. In the context of global racism and militarization, Muslims are compared to American Indians and are thus regarded as deserving genocidal violence. In a logic that seeks to justify state-sanctioned and socially sanctioned forms of killing, the attacks on September 11, 2001, on American soil by a non-state actor are being recast as a reference to reclaiming the supremacy of U.S. state sovereignty, an idea institutionalized in the genocide of American Indians that was imagined as protecting people and territories under the benevolent interest of American empire. Afghanistan, Iraq, Palestine, Lebanon, Syria, Iran, and Pakistan are all imagined as the "Indian Country" of twenty-first century American imperialism.

It is important to note that "Indian Country," and similar vocabulary drawn from western cowboy-and-Indian films, were also used by U.S. military personnel in reference to the Vietnam War (Drinnon 1990, 368–70, 451; Dunbar-Ortiz 2003, 2004). Through the landscape of a genocidal "Indian Country," U.S. soldiers employed the term "gook" in Vietnam as they do in Iraq and Afghanistan with the term "haji," an Arabic honorific for Muslims who have performed the religious pilgrimage to Mecca, that is made into a similarly derogatory and racialized epithet.[10] In this reframing of racial geography to achieve the American empire's global ambitions, therefore, enemies are renamed by transferring U.S. racial histories to international locations.[11] A rearticulation of the Middle East through motifs related to the conquering of "Indian Country" in the Old West is also prominent in the rhetoric of settler colonialism employed by Zionist immigrants reclaiming Palestine from Arabs (Salaita 2006b).

As Richard Slotkin (1973, 1986, 1992) has demonstrated, the U.S. war machine historically has used the myth of the American frontier as an ideological rationale to justify the aims of empire. The global War on Terror is not only about maintaining a sense of domestic security for the U.S. nation-state through imperial intervention; it also transcends spaces of domestic and international sovereignty by imagining enemies beyond the nation-state's boundaries. Ensuring homeland security requires racially translating foreign bodies and places into American idioms and domestic histories, which, in turn, requires making enemies visible abroad and at home. Such militarization is a complex process encapsulated in the imagination of imperial histories, racial geographies, and violent state policing (Hardt and Negri 2000, 2004; Harvey 2003). This is how "Indian Country" becomes a device to frame the enemy under the terms of panic, threat, peril, evil, and terror. Because "the Muslim" as a concept is far from coherent, it must be made into a legible racial category—albeit one that combines religion, nationality, and culture in a broad classification. Imperial racism makes claims of exceptionalism through racism without race (Hardt and Negri 2000) and the ability to do better than other models of empire (Stoler 2006). Hence, America's claim to exceptionalism involves constant nation-building and imperial statecraft by manufacturing enemies in wars of security at home and overseas. Using the term "Indian Country" is an important device in mythologizing U.S. empire via fictionalized claims to sovereign power, and it demonstrates an imperial logic of representation and meaning making that are central to racializing Muslims as visual targets of imperial spectacle.

Representing Targets: Imagining a Muslim Racial Formation

Throughout its history, the formation of the U.S. empire has depended on multiple, overlapping cultural technologies (Kaplan and Pease 1993). Racial profiling, policing, and the surveillance of immigrant communities are enabled by employing the concept of culture in a variety of ways. This is not only the singular idea of culture that can be bounded, contained, and readily defined but a constantly shifting and dynamic conception of culture that adjusts to imperial agendas. For the law to have an object of restriction, and for the state to have a foe, the constructed enemy must be made legible and identifiable in a common vernacular. It is in this sense that the visual cultures of popular representation create and target "the enemy" not only through images and appearances, but also through the meanings that are created when those images are juxtaposed within cultural, political, social, and historical frameworks.

In his influential book *War and Cinema* (1989), Paul Virilio argues that film representation is instrumental to the process of making targets of war, both real and imagined. As Virilio argues, technology is itself central to the violence of the screen that is transposed onto bodies in real time. This process of image making is a tactic of the war machine that seeks to control the production of the spectacle of new and different representations, whether it be of war or the enemy (Virilio 1989, 5). Influenced by Virilio's argument, and by Virilio's later invocation of the "information bomb" as a mode of representational warfare, espionage, and deception (Virilio 2000), Rey Chow (2006, 36) argues that "war and knowledge enable and foster each other primarily through the collective fantasizing of some foreign or alien body that poses danger to the 'self' and 'eye' that is the nation." In Chow's usage, the "eye" is the technology of framing the target as a dangerous monstrosity, which then justifies, citing the moral obligations of the state to its citizenry, the use of violence in war, and the production of representations of enemies. It is in casting the enemy as a foreign and racialized alien, often read as "immigrant," that the moral justifications for violence and war are made palpable for consuming publics. This is not merely a false representation; it is an active form of producing racialized subjects.

Certainly, there are no guarantees in how representations signify meaning because meaning can be constructed, manipulated, and restricted. As John Tagg (1988) has demonstrated, in the historical use of photographic representations, signification has been highly manipulated to provide a sense of objective fact. In other words, images have been made not only through what is depicted but also through the process of image making itself. It is this process, I argue, that reveals an important aspect of race making in visual culture. Through the mediation of the popular cultural forms of photography, television, and film, the figure of the Muslim is constructed as an enemy target.[12] As Tagg (1988, 2–4) argues, photography—and, by implication, film—is constructed, controlled, and limited by the technological changes that are part of the process of manufacturing images. Portraits, mug shots, passport photos, film stills: All provide readings as a disciplinary method of dividing the body as an object into parts and studying them as a series of indexical images (Tagg 1988, 7–8). This process of producing representations is thus divided into two parts: the constraints imposed by the technological medium, and the social practices of manipulation that suggest meaning.

In what follows, I examine the construction of the racialized Muslim as imperial spectacle in what Fatimah Rony (1996, 9) has called ethnographic cinema, an important technology and social practice from which categories such as "race and gender are visualized as natural categories . . . [at] the intersection between anthropology, popular culture, and the construction of nation and empire." Ethnography and cinema, in this argument, share a legacy of attempting to capture cultural essences through evidence such as cultural and religious practice, social and kinship networks, food, dress, social institutions, and other objects of the ethnographic gaze. For Rony (1996, 8), ethnographic cinema includes " 'art' [films], scientific research films, educational films used in schools, colonial propaganda films, and commercial entertainment films." Ethnographic cinema thus is a racial and cultural archive of visual representations that, in the post–9/11 era, conjures racial threats out of Muslim populations. Visual culture and media, whether based in fact or in fiction, imagine an enemy target out of the figure of the racialized Muslim, who potentially poses a danger to U.S. security.

Specifically, I argue that the television miniseries *Sleeper Cell* and the Hollywood film *Syriana* are elements of an ethnographic cinema that indexes the global War on Terror using the terms of the U.S. racial scheme and a broadly constructed global racial system. *Sleeper Cell* and *Syriana* contribute to the logic and the rationales that imagine Muslims and Islam as threatening by rear-

ticulating the cultural history of the U.S. with reference to militant black nationalism, multiculturalism, the politics of racial casting (Shohat and Stam
1994) and racial passing, the use of racialized geographies, and references to
class warfare. I end this chapter by reflecting on these issues in the film *Children
of Men* as a future present.

Visual Partitions: From Palestine to Pakistan in the Multiracial Imagination

Sleeper Cell premiered in 2005 and ran for two seasons in the midst of the post–
9/11 boom in terrorism-themed films, documentaries, and television shows.[13]
The critically acclaimed series, which aired on the Showtime cable-television
network, drew on social issues that originated in the post–Civil Rights era of
the late twentieth century to evoke the Age of Terror of the twenty-first century.[14] Set in race-divided and class-divided Los Angeles, an urban metropolis
rife with plots to subvert modern ideas of progress, it featured as its main
character an undercover FBI agent named Darwyn al-Sayeed, an American Muslim who has been planted in a terrorist sleeper cell. His objective is to infiltrate
the cell by gaining its members' trust, find out the means and intended sites of
its terrorist activity, and, ultimately, foil its plans.

The opening episodes of the first season introduced viewers to another
character: an African American Muslim inmate, played by Albert P. Hall, who
works as a prison librarian and serves as the contact to civilian sleeper cells.
Hall has appeared in a number of major war films, including *Apocalypse Now*
(1979), as well as in the third season of the popular television series *24* (2004).
Further, he has played two highly significant movie roles that represent African
American Islam: Elijah Muhammad in the film *Ali* (2001) and Baines in Spike
Lee's *Malcolm X* (1992). In *Malcolm X*, Baines (a composite character) is a black
inmate who introduces Malcolm Little to the teachings of the Nation of Islam in
which he functions as a sort of prison intellectual and conveyer of religious
knowledge. The similarity of this role to Hall's role in *Sleeper Cell* is striking, not
only in the development of a stock character by a single actor, but in the
ideological shift in U.S. attitudes toward Islam that these two different portrayals mark—that is, the transition from fear of the black nationalism of
Malcolm X to the dangers of post–9/11 multicultural and multiracial Islam.

In the post–9/11 version, American Islam is represented as superficially un-
threatening but ready to surface at any moment through a network of quiet,
underground sleeper cells. The themes connected in these two characters

played by Hall are the militant antiracism and anti-imperialism of the Nation of Islam and the idea of militant terrorism that is assumed to be a strand of Islamic fundamentalism within contemporary American Islam. The subtext, in other words, is that diversity stimulates an anti–Americanism that has long been present among American Muslims, whether they are African American or immigrants. The characters portrayed by Hall are significant in that, in the American imagination, they raise the multiple specters of race wars, liberation and civil rights, multiculturalism, and anti-imperialism, all of which are read as potential terrorism in the *Sleeper Cell* series. In the context of the rise of the Nation of Islam in the era of the Civil Rights Movement in the U.S., Islam is a militant form of liberation; in the context of post–9/11 America, Islam implies the racial, religious, and social threat of terrorism.[15]

Sleeper Cell is careful to parse this narrative by depicting mainstream Islam set against the dangers of radical Islam. The characters in the sleeper cell of both seasons are mostly new converts or recent reverts to Islam who, overtly, are subjected to some form of abjection. For example, the first season features a Bosnian Muslim who suffered through the genocidal war in the Balkans and who is seeking revenge against the U.S. government because he believes it failed to save his family because of their religion; a French convert who seeks to prove his devotion to Islam to his estranged Moroccan girlfriend; and a white American convert who, apparently, is rebelling against his mother, a feminist professor at Berkeley. The second season—featuring a female convert from western Europe who is a rape survivor; a Latino Muslim who is a former gang member; and an Iraqi brought up in a wealthy family in the U.K. who is struggling with his homosexuality and displaces the stigma to the war in Iraq—raises the bar in terms of the multiracial threat of Islam by employing a pantheon of non-normative characters. The show has been lauded for its depiction of diverse characters, even though these figures represent well-worn threats imagined via race and sex panics and offer pseudo-psychological frames that are based on interpreting Islam through models of sexual repression and unresolved rage. Within the quasi–Freudian frame, these archetypes offer easily intelligible explanations of terrorists' intentions while blaming liberal multiculturalism for unleashing diversity.

Sleeper Cell's main character, Darwyn al-Sayeed (played by Michael Ealy) is a second-generation African American Muslim who embraces orthodox Sunni Islam and has parted from the radical view of his father, who is a member of the Nation of Islam. As the heroic mediator of the show and its multicultural and multiracial cast of characters, Darwyn represents hope for American Islam—a

Darwyn al-Sayeed meets Farik al-Faris in a synagogue in the first episode
of *Sleeper Cell* (created by Ethan Rieff and Cyrus Voris).

kind that serves the security interests of the U.S. government to save human
lives—while grappling not only with his faith but also with misinterpretation of
it by his co-workers in the FBI.[16]

The dynamic of historical evocation via stock characters and actors' film-
ography is manipulated throughout *Sleeper Cell*. The episode "Al-Fatiha" ("The
Opening," also the title of the first chapter of the Quran) introduces viewers to
another character, Faris al-Farik, the leader of the sleeper cell. Darwyn is sent
by the Librarian (Hall) to a synagogue to meet Farik, who is using the purportedly ideal cover of an American Jew. Farik portrays himself as a model
citizen, dressing in fashionable suits and, in his spare time, coaching Little
League baseball. He also runs a private security agency, perfect for penetrat-
ing potential enemy targets—in this case, locations the sleeper cell will target
as sites of mass destruction. After a first, heated encounter at the synagogue,
Farik and Darwyn meet at a doughnut shop, where they discuss their roles
in the cell. The encounter opens with a discussion of racial appearance and
stereotype:

Darwyn: Shouldn't you be eating a bagel?
Farik: Most people from the Middle East look alike, sometimes even to each
    other. I've passed as Persian, Turkish, Coptic Christian, as well as Sephardic
    Jew. Don't African Americans have a long history of trying to pass for white?
Darwyn: I don't.

Though the discussion starts with a cultural stereotype (Jewish foodways as represented in a bagel), it quickly transitions into a comparison of racial assimilability and dissimulation of the Arab and Muslim body and African Americans' desire to racially "pass." In the logic of the show, this is the quintessential act of members of a sleeper cell: the ability to embed themselves in an unsuspecting community. Here, passing is a form of dissimulation in which race is mobilized for an ambiguous racial figure. Indeed, Arabs often have been cast as racially unclear, with a fraught relationship to whiteness.[17] Farik, who supposedly has Saudi Arabian origins, is played by the Israeli actor Oded Fehr, who is well known for portraying Ardeth Bay in *The Mummy* (1999) and *The Mummy Returns* (2001)—that is, another pseudo–Arab character, represented through the symbols of ancient Egypt and Islam, and, perhaps, a stock character of what Sunaina Maira (2008a, 334) calls "racialized Arab-face." The issue of passing also relays racial authenticity not in matters of cultural performance—in other words, how black, Jewish, or Muslim you are—but in matters of cultural intention. That is, identity is a practice, not just an appearance. In the allegorical context of the show, this shifts the idea of racial visibility to a broad set of traits, from phenotype and appearance to cultural practices and social kinship networks, to reimagine racial targets of surveillance, regulation, and policing.

The process of casting actors is only partially in dispute here; more accurately, I want to highlight the ways in which unacknowledged histories are embedded in such choices to further reinscribe political and social conflict. For example, the accuracy of Fehr's depiction of the Saudi Arabian character Farik is not as much of an issue (although most Arabic speakers notice that his accent is unusual) as the history and calculated grammar that is evoked by an Israeli portraying an Arab terrorist. Racial passing and ambiguity is triply played on in the dialogue quoted earlier in that an Israeli actor is portraying an Arab Muslim who is impersonating a Jew. It is not just any actor playing this character; hiring Fehr represents a culmination of choices based on the production and direction of the series as it overlaps with the written script and the chosen actor's performance. In this sense, historical interpretation is both hidden and in plain sight—much like a sleeper cell. The most immediate historical reference in this twist of casting, of course, is to the Israeli–Palestinian conflict, in which the Arab is viewed as a rational and calculating menace to modern secular society. Although such conflicts are discussed throughout the series, the debate is framed in a narrow and simplistic way that justifies imperial violence against the unjustified actions of terrorists.[18] In fact, the issues of Palestinian autonomy and Israeli colonial occupation are given scant space in the show; instead, the conflict is embodied in the Farik/Fehr character, which, in turn, is resolved through irrational violence. As neoliberal history via Hollywood, the show draws on Orientalist fear and stock characters such as the "evil Arab" (Semmerling 2006; Shaheen 2001, 2008); thus, its narrative of Islamic terrorism inevitably falls into a dyad in which the Israeli state is portrayed as an innocent entity associated with democracy, secularism, and rationality, while Palestinians are portrayed as reactionary, emotional, and violent and conflated with Islamic radicals and terrorism. The apparent symbolism of Palestine recasts conflict, struggle, and autonomy as the perils and threats of immorality, violence, and terrorism. Palestine is an embedded symbol of terror in the complex associations that figure Islam and Muslims into a racial formation.

This mechanism of portraying "Middle Eastern" and "Muslim" stock characters is also employed in relation to the partition of India and Pakistan. A number of actors of Indian origin have portrayed Muslim characters and, interestingly, Latino characters, perpetuating the kind of phenotypic racism that casts "Muslims" as brown-skinned and signifying a similar displacement, or in between-ness, in the U.S. racial scheme.[19] The profile conflates those who hail from India with those from a broad geography of the Islamic world most readily combined with the abstracted Middle East. The casting of these actors in a wide spectrum of identities, from Pakistani and Indian to Muslim, Hindu, and Sikh, follows the idea that South Asian Americans have a uniform, stereotyped appearance based on cultural attributes that vary depending on ethnic, national, or religious community. As an example of racial dissimulation, such casting reifies performances of racial passing as Muslim, Arab, Middle Eastern, or, simply, "Islamic terrorist," thus articulating these assumed identities as authentic. In addition, many of these actors have a diasporic personal history that reinforces notions that they are conversant in multiple social milieus and can tune their portrayals for the widest audience consumption. In other words, diasporic portrayals, which often contain multiple inflections of assumed locations, come to represent the authentic immigrant. Thus, as an example of what Shohat and Stam (1994, 189) call "the racial politics of casting," using South Asians as stock characters of Arabs and Muslims is not so much about an actor's ability to portray complex characters with multiple temperaments as it is about being able to reflect multiple racial and ethnic groups that fit broad stereotypes of populations to affirm racialized ideas of culture, comportment, and bodily ascription.[20] In producing this illusive "reality effect" via realistic depictions that use actors to convey racial authenticity (Shohat and Stam 1994, 180), stock characters and portrayals of 9/11-themed material is part of a didactic exercise in profiling the racialized Muslim.

Thus, In the post–9/11 era, the Muslim racial formation conflates Arabs and South Asians so that actors can play a broad spectrum of roles and representations. The histories that underlie narratives based on domestic terror schemes in the U.S. thus represent the full scope of the Muslim Middle East. Racial ambiguity and dissimulation are devices from which to racialize cultural, societal, and historical difference from the perspective of American imperial interests that requires a visible target—that of the racialized Muslim.

The Pakistani Labor Migrant in the Global Racial System

In the otherwise laudable film *Syriana* (2005), directed by Stephen Gaghan, the Middle East is portrayed as a place where Muslims of different backgrounds, whether Arab, Iranian, or Pakistani, coalesce into a unified racial figure.[21] The world of Muslims in the film's narrative is driven by oil, drugs, arms, labor, Islam, terror, and capital, in which the extremes of wealth and poverty are made apparent through competing geopolitical interests and transnational labor migration. As a portrayal of how globalization intersects a number of complex issues, *Syriana* presents a dazzling array of social and political problems with unusual nuance. In particular, it dramatizes class differences among various factions of the Muslim world in a realistic spectrum that encompasses drug-addled parties in Tehran, arms dealing by Hezbollah, oil politics in the Arabian Gulf, and, finally, the harsh lives of transnational workers. The last category functions to explain terrorism on the ground—that is, the recruiting tactics used to motivate youth to engage in violence. Unfortunately, the film's narrative rehashes the hackneyed explanatory framework of class warfare and ultimately falls short of providing what could have been an illuminating foray into the motivations behind, and devastations of, transnational labor migration.

Historically, labor migrants began going to the Middle East from various parts of South Asia in the first half of the twentieth century and have been going en masse since the early 1970s (Vitalis 2007). Labor migrants reflect the need in the Arab Gulf states for a foreign workforce to occupy the middle and lower tiers in such parts of the service economy as the oil fields and massive construction projects, as well as in professional fields such as engineering, health care, and information technology. Building entire cities from the ground up, South Asian laborers have been an integral part of development of the Arab

Workers waiting for buses surrounded by early-morning fog in *Syriana*
(directed by Stephen Gaghan).

Gulf region. Indeed, much of *Syriana* was shot on location in well-known worker camps outside Dubai, in the United Arab Emirates, to add a sense of ethnographic realism to the narrative.

One of the film's subplots focuses on the problems of a teenager from Pakistan who is increasingly disaffected with his life as a labor migrant. He, along with his father, faces humiliation through limited opportunities and degrading work conditions. In a scene that follows their dismissal from jobs at the oil fields, the father and son are beaten for speaking while standing in line to update their immigration papers—a depiction of the everyday brutality involved in the tight regulation of immigrants in a highly disciplinary police state. The father dreams of the snowcapped mountains of Pakistan, an allusion to the North-West Frontier Provinces, an area the U.S. media often represents as offering refuge to Islamic militants such as Al-Qaeda and the Taliban. Yet for him the dream of economic freedom is tied to family reunification and the aspiration to earn enough money to buy a home. The seeming impossibility of achieving this in the face of the hardships of working in a foreign country contributes to the son's desperation and, seemingly, to his susceptibility to militant Islamists seeking impressionable youth—an overly simplified resolution that does not question its own assumptions.

The code of this narrative thread in the film establishes the notion of "dangerous nationalities." Among the range of South Asian labor migrants living in the Gulf region, it is Pakistanis who emerge in the firm as dangerous and susceptible to Arab-led Islamic militancy. This logic is pervasive in defining these labor migrants as a whole. For example, one character who appears in a scene with an official wearing the head garb and beard of an Indian Sikh is credited not as an Urdu, Hindi, or Hindustani translator but as a "Pakistani" translator. Later, viewers are shown Pakistani youth at *madrassas* (Islamic schools) led by militant Arabs preaching anti-capitalist, anti–Western messages in favor of an Islamic utopia. A long list of visual cues and popular culture references in *Syriana* signal not only that Pakistan has becomes a central part of the Muslim world, but that it is responsible for the dirty work of Islamic militancy, an ironic parallel to the role of Pakistanis in the Gulf as a laboring class that does the muscle work for Arab bosses. In this imagined world, Pakistanis are not from the Middle East, but as guest workers they have become part of an indistinguishable Middle East ruled by their Arab co-religionists.

Syriana certainly should be applauded for its attempt to present a complex Muslim world divided by religious sects, ethnicity, nationality, and economic standing. Yet little differentiates the characters in the film aside from a classification of the dyads of Muslim/Arab/Pakistani versus American, wealthy versus destitute, and corrupt versus militant. From the perspective of U.S. foreign policy, geostrategic security translates into a map of political and economic interests. As a CIA official says in the film:

> India is now our ally, Russia is now our ally, even China will be an ally. Everybody between Morocco and Pakistan is the problem. Failed states and failed economies, but Iran is a natural, cultural, ally of the U.S. Persians do not want to roll back the clock to the eighth century. I see students marching in the streets; I hear [President] Khatami making the right sounds. And what I'd like to know is, if we keep embargoing them on energy, then someday soon, are we going to have a nice secular, pro–Western, pro-business government?

As a cultural mapping of the Muslim Middle East, North Africa, West Asia, and South Asia form the boundaries of a world that is not noncompliant with the interests of the twenty-first-century U.S. empire. In what is often described in film reviews of *Syriana* as a confusing narrative and a barrage of characters,[22] the figure of the Muslim ends up uniformly racialized as a problem. The Muslim social and cultural world is thus understood through the racialized tropes of Islam and oil glossed in the geostrategic terms of energy, governance, and economy. In this framework, arms, drugs, terror, and labor migrants are all assimilated into a single type of illegal and criminal commodity. As markets and economies that do not cooperate with the neoliberal marketplace crafted in U.S. empire, the countries in these diverse regions are made into problems that require economic sanctions and embargoes that justify violent military force.

Pakistani teenager at the helm of a boat becoming indistinguishable from a missile in *Syriana*.

In this logic, the potential to do harm through terrorism is regarded as a social and cultural attribute. In the emerging Muslim racial scheme, this potential is found in the bodies of those who are read as Muslim based on phenotype, dress, and bodily comportment, as well as religious belief and practice, and then essentialized as potential terrorists. In the biological metaphor of naturalization, cultural and social traits can be transmitted—that is, terror and its ideology are understood as socially and culturally learned and simultaneously internalized in the body. The metaphor becomes quite literal when the body is used as a weapon or instrument of terror. Indeed, in one of *Syriana*'s scenes, the Pakistani youth and a friend undertake a suicide mission by driving a missile-laden boat into a U.S. naval ship. By working against a logic that regards corporal essentialism as counter to the idea of learned behavior, the racialization of Muslims in *Syriana* incorporates both to exemplify how ambiguity is used to racialize religion (Bayoumi 2006).

In the context of the Muslim world, arguing against the U.S. empire's worldview or feeling alienated under capitalism immediately signifies the anti–American attitude that naturalizes terrorist violence. Indeed, in the suicide-mission scene in *Syriana*, the boys' bodies themselves act as instruments of rage and violence against a system that has marginalized them. Yet such an analysis is far from apparent, and although the act itself is supposed to speak for itself, it remains quixotic and inexplicable. In this sense, terror and violence are coded as part of a spectrum of general disenchantment among Muslims that requires vigilance. It is with this in mind that the established rubric of the domestic War on Terror mandates that migrants from the Muslim world become the primary targets of controlling terror. Specifically, South Asian workers in the Arab Gulf are imagined as the same migrants who go to Europe and North America, and as part of an endlessly expanding threat of terrorism.

The migrant is associated with criminal activity via a system of racial profiling that imagines culture and capital in terms of transformative power and imminent transportability. That is, associating with certain ideas, people, and resources has the potential to lead to terrorist activity in which the immigrant is imagined as a container and carrier of a violence-prone ideological disposition. In this conception, the body of the Muslim migrant translates into the interchangeability of terror objects in which resources can be exchanged or transferred into other commodities that might end in acts of mass destruction. Thus, for example, an innocent donation to an Islamic charity at a mosque can lead to the purchase of weapons for terrorist activity, further leading to a string of metonymic equivalences in which intention is placed on to the act of trading one commodity form for another. This analogy of exchange is translated to racial, ethnic, religious, and national characteristics so that fungible assets become another way to think about social and cultural traits that can be transmitted and passed on through learned behavior.

Migrants from the Muslim world, then, are imagined as dangerous in their unpredictable allegiances and potential to enact terrorist violence. The process in which arms, drugs, terror, and immigration are portrayed as commensurate with one another is rooted in state-sanctioned practices of racial profiling that signal an elaborate process of racialization based on chains of meaning in which the arduous life of labor migrants makes them susceptible to criminal and terrorist acts.

Discontent: Muslim Futures

The film *Children of Men* (2006), directed by Alfonso Cuarón, presents an imagined future set in the year 2027. Humanity is in crisis because human reproduction apparently is no longer possible. The central theme concerns saving the life of a young black woman who is miraculously pregnant (a reminder to the viewer of the racially, gendered, and sexualized economy of enslaving Africans). In this dystopic future, the division between the haves and the have nots is striking. For the wealthy elite, art has no historical meaning or value; those who must survive without amenities live in shantytowns and are forced to deal with kidnapping and urban warfare. The countryside is abandoned as a wild space marked by anarchic unpredictability. In the imagined future of *Children of*

Men, urban landscapes are a war zone whose inhabitants live under a constant state of homeland security; urban spaces uniformly have been transformed into detention camps, a metaphor for places such as Baghdad and Kabul that are suffering the perilous consequences of the nonfictional global War on Terror.

Children of Men projects elements of the contemporary present into the future to describe the consequences of historical amnesia, both to underscore the potential danger of forgetting history and to point to the progressive destruction of human, ecological, and technological relationships in the contemporary world. The film's future world is marked by mass migration, ecological despair, normalization of the police and warfare state, paranoia, and technological stagnation. Everyone is an immigrant, and birth is overwhelmed in the violent ravages of a permanent war on terror. The security state, facing extinction, has become a military state that resorts to violent policing in an all-out struggle for survival.

The brilliance of *Children of Men* lies in its ability to present a future saturated by the present; it foretells encounters with the police state and dissenting protesters in permanent struggle. For example, it portrays members of a resistance group, "The Uprising," wearing Islamic dress; graffiti and placards in Arabic are visible, and recognizable, as forms of protest associated with the Palestinian struggle. In fact, the Arabic word "Intifada" is written on the walls in a detention-center scene, pointing to the transformation of Muslim bodies into racialized groups of resistant agency in the context of a militant police state.

Migration and globalization thus are problems of containment. The migrant becomes an easy target for fabrications of terror and the hubris of empire. Activists for the future of humanity who turn present-day fears of so-called global security on their head are labeled terrorists and must cohabitate in spaces of migration with other enemies of the state in a system of detention centers run by "homeland security." An overabundance of migrants in the global North recalls contemporary fear mongers of the Christian right who claim that a demographic winter is coming in which migrants will outnumber all others because reproduction rates are falling;[23] ideological divides are thus conjured through class, race, and religion. The future imagined in *Children of Men* is an Orwellian world in which the only crime—or all crime—is translated into terrorism. In other words, migrants are terrorists until proven otherwise. This is a condition in which technology is used to assuage fears of migrants and terrorists and the looming figure of Islamic radicalism. As a response to security fears that operate without context, historical memory is buried in the collision of imperial

The future of global security dissent: Protest scene in *Children of Men*
(directed by Alfonso Cuarón).

expansion and the ravages of neoliberal capitalism. Thus, the failures of the
present become the dystopia of the future. And the future of the figure of the
Muslim is very much located in present migration, terror, and racism.

Conclusion: Consolidating the Racialized Muslim

In the immediate aftermath of 9/11, as everyday racial violence in the form of
hate crimes against Muslims, Arabs, and South Asians increased, working-
class migrants became the central targets of the U.S. security state, which used
systems of detention and deportation to control immigration.[24] As a lingering
threat of the figure of the racialized Muslim, transnational workers are the
hardest to imagine and codify in processes of globalization. This is partially an
act of concealing working-class lives, but also a basic misunderstanding of
how such transnational laborers are incorporated into the system of globalization. Labor migration throughout the twentieth century became part of a global
racial system that depended on the dictates of the global economy and newly
configured forms of social stratification. Working-class migrants across the
globe are racialized by imperial economies that extract surplus value as new
forms of sociality and subjectivity are constructed. Racializing the figure of the
Muslim and placing Pakistan into a geographic logic of the Middle East serve
the purpose of creating a visible population as a racialized threat.

The use of ethnographic cinema as imperial spectacle for the aims of U.S.

foreign policy derives from a history of geopolitical strategies of containment and economic control (Little 2002; McAlister 2005; Shohat and Stam 1994). The consolidation of a Muslim racial formation in post–9/11 ethnographic cinema demonstrates how Arabs and South Asians are combined into the racial figure of the Muslim. As emblematic problems in the War on Terror, Palestine and Pakistan are used to reconfigure the geography of the Middle East and the Muslim world to construct targets, enemies, and racial figures. This racial scheme mobilizes a logic based on essentializing phenotypic attributes such as skin color, along with notions of religious comportment, dress, and cultural practice. The examples of visual culture examined in this chapter point to the fear of multiculturalism in this Age of Terror that creates a wide range of terror threats. The narrative anxieties evident in *Sleeper Cell* and *Syriana* speak to the ambiguity of the racialized Muslim figure in its multiracial diversity even as their implied analyses of post–9/11 terror fail to account for that complexity. Instead, their portrayal of histories of conflict with the American empire, which emerge out of the confluence of oil politics, Islamic ideology, and transnational labor migration, further naturalizes the connection of terrorism and Muslims through a logic of covert cultural racism.

Although I argue that there are particular devices and strategies for manufacturing the racialized figure of the Muslim through imperial spectacles such as dissimulation, passing, multiracialism, and class warfare, these ideas draw on historical processes of subjugation at work in the U.S. racial formation. The process of consolidating an idea of the racialized Muslim involves conflating multiple populations in relation to histories of racialized oppression in the U.S. This involves imagining a broad geography of the Islamic world that places Palestine, Iraq, Afghanistan, and Pakistan, in a central position in the global War on Terror. Pakistan is recast as part of the Middle East through imagined geographies of conflict and through the construction of the figure of the Muslim in the global racial system. Thus, conflating such diverse populations as Arabs and South Asians into the racialized "Muslim" produces a visible target of state regulation and policing for consuming publics. The future of such logic is indeed dystopic and fraught with decay and historical amnesia, as presented in *Children of Men*.

To illuminate the complexities of migration in the global economy, I now turn to the specific study of transnational labor migration from Pakistan. Beginning at the source of much of this transnational work, I examine how the migration industry lures workers into overseas travel and how state practices of producing and regulating labor migration are part of the global racial system.

PART TWO

Globalizing Labor

FOUR

Labor Diaspora and the Global Racial System

On 5 August 1972 Idi Amin informed his country that "Asians came to Uganda to build the railway. The railway is finished. They must leave now." The state shortly thereafter expelled 50,000 Asians. We tend to remember this act only as an example of Idi Amin's heinousness, and we forget the hand of the British, who did two things: They created the idea that desis are only temporary workers whose culture is so transient that they can only make their lives in their homeland, and second, they made it very difficult for the Asians to enter Britain (whose "Commonwealth" was shown to be an utter sham by this episode). The social being of the desi is structured by this imperial racism.

—Vijay Prashad (2000, 100–101)

Driving in Lahore can be an adventure. The drivers' aggressiveness makes the cars seem like toys on a racetrack, particularly on the main thoroughfares that lead from the old city to the suburbs. When you enter a particular neighborhood, you also enter a puzzle with its own logic, in which street names and building numbers are not always sequential. On my way to meet the director of an overseas labor agency in the Model Town neighborhood, a colonial garden city built as a housing cooperative in the 1920s by well-to-do Sikhs, I got lost. Yet earlier in the week, I had found the location with little trouble. When I arrived for the first meeting, I waited alongside prospective labor migrants for a few hours before being told that the director I had come to meet would not show up. Traveling to the second meeting, I could see the street I needed to be on but kept running into streets that led in the wrong direction. With the mid-afternoon heat bearing down and my internal clock ticking, I started to get nervous about missing the meeting, so I decided to park and walk, making it to the building only forty-five minutes late.

Entering the office I exchanged salutations in Urdu with clients who recognized me from my earlier visit. They had been waiting since early morning, as they often did. The all-male clientele usually sat and exchanged stories or played cards until the director appeared. When they wanted food, they walked to a cheap eatery up the street. Many of these prospective labor migrants had come a long way, from villages and small towns, or were staying with relatives in the city until they found work. Some had been recruited by agents in their hometowns and sent to the offices in Lahore. As the capital of the Punjab Province, and with an international airport, Lahore is a major Pakistani hub for transnational labor migration.

I walked up to the secretary, also male, who looked amused and casually informed me that the director, who was a lawyer, would be stuck in court all day, although he might still show up. Exasperated, I sat down and decided to make the most of it. I had been in this situation quite often: Waiting is a common feature of dealing with any bureaucratic structure. During my field-work, I had visited many government offices and independent agencies that dealt with overseas migrants in Pakistan. Many of those offices are located in commercial and business districts; this office, though, was in a converted home in a residential area. The entrance and drawing room had been reshaped into a waiting area with seating, although most of the clients sat on the carpeted floor. The adjoining dining room and kitchen served as reception and storage areas, with pots of chai simmering for most of the workday. The master bedroom was the director's office.

Aside from its remote and hard-to-find location, what set this agency apart was how long it had been in business, the expensive advertisements it placed in Urdu and English newspapers, and the fairly lucrative and dependable con-tracts it obtained for its clients. It had started in the early 1970s mostly by delivering workers to the Middle East and had come to serve a cross-section of clients seeking jobs that ranged from unskilled and manual labor to profes-sional technical work. In a market where such firms turn over quite rapidly, this agency had developed a reputation for reliability.[1] One of the company's adver-tisements that ran almost weekly in the local Urdu and English newspapers promised opportunities in the U.S. The ad was hard to miss: It prominently featured an American flag.

I struck up a conversation with the secretary and the director's assistant, both of whom had worked abroad and had since become trusted employees of the broker. I asked them about their experiences abroad and then let out the question I had been dying to ask: why the American flag in the ad? Official government statistics, after all, told me that such contracts are rare compared with the hundreds of thousands available for work in the Middle East.[2] The response was simple: "This is everyone's desire. It's a possibility as long as you keep working and get experience by going abroad." I sensed that the answer was meant mostly for the clients, so I pushed a bit by asking whether they knew anyone who had gone to the U.S. Both said they knew lots of people, although they did admit that few had gotten such a contract through their office. I was certain the reception room was perking up; the assistant was, too, who felt that in his boss's absence he needed to clarify:

> Pakistanis have been working abroad for a long time, well before all of these jobs in the Gulf. All of us still want to make it to a place where the possibility of making a decent living is possible. Today that is the States. People also go to the U.K., Australia, Japan, but the dream is America. Before, during the time of the British, our people used to go wherever we were sent. We would end up in Uganda, Kenya, Fiji, or Mauritius and then come back, but a lot of those people never came back. They found a good life. Anybody who comes into this office is looking for the same thing.[3]

This was a fairly strong statement of sentiments about transnational labor migration I heard over and over from migrants themselves. Many Pakistanis have relatives or friends who have left for the U.S., Europe, or other points of the diaspora; migration thus is a common theme among the Pakistani middle class. The dream of migration, cultivated through word of mouth and prominent in Pakistani television serials, Bollywood films, and South Asian popular culture outlets, is pivotal in the mobilization of the transnational workforce. Even though I knew the history of Pakistani migration, I wondered about how exactly it created a sense of place and destination for potential migrants. More broadly, I wondered how the desire to achieve and maintain middle-class status by traveling to work abroad has been produced through historical constructions and systems of patterned labor migration and, ultimately, how this has been controlled by mechanisms of the state.

The director never showed up for our scheduled meeting. A few weeks later, however, he appeared after hearing I had been frequenting the office. During our eventual meeting, I heard much that I had heard before. In fact, the information was starting to sound rote—perhaps part of a standard script provided to labor migrants. He told me about contracts and the supervision of sending and receiving countries; he regaled me with stories of his company's success; and finally, he provided yet another lesson on the history of labor migration from Pakistan to other parts of the world. All of these stories conveyed ideas of possibility and prosperity achieved through perseverance and hard work. He was not the first to draw deliberate comparisons between the migration of indentured

Pakistani laborers under colonialism and contemporary migration, which is jarring not only because the "golden dream" metaphors developed by colonial agents continue to be used, but also because this narrative masks the true conditions of labor migration that make workers vulnerable to exploitation.

Risk and danger for labor migrants, a structural feature developed through the formalization of the market economy and state regulation in the colonial period, have intensified under the regimes of terror control in the post–9/11 era. As I discussed earlier, constructions of the Pakistani migrant as threatening develop out of a particular history that selectively places labor migration in a number of categories that serve the purpose of regulating states' borders (Sassen 1988, 1998). Coupled with a history of the race concept that makes "the Muslim" into an enemy category, labor migration is divided into a schema of formal and informal labor that imagines transnational workers and migrants as part of a clandestine, underground shadow economy that is easily recast as illegal, criminal, and terrorist in the War on Terror. The blurring of formal, temporary, and informal labor markets informs the widespread fears, panics, and perils that surround the Muslim/Pakistani labor migrant.

In what follows, I recount the historical trajectory that connects the period of colonial indentured migration to contemporary labor migration that pushes workers to the Middle East even as they imagine greater possibilities, such as traveling to the United States and Europe. These experiences of migration from Pakistan are structured through social encounters with other workers, employers, employment brokers, and the state. Transnational migration is an element in the shifting notions of social stratification that divide workers into a labor diaspora that has become part of the global racial system. I examine how labor migrants analyze social hierarchies in terms of a raced and classed masculinity and conclude by showing how some migrants turn to Islamic revivalist organizations to mitigate such experiences through the moral production of religious reasoning.

South Asia and the Formalization of Labor Diaspora

The history of how South Asian labor migration grew into a larger labor diaspora within the modern global racial system starts with the colonial project of indentured labor migration that began in 1838 and ended in 1917. Indentured labor filled a gap created by the abolition of slavery in the British Empire and the resulting labor shortages in the colonies of the Caribbean, Africa, and the Indian Ocean region. In this period, more than 1.5 million men and women from the Indian subcontinent went abroad to work on plantations in the Asian Pacific region, East Africa, South Africa, and the Caribbean (Northrup 1995, 20–21). As the British Empire expanded, this mobile workforce became pivotal to its success as a model of global imperial capitalism. The Indian subcontinent soon became an important hub in which people, institutions, goods, and ideas circulated as part of Britain's regional and global imperial project (Metcalf 2007).

Among the important British exports from the Indian colonial center, alongside the reserve workforce, were experiments in colonial statecraft, governance, police enforcement, and military rule. They created important parameters for, and precursors to, contemporary contract-based labor migration. Through varied policies of governance, the British Raj sent indentured workers to other parts of the empire, establishing official patterns of migration; through this institutionalization, it also made other historical trade and migration routes used by South Asians extra-official—that is, it placed them outside the purview of colonial sovereignty. Some indentured laborers followed existing regional routes, often mapping local migration patterns as concurrent with imperial interests, as trade destinations in the Gulf region such as present-day Saudi Arabia and Iraq show.

The indenture period also formalized the transnational labor market by instituting components of contracting and subcontracting as a neoliberal economic strategy; by creating a massive, temporary reserve workforce; and by generating new categories of "legal" and "illegal" migration with the new frame of a global racial system. The colonial state employed a legal apparatus that formalized migration based on contracts and institutionalized a recruiting system based on brokers, agents, and a system of disciplinary and bodily practices to examine prospective laborers. The formalization of the latter systems specified ranges of practice deemed legal and illegal as part of the formation of a formal and informal economy.

In the early colonial period, indentured labor was defined as temporary work and restricted by the state to periods of about five years. As experiments with this form of labor continued, it became clear that indentured labor easily blurred into an informal and unregulated economy even under the aegis of contractual guarantees and protections (Carter 1995; Kale 1998; Lal 1983; Look Lai 1993; Ramdin 2000; Tinker 1974, 1977). In these circumstances, temporary wage work was easily obtained outside the bureaucracy's supervision of official labor migration; it was also easily corrupted through the exploitative practices of colonial plantation owners who flouted official regulations. The boundaries of legality, as I argue more thoroughly in chapter 5, are blurred not only through the selective enforcement of regulatory procedures that is evident in contemporary labor migration practices, but also in the production of figures and subjects of illegality. Many of the laws and structures used to control migration in the contemporary period are drawn from colonial indenture practices, particularly bureaucratic and legal institutions such as recruiting agencies and migration laws that were developed to control migration. For example, many of the current laws regarding transnational workers from Pakistan refer to, or are the same as, laws drafted in the colonial indenture period (Gilani 1985).

The indenture period also formalized a depot system that served to regulate the bodily and biomedical condition of migrants, constructing a racial logic of suitable work based in colonial ethnology and producing an awareness among migrants of the work and geographic conditions colloquially referred to as the Girmitiya, a term referring to the colonial period of indentured labor migration. Becoming a formal market meant that labor migration was officially sanctioned by the British colonial state, and it was through this official recognition that the conditions of the informal market were simultaneously established. From the nineteenth century into the twenty-first century, the gap between "formal" and "informal" expanded through the processes of globalization and capitalist accumulation, which increased the demand for transnational workers who were desperately needed to build colonial, industrial, and postindustrial societies. To control migration flows, the state developed an arbitrary system of regulation that deemed migrants legal or illegal based on a historical and political context.

It has been suggested that the colonial indenture period should be understood as separate and distinct from postcolonial South Asian migration (Ghosh 1989; Mishra 1996). I argue, in contrast, that through the logic of formal and informal markets, the conditions of contemporary transnational contract-labor migration parallel those of colonial indenture. As Vijay Mishra argues the distinction between *diasporas of exclusion* grounded in hierarchies of domination under imperial and colonial control and *diasporas of border* that are emblematic of the cultural politics of hybridity in the postcolonial era (Mishra 1996, 2006) is an important historical device to separate these two periods based on the differences in systems of power and formation of diasporic identity. However, it also obscures some of the present historical connections and continuities.

Separating transnational migration into periods of exclusion and border is most useful when comparing diasporic populations formed from indentured labor migration in the colonial era with the professional, middle-class diasporas in the U.S. and U.K. since the Second World War. This comparison, however, ignores the complexity of working-class migration and labor diasporas that historically have emerged from South Asia. It also fails to articulate the continuities of state regulation and an analysis of power over historical time that have made migration a central aspect of South Asian and global history (Kalra 2009; Talbot and Thandi 2004). Structural market conditions that seek to exploit workers for maximum labor value have become a transnational phenomenon, but so have forms of labor-migrant consciousness and resistance strategies. Just as indentured laborers in Fiji constructed the imagined Girmitiya identity of resistance (Lal 1983), acts of organized struggle are now taking place among transnational workers in seemingly divergent regions of the globe, from the Middle East to North America (Das Gupta 2006; Mathew 2005). For certain contemporary labor diasporas, surviving the continual and brutal violence of the global racial system and the exclusion represented by border policing requires such strategies of imagination and polyculturalism (Maira 2009; Prashad 2001).

In addition, from the critical standpoint of political economy, these two histories are related through the imperial goals of empire building—from the age of British Empire to the current American imperial formation.[4] Under the British Raj, migration to and from the Indian subcontinent depended on direct capitalist expansion into new markets and military recruitment; in the postcolonial era, however, the process of empire building extends this market logic through the indirect control of international financial institutions and coercive military intervention. Such shape-shifting, flexible modes of empire and production, which drive workers increasingly to escape unemployment, economic crisis, famine, war, and other dire situations in their home countries, have caused labor migration to become increasingly transnational and, consequently, more vulnerable to excessive exploitation (Hardt and Negri 2000, 155, 253).

The current phase of American empire has extended this logic into creating informal colonies through a neocolonial model and, more recently, into a directly imperial one. In contemporary South Asia, the influence of the U.S. in the affairs of Pakistan and Afghanistan is part of this imperial logic. As a client state receiving U.S. economic and military aid, Pakistan continues to be subject informally to the ambitions of American empire that seek to secure regions from the Middle East to South Asia not only to guarantee resource extraction, but also to regulate transnational migration through the War on Terror (Ali

2008; Siddiqa 2007). In the context of imperial formation, the Pakistani labor migrant is a feature of a global racial system, and of a South Asian diaspora, in which work, labor, and migration are imagined in the terms of a fixed and racialized personhood.

Beginning in the colonial indenture period, the state system of controlling migration has generated techniques to produce migrants to meet economic and political needs. These techniques are now instrumental in constructing the figure of the migrant in the global racial system. In the contemporary period, the Gulf region has become a primary feeder of South Asian labor migrants to other destinations, including Europe and North America. The Gulf countries began serving as a hub as early as the 1930s, when South Asians traveled to work in the oilfields of Saudi Arabia, initially under the British and later under terms brokered by the United States and the Saudi government to trade oil for American military training and arms (Vitalis 2007). Movement between South Asia and the Gulf reached mass-migration levels in the 1970s, and the region continues to serve as a destination for working-class migrants from South Asia. In the past thirty to forty years, the Pakistani state has become increasingly involved in the production of labor migrants and in transnational migration that has generated a labor diaspora comprising millions of workers.

The system of indentured labor formalized through imperial expansion across Asia and the Americas provides an important point for comparative studies of world regions and the formation of a global racial system, from British colonialism to American capitalism. Recent studies, for example, have identified the racialized category of the coolie as central to defining meanings of indentured and immigrant Asian labor in nineteenth-century America (Jung 2006; Yun 2008). Similarly, such a framework continues into the present in the racial construction of labor migrants from Pakistan as Muslim, illegal, and criminal. Such a diaspora is not only a labor supply that enhances economic and social development, as much of the research on international migration has argued, but also an integral aspect of the global economy.

Labor migration today is tethered to a global racial system that manufactures meanings and representations from dynamics inferred from a South Asian labor diaspora engaged in multiple patterns of migration, including seasonal, step, circuit, and circular. Further, migration to the northern countries of Europe and North America is qualitatively different from migration to the Middle East. So for labor migrants, seeking work invokes a consciousness shaped by the terms set by multinational capital and transnational labor in which individual workers pursue specific forms of social and cultural capital. In tracing the work narratives of male Pakistani labor migrants, I examine the formalization of the official market for transnational labor from the perspective of the creation of a migration industry and the production of transnational modes of workers' consciousness that relate to labor conditions, transnational identities and masculinities, and encounters with risk and racial violence.

Recruiting, Racial Ethnology, and Worker Consciousness

The experiences of indentured migrant laborers from South Asia and other regions stand in stark contrast to the violence of the forced migration inflicted on millions of enslaved Africans. After slavery was abolished in the nineteenth century, Britain was able to continue its empire-building project primarily by recruiting Indian and Chinese labor under indenture contracts (Jung 2006; Look Lai 1993). The labor contract became an important site to define work and, significantly, the rights associated with work, thus allowing the state to intervene in cases of malfeasance. And the depot system institutionalized the process of recruiting prospective laborers.

The depot system involved a system of brokers, agents, and recruiters who worked on behalf of the state to find suitable workers. The depot itself was a waiting station in which the discipline and bodily health of workers was tested via regimented schedules based on colonial epidemiology. By the 1850s, major depots had been created in Calcutta, Madras, and Bombay and, soon thereafter, in Lahore and Karachi, and agents were being sent to villages and towns to recruit potential laborers. The state mandated that an emigration agent oversee both the recruiting of laborers and the appointment of recruiters, who were required by law to obtain licenses from the Indian Protector of Emigrants. Until they embarked on their journey to colonial plantations, migrants were housed in the depots, where they were brought into the subjectivity of indenture. As Hugh Tinker (1974, 137) wrote about this moment: "The labourer was ready to begin the process of becoming an indentured coolie; henceforth he was just one of many human parts in a vast assembly process." This subject formation revolved around ensuring the health, well-being, and productivity of the labor migrant. Workers were put through a course of inspections, documentation, and disciplining by agents and recruiters (Tinker 1974, 137–42). A variant of this depot system is still used in many sending countries to control the flow of migrant labor.

Under the British Empire, labor was imagined as a dynamic category based in historically contingent meanings and conceptions. It functioned as a kind of experiment in the colonies to test the limits of such abstract concepts as freedom, reason, and liberalism, with which the metropole would ultimately consent or disagree (Bagchi 1999; Chakrabarty 1989; Fernandes 1997; Kale 1998; Mehta 1999; Prakash 1990). Rising political opposition, for example, eventually led to the abolition of slavery, and the same would happen with indenture. "Free labor," based in colonial assumptions about freedom and the necessity of work, and the paired category of "bonded labor," which tied work to contractual service, were important terms in conceptualizing the indentured workforce. The idea of freedom to work was constructed in opposition to the outlawed practice of forced enslavement and presupposed the free will of the individual to enter into a work arrangement that offered a wage. The responsibility was thus placed on workers to enter into bonded agreements; the bond or contract, in turn, transformed indentured labor into a mutually agreed arrangement in which remuneration that usually included wages, housing, transport, food, and other necessary goods were promised in exchange for the timely completion of mandated work.

This formal arrangement, though, continued to have structural repercussions in the creation of official and unofficial marketplaces to sell labor, and the shifting meaning of the term "labor" enabled the state to control populations efficiently, especially in terms of expressing dissent and protesting work conditions. In other words, as the state's category of free labor shifted, new forms of social control were implemented to maintain an efficient and docile workforce, and the responsibility for migrants' well-being gradually was transferred from the colonial state to the workers themselves. The view that labor could be shaped to serve the particular needs of empire was an outgrowth of Taylorist systems of quasi-scientific management that depended on efficient categorization to create, maintain, and ultimately dispense a particular labor supply. Crafting a workforce meant meeting certain requirements through recruiting.

Before the colonial state intervened to establish a formal, regulated market, indentured migration followed patterns initiated during slavery. The regulatory apparatus that encouraged this early migration was based on coercion and exploitation. Creating a formal market established an official migration industry that served the purpose of regulating both the colonial economy and a direct regime of accumulation. In 1837, the colonial government of India passed the Emigration Act, which introduced the recruiting of Indian laborers to work on plantations in Britain's outlying colonies. The act stipulated that an intending emigrant must appear before an office designated by the Government of India, along with the emigration agent, who was required to produce a written statement of the terms of the contract. The length of service was to be five years, renewable for further five-year terms. The emigrant must be returned, at the end of his service, to the port of departure. The vessel taking the emigrants was required to conform to specified standards of space, dietary, etc. Each ship was required to carry a medical man to care for the coolies. An omission from the Act was the absence of similar requirements for the ships bringing back time-expired men to India. (Tinker 1974, 64)

The mandate to send workers to colonies without return was met with popular protest and agitation. Opponents, who drew inspiration from the antislavery movement, argued that regulated indentured migration, even with contracts, was state-sanctioned slavery. Also, the initial act contained sufficient ambiguity to make the potential for exploitation greater. For example, although the act specified conditions for transportation, they were fairly arbitrary and did not protect laborers from accruing debts through the commonplace practice of taking out high-interest loans with brokers and lenders. And leaving return passage out of the act, a key omission, created communities of permanent migrants in colonies because it placed the burden of paying for return transportation on workers who not only were paid meager wages but were remitting most of the money to their families in the home country.

Colonial preferences for workers were based on typologies of social difference generated through a complex racial ethnology that mobilized discourses of race, ethnicity, religion, class, gender, and sexuality to categorize populations through imperial ideas and sentiments (Stoler 1995, 2002, 2009). After the historic Mutiny of 1857, in which Indian soldiers recruited by the British East India Company started an uprising that led to widespread civilian rebellions, the British reorganized the Indian army along the lines of the fictitious "martial races," categories that the British defined through biological and cultural notions of race and masculinity (Puri 1983, 19; Streets 2004). Drawing on racialist theories and colonial knowledge, for example, the British defined Punjabi Sikhs as bold warriors, in contrast to Tamils from southern India, who were defined as weak and untrustworthy. Further, recruits from the Punjab Province were viewed as strong fighters yet docile in nature, making them ideal subjects who would follow orders, particularly when policing Indian civilians. Punjabis' experiences fighting abroad on colonial military expeditions were subsequently transposed onto worker-recruiting schemes (Metcalf 2007).

As Mustapha Kamal Pasha (1998) has argued, this process of recruiting, from the military sphere to labor schemes, required a structure of Orientalist racism. First, the recruiting of Indians into the military established a relationship between the colonial state apparatus and local Indian populations. Using principles of selection grounded in Orientalist ethnological categorization, colonial officers thus divided populations and simultaneously controlled them using native soldiers; this ultimately extended into the recruiting of certain groups as indentured labor migrants. Moreover, many indentured laborers came from agriculturally depressed areas prone to famine and thus could provide surplus seasonal labor in times of scarcity.[5]

The labor contract, however, was also instrumental in forming workers' consciousness (Lal 1983; Mishra 2005; Prashad 2000)—specifically, a "Girmit consciousness," named for the *girmit*, or the agreement South Asian workers in Fiji signed to return to their homelands when they completed their term of colonial indenture, reflecting their desire to obtain capital through transnational labor migration and developed in response to the exploitation of workers. For the Girmitiya, as these workers came to be known, the formal labor agreement constituted a specific relationship to the British Empire based on the exchange of labor for a guarantee of social and economic rights. Through layers of exploitation and deceit, however, the colonial edifice came to represent the trauma of migration.

The term "Girmit" thus was derived not only from agreement but also from betrayal. The racialized process of recruitment, deception by brokers, indignities of the depot system, hardships and suffering of plantation life, and corporal punishment were all elements that represented the idea of *non-agreement* in a hybridized *girmit* that was transposed into the affective being and working bodies of the Girmitiya. In this way, the girmit represented the unknown realities that became a condition of the Girmitiya in an ontological and affective formation whose expressions remained rooted in the unspeakable agonies of labor migration (Mishra 2005, 31). Complex forms of worker consciousness continue into the postcolonial period in which the promises of migration are contradicted by the risks and vulnerabilities of the experience of labor diaspora. The indentured Girmitiya, as an embodied consciousness of promise and betrayal, persists in contemporary working-class migrations as an affective condition of laborers' life worlds through the imaginaries of diaspora and exploitation that I discuss more fully in the next chapter.

In 1917, indentured migration sanctioned by the British Empire came to an end. The outcry against indenture by Indians in public debate had gained momentum, and the changing political economy of labor migration was becoming less profitable to the British. Simply put, the indenture system was not worth the argument. From the time the British indenture system was abolished until the Second World War began, the international labor market shifted to other patterns of migration in which state management was less formal. The global economic downturn of the interwar period brought less demand for laborers across borders, but it also marked a new era of experimentation with transnational workers from the Indian subcontinent, particularly in Africa and the Middle East. By the end of the 1940s, the rebuilding of the global economy and the rapid industrialization of several regions of the world required the large supplies of transnational labor that subsequently emerged as the standard solution to crisis in the world economy. Through this period of shifting structures of labor recruiting, a clear pattern of postcolonial labor diaspora began to emerge that would send workers from South Asia across the globe.

Globalizing Labor through Official and Underground Markets

In the early 1930s, South Asian labor migrants were recruited to work alongside Arabs, Europeans, and, later, Americans in the newly discovered oilfields of the Middle East. In the beginning, British oil companies implemented racial systems of labor control that benefited from the lessons of the indenture model. Americans later equally borrowed from Jim Crow systems of racial segregation and domination developed in the post–Reconstruction South to divide labor camps and subjugate workers (Vitalis 2007). Complaints about the mismanagement of contracts, the mistreatment of workers, harsh conditions, and violations of human rights steadily increased, and the first organized workers' strike in Saudi Arabia took place in 1942 at a construction site. The first outbreak of labor unrest involving an American-run oil refinery occurred in 1945 (Vitalis 2007, 92–93).

Further, by the late 1950s, large numbers of South Asians, many of them from Pakistan, had been recruited to Britain to fill labor shortages created by the Second World War. Much of the work was in the industrial sector, mostly in factories and mills (Werbner 1990, 2002). Pakistanis also traveled to the U.S. in large numbers after the Immigration and Naturalization Act of 1965 shifted preferences toward educated professionals; even more made the journey in the 1990s under family-reunification policies and travel visas (Prashad 2000, 78–79). North America has always had particular appeal for educated workers because of its need for highly skilled technical professionals and because it offers the promise of upward mobility. Because they are perceived as providing greater access to capital and resources, Europe and the U.S. have become symbols of wealth and opportunity in the imagined frameworks of potential migrants.

Throughout the second half of the twentieth century, a complex class formation emerged in the Pakistani diaspora in which working-class migrants—those who could not secure official passports and visas or did not possess highly prized and needed skills—traveled to secondary and tertiary locations to pick up skills and experience and establish social networks.[6] Southeast Asia, the Persian Gulf, and Indian Ocean regions became hubs of migration that welcomed less skilled and less affluent foreign workers to meet the needs of a complex service economy that required professionals, but also domestic workers, manual laborers, and guest workers in much larger numbers. These destinations mapped the patterns of the dynamic labor diaspora that has emerged as a central part of the global economy.[7]

By the 1970s, the migration of South Asian labor to the Middle East as temporary workers had reached massive proportions (Addleton 1992; Gardezi 1995). In Pakistan, migration for the most part was not regulated by the government until 1979, when institutions were established to oversee and protect overseas Pakistanis. Until that moment, much of the migration to the Middle East from Pakistan was informal and relied on personal networks based on word of mouth and kinship (Abella 1987). Throughout the 1970s and early 1980s—and more recently in the 2000s—the majority of labor migrants from Pakistan have been male and employed as temporary workers in the middle to lower tiers of the service economy. They worked in fields that ranged from construction and oil refining to driving and semiskilled air-conditioner maintenance. When the state began taking an interest in labor migration in the late 1970s, it initially became involved in facilitating state-to-state contracts and controlling remittances (Arif and Irfan 1997; Azam 1995; Irfan 1986; Kazi 1989). For the state, labor contracts represent a boon to the national economy (Azam 1995). Indeed, as one economist argues, remittances from workers in the Gulf kept the military regime of Zia ul-Haq afloat through the 1980s and continue to have a significant influence on the Pakistani economy (Zaidi 1999, 431).

Providing avenues of migration to the Middle East, however, also became a way for the Pakistani government to export domestic labor unrest and demands to reform labor laws. The boom in labor migration to the Gulf from the late 1970s through the 1980s occurred alongside upheavals within Pakistan that led to the formal liberalization of the economy in the 1990s and the consolidation of the military's stronghold in the social, economic, and political spheres (Donnan and Werbner 1991; Siddiqa 2007). In this process, people from a wide range of class positions—from the former peasantry to the landed and educated middle classes—entered the transnational working class.[8] This was a significantly different phenomenon from the migration of educated, middle-class professionals with access to the resources, cultural capital, and social networks needed for travel, education, and work abroad.

So-called temporary guest-worker systems in the Gulf blur easily into the informal economy. This flexible condition is widely accepted to maintain a reserve of temporary workers who can quickly be deported in times of crisis (Willoughby 2006), and this has become a general pattern in the global economy. In the twenty-first-century War on Terror, when labor migrants are broadly racialized and criminalized through the rubric of the informal economy, this allows host countries to define transnational migrants either as temporary and necessary or as part of clandestine and illicit networks of trafficking, depending on the circumstances. From the perspective of host countries, the proliferation of this transnational working class is ultimately about containing the reserve labor force in the global market. Because this process of control is largely enforced on a male workforce, masculinity becomes a site of regulation. In Pakistan, male workers historically have been the target population in the creation of the transnational labor market. Indeed, Pakistani government officials often cite the exploitation of women from countries such as Sri Lanka and Bangladesh to justify the country's all-male transnational workforce.

Female transnational workers, in fact, have been a driving force in changing the domestic economies, and restructuring of families in, India, Sri Lanka, and Bangladesh. Pakistani officials, however, often counter examples of such positive change by arguing for the need to protect the honor of Pakistani women. The circulation of media reports about the abuse of women employed as domestic workers, particularly in the Middle East, North America, and Europe, is one technique used to control gendered migration. In host countries, media coverage often focuses on the dangers of *labor migrants*, whereas in home countries, the stories evoke the dangers of the *labor migration process*. These narratives highlight not only transnational workers' vulnerability to exploitation, but also their vulnerability to racial and cultural assumptions. It is in this sense that labor migration for women in Pakistan is imagined as suitable only for those of middle-class, professional standing and not for the working class.

This gendered control of the Pakistani transnational labor market has led to a domestic economy that relies on remittances from male workers overseas and a feminized agricultural sector, as women and children are often left to tend to farming and other pastoral work (Kazi 1999). In the 1980s and 1990s, remittances helped to created a new rural middle class in Pakistan that could participate in conspicuous consumption both through duty-free shopping in the Middle East and at new retail centers in cities throughout South Asia. Money moved domestically and regionally in traditional ways, through government-controlled banking systems and tax structures, but also through non-traditional means such as informal money-transfer schemes.

Much of the debate surrounding the economic role of labor migration has centered on the material benefits gained by labor migrants. On the one hand, remittances sent back to Pakistan have played an important role in the national economy, as it has in other South Asian countries (Bagchi 1999). Some argue, however, that despite its short-term benefits, it is not a long-term strategy in providing income for labor migrants (Addleton 1992; Lefebvre 1999). Although there is merit in this argument, labor migration itself is based on short-term alleviation of shrinking incomes and dwindling living standards by providing access to temporary wage work. Transnational labor migration also has played an important part in economic development for working-class migrants. Many previously unskilled migrants were able to accrue enough money through the cash provided by remittances to start small businesses. This upward mobility has had an enormous impact on the Pakistani economy by broadening the distribution of capital (Gardezi 1995).

The Pakistani state has a vested interest in regulating the labor migration industry. Foremost, from the state's perspective, is the solution transnational labor migration provides to the domestic problems of underemployment and unemployment. Labor migration also creates jobs at home by supporting an independent and private industry of contractors who manage the system. Pakistan, as a sending country, is also interested in regulating the flow of remittances, which make up a significant share of the gross domestic product (GDP). Since 1980, remittances from transnational workers have represented anywhere from 3.3 percent to 8.9 percent of the GDP, and the percentage has been rising rapidly since 2001.[9] The percentage dipped in the early 1990s—a time of economic crisis in the Middle East brought on by the first Persian Gulf War, which reduced the demand for labor migrants, and of structural adjustment in Pakistan, which reduced the overall effects of remittances in the domestic economy.

Because migrants use both formal and informal banking systems remittances are notoriously difficult to track. The volatility of the banking system in Pakistan and constant collapses of the rupee add to the difficulty of obtaining reliable figures. In 2004, however, when the Pakistani government initiated schemes to promote the use of the state banks in an effort to curb smuggling and money laundering, remittances through official channels totaled almost $4 billion, and remittances through unofficial channels were estimated as high as $15 billion to $20 billion. In 2008 alone, remittances received from Pakistani transnational migrants easily reached more than $1 billion from the U.S., the U.K. and European Union, and United Arab Emirates each.[10] Economists estimate that the official figures represent, at best, half of the remittances that actually enter Pakistan. Much of the disparity results from workers' use of unofficial money-changing systems and informal banking networks, called hundi in South Asia and hawala in the Middle East, that charge lower fees than banks.

Since the late 1990s—and increasingly after 2001—the U.S. government has increased its efforts to track global financial flows. In response, the Pakistani government has tried to eliminate the informal money-transfer systems, both to alleviate the accounting problems created by a dual banking system in which large amounts of currency enter the country without benefiting the state and to create more accurate paper trails to make alleged criminal activity traceable. Along with migrants, smugglers and traffickers use the informal money exchange and money transfer systems. Without doubt, terrorist networks are part of the new international economy alongside the markets of exploitative capitalism legitimized by the state (Napoleoni 2005).

Labor migrants are often the biggest victims when ideas about these systems are collapsed. The informal economy places transnational workers, and their money, in global markets that are described variously as "clandestine," "underground," "black," "gray," and "shadow." This is how Pakistani migrants who use informal systems to obtain employment, transfer money, and purchase commodities become identified as racial deviants who must be policed and regulated in the War on Terror. As recent ethnographic work has shown, transnational networks of crime, money, and power are increasingly blurred through the contemporary modes of the global economy (Nordstrom 2007). The formal and informal elements of the Pakistani transnational labor market are central to understanding the elements of the state that I elaborate in terms of the enforcement of the law, the concept of illegality, the legibility of documentation, and the attempt to control migration flows.

In the 1980s, an important scholarly literature developed on the effects of migration on economic development throughout Pakistan that made direct policy suggestions to improve and facilitate labor migration (Arif and Irfan 1997; Azam 1995; Irfan 1986; Kazi 1989). This state-sponsored research, however, was gradually abandoned in favor of studies aimed to procure foreign economic aid to alleviate poverty.[11] Simultaneously, labor recruiting in Pakistan was privatized—that is, handed over to independent employment agencies. As the process of international migration expanded and normalized, transnational migrants emerged as a complex population with shifting class status and positions.

Historically, the Pakistani state controlled and regulated formal labor within the domestic economy to supplant the power of trade unions.[12] In its sixty-plus years of existence, the Pakistani state has consistently battled against trade unions and all but decimated organized labor (Ali 2001; Shaheed 2007). The disempowerment of trade unions placed the regulation and control of formal labor solely in the hands of the state. As a result of the Green Revolution of the mid-1960s and the shift to neoliberal strategies in the early 1990s, domestic workers increasingly have felt the highs and low of the economic market. Further, the government's reliance on multinational capital in the form of tied credits and loans from international agencies such as the World Bank and the International Monetary Fund has left the domestic market open to massive fluctuation and high unemployment, leading to an economy that is prone to crisis (Zaidi 2005). Planned industrialization failed to take off in Pakistan; this, coupled with the state's tight control of the formal labor market, resulted in chronic high unemployment and underemployment, a phenomenon that also affected the domestic middle class. For its part, the urban working class in Pakistan, displaced from agriculture and existing in an indeterminate industrial economy, has become surplus labor.

Moreover, the dominance of the military in Pakistan has created an unusual class structure in which civilian wealth is buffered by a military class. Capital is absorbed into an invisible economy in Pakistan that creates independent wealth for members of the military, especially after they have returned to civilian life (Siddiqa 2007). So-called milbus (military business) not only channels resources toward the military class; it also obscures how those resources are concealed in the corporate sector. Military capitalism is self-contained and is not transparent. It provides privileged access to assets for a select group of beneficiaries who dominate the marketplace and, in turn, perpetuate the need for a military-industrial economy. Within this system, even remittances from transnational workers, spent in the artificially inflated domestic real-estate and consumer-goods markets, guarantee the capital growth that keeps milbus functioning and dominant in state and domestic affairs.

The inadequacy of education is another important variable that promotes overseas migration (Hoodbhoy 1998). Class background is an important factor in gaining access to migration and overseas work. For unskilled migrants, labor-intensive and temporary work in fields such as construction is often readily available. Obtaining coveted higher-skill and higher-status positions within the service economy, however, requires greater levels of social capital. For the professional classes overseas, getting a job often depends on access to the resources of education and the liquidity of capital assets of the middle classes.

Constructing a male and working-class pool of transnational labor is thus integral to diffusing the constant crisis of the Pakistani state and its inability to stabilize the domestic economic and political system. By configuring exportable labor as male and working class, the state also is able to reproduce patriarchal forms of capital accumulation within its modern restructuring of neo-patriarchal social forms (Sharabi 1988) in which women are taking a larger role within the domestic economy and the transnational family is being normalized. Thus, Pakistani working-class transnational migration is navigated largely by men in a context in which masculinity is reproduced through normalized social patterns even as the state generates new cultural formations.

Within the Pakistani transnational migration system, the terms of labor contracts are often set by overseas employers in collaboration with the government. Calls for employment are then turned over to subcontractors in the private sector. It is such labor schemes that often connect transnational workers to the global North—to countries in Europe and North America that increasingly seek migrants from the educated and professional middle class. Alongside these shift toward liberalization in the national economy, the Pakistani state has pursued international migration strategies that rely on minimal regulation based on the theory of market self-correction. Private recruiting agencies, which are referred to as "body shops," lease workers' services under the terms technically set by transnational employers and the state. Under such guest-worker arrangements, the governments of the sending and receiving countries become responsible for overseeing this activity and intervene mostly in conditions of labor unrest or in response to legal complaints. The shift from labor contracting to subcontracting thus institutionalizes the temporary status of the work and makes it nearly impossible for labor to organize under the formal protection of government regulation offered to domestic trade unions (Stalker 2000).

The Pakistani state continued to oversee labor recruiting throughout the 1990s and deployed some migrants through government agencies that directly administered work contracts with other countries.[13] This regulation was highly casual, though, and for the most part the government intervened only in cases of malfeasance that labor agencies failed to address. Initially, streamlining the labor-recruiting process proved difficult because of the many available ways to obtain transnational contracts—for example, through the state, through labor agencies, and independently through social networks and previous experience. This also added to the difficulty of enforcing regulations that protected contract workers.

Thus, as in the colonial era, the current recruiting system for transmigrant laborers takes two forms: as a state-sanctioned legal practice and as an extra-state practice that produces illegality. In both forms, the state ultimately benefits—economically, from remittances and the resulting flow of foreign capital into the domestic economy, and politically by alleviating the need to develop an infrastructure to ensure employment within Pakistan. In addition, it allows labor migration to be viewed as a non-permanent, temporary condition in which workers are repatriated when they complete their terms of service. Labor migrants are often maintained as non-permanent residents in the Gulf region through legal policies that regulate and enforce their status as guest workers. This system is not easy to maintain, however, and they find their legal status shifting through selective enforcement and the pressure many countries feel to build a semi-permanent reserve labor force. Hence, migrants are often encouraged to prolong their contracts or to go from contract to contract, creating a community of workers whose status is uncertain and in which the enforcement of immigration regulations depends on the state. The boundaries of workers' status, then, are porous in the legal sense of nation-states' sovereignty, under which foreign workers are integral to state projects unless and until changing conditions make them disposable.

The patterns and processes of global migration that originate across South Asia are complex and intertwined with a number of regions and destinations that are broadly imagined in the migration industry. The brain drain that continues to draw highly educated professionals from South Asia to Northern countries is now complicated by a robust technology industry in India that depends on a local workforce.[14] In contrast, the driving of surplus laborers into the global market has also created what might be called a brawn drain from South Asia. In broader terms, the process of transnational migration transformed patterns that imagine a labor diaspora linked to the homeland through social, cultural, and economic ties. Workers are often caught between short-term and long-term goals that generate set patterns and particular imagined transnational landscapes.

Within the complex system of temporary and seasonal migration, as well as more permanent step, circular, and radial migration, workers rely on shared knowledge of the experience developed through networks of affiliation and sociality. For labor migrants, the social elements of migration are a central part of imaging the global landscape of possibility and prospects. Relationships are forged and used to facilitate navigation within the migration industry and the labor diaspora. In this way, transnational labor migration produces complex migrant subjectivities through active forms of imagining and representation. This subject formation is centralized through not only state power but also through complex systems of sovereignty of dispersed and imposed power that operate through non-state actors. Brokers and agents, employers, state officials and bureaucrats, security and police officials, landlords, local citizens, and fellow workers are all part of the cast of characters involved in the deployment of the transnational migration industry. That industry, in turn, wields power based on a number of points of reference. Through recruiting, contracts and agreements, visas and other documentation, work conditions and grievances, debt and remittances, and deportation and detention, labor migrants are structured into a system that limits their life worlds.

Pakistani labor migrants working in the Gulf region, for example, follow a particular pattern of ethnic and regional recruiting. The majority come from Punjab Province, followed by the Khyber-Pakhtunkhwa Province and Sindh Province, a demographic that is consistent with the population size of each of these provinces.[15] According to the patterns instituted in the indentured period, Punjabis and Pashtuns from the Khyber-Pakhtunkhwa Province (the "martial races," as discussed earlier) are preferred as a labor force because they are regarded as hardworking and, for the most part, docile. In the postcolonial era, however, Gulf Arabs often view workers from Pakistan as vulgar and uncivilized, perpetuating the legacy of imagined inferiority of these laborers based on class status and social position. Contrary to this depiction, Pakistani workers have a complex understanding of their work, social relationships, and connection to their Arab co-religionists.

Those who enter the transnational labor market do so for a variety of economic, social, and political reasons. Young men from urban middle-class backgrounds, who often seek the pleasures of migration and travel, stand in stark contrast to those from Pakistani villages and rural areas who see migration in the immediate economic terms of providing food, clothing, medical care, and other necessities and amenities for their families. Urban middle-class youth often conceptualize entering the service economy in terms of *aish karna* and *aiyashi*, Urdu words that can connote seeking fun, a pleasurable life, sensual enjoyment, and even carnality. This, in turn, can also be associated with *tamasha* (spectacle; jestful fun), a vital source of public pleasure in Pakistan.[16] Tamasha, visible in celebrations in the cities of Pakistan during national and religious holidays, in the sports culture of cricket, and in party politics and religious factionalism, also connotes a masculine public space that is often raucous and requires feats of intense physicality and skill.[17]

The idea of having fun by engaging in labor migration also invokes consumption. Dubai, for example, provides not only work and wages to support households but also the luxuries of shopping, hotels, restaurants, and nightclubs. The often unspoken subtext at play here is access to sexual pleasure and liberty. For middle-class youth with the means to migrate abroad, cities such as New York and London are also synonymous with these kinds of pleasure. Because domestic jobs for the educated middle class are scarce, migration thus becomes a viable trade-off of the comforts of home, family, and ties to a national homeland for access to the pleasures and enjoyments of living in a foreign country.

In contrast, limited access to education and jobs for the lower middle class and working class in Pakistan preordains the need to obtain transnational work to support households and meet obligations to extended families. For these groups, "pleasure," "work," and "masculinity" are often defined through the acquisition of cultural and social capital. Yet even this bifurcated explanation of "pleasure" in migration is far from easy to assess: Engaging in aiyashi abroad is a common imaginary for labor migrants across class position, as are ideas about providing for households as working male heads of families. The key differences lie is how these groups present and play out these imagined roles in, and purposes of, migration.

Many Pakistani labor migrants spend part of the year working in host countries, then return to their families for extended periods. This has dramatically altered the social landscape of familial and relational ties. How well a migrant can maintain his transnational family often depends on the term of the labor contract (i.e., how "temporary" the job is) and which service-economy jobs are most easily obtained. Further, in the complex representations that surround labor migrants and their desires for middle-class status, they are often imagined as abnormal—sometimes as racial and sexual deviants who endanger elite notions of the bourgeois family. The impermanence of work and family life that transnational migration brings thus has produced affective registers that disrupt normal conceptions of respectable domesticity enabled by middle-class heterosexual marriage (Shah 2001). Acts of migrant homosociality—residing in mainly all-male dormitories, maintaining close ties through social camaraderie, and the production of migrant masculinities—are part of an imagined alternative that Nayan Shah refers to as "queer domesticity." In this configuration, the term "queer" refers not only to sexuality but also to non-heteronormative social relationships that "question the formation of exclusionary norms of respectable middle-class, heterosexual marriage" (Shah 2001, 13). Rendering "queer" broadly to incorporate both homosociality and homosexuality—and consequently viewing the combined concept as socially deviant—constructs sexuality as a referent of visible racial and classed abjection. This is a central feature in the construction of labor migrants as an epidemiological threat to national populations, in turn reinforcing their construction as dispensable and deportable. For example, reports have circulated that early cases of HIV in Pakistan originated with male labor migrants who had been deported from the Middle East (Shah et al. 1999).[18] Workers seeking visas to work in the Gulf are regularly tested for HIV, but many who are HIV-positive have resorted to sending others in their place to complete the medical checkups. As a result, the number of HIV-positive migrants in the Gulf has risen, and journalists have documented threats by the authorities that workers who do not accept immediate deportation back to Pakistan will be subjected to lethal injection.[19] In this context, migrant workers are imagined as potential carriers of disease that threaten the host and home nations, as well as the reproduction of the healthy heterosexual family. The homosociality of the labor migrant is interpreted as the social capacity for deviant sexualities that engage in sex work, transgender sexuality, and homosexuality.

At the same time, queer sexual migration from Pakistan, a significant subculture, has mostly gone unstudied. Diverse sexual practices, from sex work to same-sex liaisons and transsexuality, are present both in Pakistan and in the diaspora. Instead of providing a liberating framework of access to sexual desire and complex forms of gender performance, such potential social relationships are placed outside the bounds of normative heterosexuality. Even though the evidence is unconvincing and mainly anecdotal that labor migrants are culpable in potential pandemics, migrants are still regarded as debased and inferior from the perspective of middle-class respectability.

To counter ideas about "threatening" forms of sociality, South Asian workers in the Gulf often adopt forms of mutualism based on supposed common interests. In its broadest form, mutuality among workers is imagined in terms that place laborers against employers. As one labor migrant named Masud explained:

> The best people I ever met when I was abroad are, like, our people [Pakistani], [and] from Sri Lanka, India, Bangladesh. They are all good people. The best, of course, are Pakistanis. We would get along because we were the same. Even though it wasn't easy to communicate because of different languages, we understood each other. We have the same culture; we like the same kind of food. We are the same kind of people. . . . The trouble was really with the Arabs. I was surprised by this, since we are both Muslims. When we worked with Palestinians and Lebanese [laborers] it was different because they mostly stayed separate. The Arab employers mistreated us. They understood us as beneath them, and . . . [t]hey would try to cheat us of our pay, and there was never any respect.

Masud came from a small village outside Rawalpindi, in Punjab Province. When he was in his early twenties, he had difficulty finding work, so a cousin who was working abroad gave him a contact at a recruiting agency in Lahore who sent him on work visas to Kuwait, Saudi Arabia, and the United Arab Emirates. After sustaining an injury to his leg, he was considered unfit for manual labor. During his last trip abroad, however, he earned enough money to buy a taxicab in Islamabad. Masud held a conception of worker's mutuality and feelings about Arab employers, that were quite common among workers in the Gulf. When I asked Masud for more details about the conflict with Arabs, he explained the thinking more thoroughly in terms of worker hierarchies:

They would call us names in Arabic we didn't understand at first. But we knew what they were saying. They would do this when they thought we weren't working hard enough, or for no reason at all. They would treat all the workers differently based on where you were from. Some of the other Arabs were treated better because they could communicate with each other. But the Palestinians were treated the worst because the managers thought they were lazy. Many of them worked harder than any of us, but they were still treated badly. We were somewhere in the middle.[20]

The power of native Arab employers over their workers derives from a widely practiced sponsorship system, known as the *kafeel* system, employed across the Gulf region. Sponsors, who usually function as contractors for employers, have great leeway in controlling the welfare of foreign workers. Sponsors initiate contracts that allow workers to enter the country; they issue exit permits; and often they have the power to bar workers from obtaining further work permits. During the term of the work contract, the sponsor collects passports and other documents to restrict the movement of workers and prevent them from fleeing. This system thus keeps workers in an exploited and vulnerable position, and it creates hierarchies among workers that sponsors can manipulate based on socially constructed typologies of ethnic and national background that are then racialized.

In the kafeel system, hierarchy is often supplemented by labor fraud in which paid wages are often far lower than those originally negotiated by labor recruiters; workers are charged exorbitant rental rates for substandard living quarters; access to medical and health care is limited; and, as noted, freedom of movement is highly restricted. Workers, in turn, often counter the discrimination they face by invoking common and derogatory terms as "Bedouin" when referring to their sponsors and employers, which implies a view of their Arab co-religionists as trapped in a tribal culture. Egyptian and Palestinian workers also are commonly viewed as part of a disdained Arab lower class. The meanings ascribed to occupation, work ethic, and cultural markers represent a social construction of labor migrants that symbolically imagines that their role in the Gulf is as a servant class. "Most people who go to Arab countries know they are going as servants [*naukar*]," a veteran labor migrant told me, "but they don't realize they become . . . slaves [*ghulam*]."[21]

At the same time, many South Asian labor migrants in the Gulf find commonalities with their Arab co-religionists. Some come to value Arab Islam as culturally superior to the practices of South Asia, while others imagine Arab

Islam as part of a diverse Muslim *umma*, or community, that was once as provincial as South Asian Islam is often regarded. Since the 1980s, labor migrants increasingly have been influenced by the discourses of Wahhabi Islam that are prevalent in countries such as Saudi Arabia, which, in terms of cultural practice, carries religious authority. Wahhabi thought has seeped into many of the practices of Sunni Muslims in Pakistan. Indeed, such changes in practice have contributed to debates over practice within religious communities in Pakistan. These discourses of orthodoxy have played an important role in working-class culture and the practice of Islam. One such consequence that is widely reported is the shift in dress for men toward the traditional conservative attire of *shalwar kameez* and the strict veiling of women (Lefebvre 1999). Migrants often superficially adopt such modes of comportment and styles of dress following extended stay in Gulf countries. This reflects not only Saudi influence but also a shift toward incorporating codes of behavior that signify discipline, a strict work ethic, and religious devotion, all of which are seen as necessary among overseas workers who in turn must negotiate discrimination and harsh treatment in Arab countries.

Transnational identities allow Pakistanis to borrow religious practices from the Middle East but also to maintain critiques of others' cultural practices. This work and social economy creates ambivalence—indeed, a disturbance—in many Muslim labor migrants' assumptions about the Middle East, in which Arabs are thought to convey the pure cultural values of Islam. When workers encounter contradictory practices by their Arab employers, they make judgments about which practices are legitimate and which are not. These diverse Islamic publics create a complex arena of cultural critique and practice that has a self-contained logic. In the example of labor migration to Gulf countries, race and class are rarely articulated through an analyses of these concepts. Indeed, for many labor migrants, for whom race and class differences are not analytical categories, religion becomes the practical discourse to explain ethical positions (Hirschkind 2006; Mahmood 2004).

Stories of such mixed treatment of labor migrants in the Gulf makes potential travel to North America and Europe even more appealing. As many imagine it, these locations are filled with opportunities. As Hansen has shown in the context of Muslim migrants in India, these global horizons lay the foundation of travel through a mixture of fantasy, lay knowledge, and narratives of experience (Hansen 2001a, 2001b). For those who can afford to travel to the U.S. on tourist and student visas, education and social networks provide access that is also interpreted as a form of status. As one migrant expressed to me, his urge to go to the U.S. was based on having a cousin who had gone on a student visa. After earning a master's degree in business administration, the cousin started a business in New Jersey, settling there in a huge house with his wife and children. One of the more alluring signs of the cousin's success, according to the migrant, was that he owned a sports car and a sports utility vehicle. A few years later, the migrant did travel to the U.S. on a tourist visa and, later, a student visa. He was working at a gas station with another cousin while attending night school to finish his bachelor's degree but later dropped out to run the gas station full time. When I spoke to him about his experience, he talked about the pleasures of living in the U.S. Later, I learned that a large portion of his earnings were remitted to his family in Pakistan, who relied on the money to survive. Thus, his narrative was glossed in terms of middle-class desire and appearances while his reality was based in responsibility and obligations to support a family.

For many labor migrants, the cultural capital gained through multiple migrations facilitates getting jobs and expands social networks. Contacts through work experience, kinship networks, and broader social networks are often the means through which transnational work is negotiated through and around the state bureaucracy. State regulation of these informal networks is nearly impossible, given the scale of labor migration. The complicated nature of obtaining the resources needed to reach migration destinations is apparent in how social and kinship networks are employed. As one Pakistani Christian whose extended family are mostly sharecroppers from a rural village in Punjab explained:

> We mostly farm small plots [in our village] and do odd jobs here in the city. I am a clerk in a college office that doesn't pay very much. That used to be enough to get by, but it's not enough to eat anymore. To get married, to build a house, this takes more. I went to the Gulf several times—Kuwait, the [United Arab] Emirates, Saudi Arabia—you name it. The work is very hard there and does not pay enough for my family to live on. Now I want to go somewhere else, like Europe or America, even Australia. But it costs too much, and someone like me cannot come up with the money to go. Unless I know someone or have a relative who has money or knows somebody else, getting money to go is too hard. I'm the oldest son in my family, so I'm expected to provide for everyone else.[22]

With a national population numbering 2 million to 3 million, Christians are the largest minority in Pakistan, though they make up only about 2.5 percent of the total population. The pressure to travel abroad is complicated by social position and the ability to amass capital resources through social networks.

Although those who have wider networks and more status may be able to obtain the finances to travel abroad, they face similar dilemmas. As a youth from a small town outside Gujranwala explained, his family expected him to go abroad wherever he could. His family were not Christian sharecroppers but Sunni small landowners who considered themselves middle class:

> I can go anywhere I want to. I just call my uncle in Karachi and I can get a ticket made. I went to Dubai last year but got sent back because of my papers. But that doesn't matter. I'll go to New York next and make enough money to come back and get married. My brother is there now, and he works with some friends. I'll do the same and come back after a few years.[23]

On another occasion, I spoke to a group of Pakistani Christians who were hoping to find work abroad. They were eager to find out how they could get to the U.S. As I explained the process, they became excited. One told me a story about a cousin who was living in Chicago and making more money than he could imagine making in Pakistan. I countered that it was difficult to get visas to the U.S. and, once there, to find work. "We could go to the Middle East, but the wages are much lower than in America," he responded. "At least in America you make a decent amount of money no matter how they treat you." Another said he wanted to go to the U.S. for a few years, then settle down in Pakistan. An important factor in the desire to migrate to the U.S. is the imagining of available opportunities and the willingness to endure hardship to have this access. In fact, the U.S. as a destination holds power over and above other sites of labor migration, including the Middle East, Europe, Australia, and East Asia. This was made apparent by a taxi driver from New York I spoke to in Lahore. He had just come back from working for nine months in the U.S. and planned to spend three months "on vacation" with his family in Pakistan, as he put it. He also had spent five years in the Middle East but said that the work conditions were too harsh. Going to the U.S. allowed his family to live a comfortable life. It was hard to be away from his family, he said, but important to their future because eventually he would be able to sponsor them to move to the U.S. He emphasized that his teenage children would have more opportunity in America than in Pakistan, where the economy and the political climate made the future uncertain.[24]

Thus, for transnational migrants, the process of imagining global destinations becomes an important part of reconciling the rigors of migrants' work with the desired pleasure and rewards of travel abroad. In the process of subject formation, migrant workers engage in a constant mapping of the labor diaspora. As much as the migrants exert agency in this process, however, structural features of the migration industry and the labor diaspora confine their life worlds to a specific set of possibilities. Although the actual experience of migration is filled with failures and disappointment, success is part of how migration is continually imagined. In the next section I trace such a migration history to elaborate such possibilities.

Race, Class, and Migration in the Labor Diaspora

Changez grew up in a small town about five hours southwest of Lahore. After completing a degree in economics in the 1970s, he tried to get a job in Pakistan, with no success. Pakistan was in the midst of a tumultuous political and economic transition. In 1977, Prime Minister Zulfikar Ali Bhutto was deposed and sentenced to death, then replaced by the military dictator Zia ul-Haq. For the next eleven years, Pakistan underwent a transition in which the government imposed a strict social program of Islamization, with included the imposition of Sharia (Islamic law). Under military rule, the economy floundered, and unemployment and underemployment reached historic highs. Like many who could not find jobs, Changez turned to the idea of leaving Pakistan. He was young, single, and needed to make an income to support his family. His father, who had worked as a railway station porter, had retired. Although he received a modest government pension, he relied on Changez, his only son, to provide future income for the family.

At first, Changez was not keen to travel abroad, but childhood friends and relatives encouraged him to rethink his position. After a cousin living in Lahore went to the Gulf and returned with reasonable earnings, Changez decided to follow suit. His cousin introduced him to a labor broker, who prepared him for his first trip abroad. He had a passport made, and the agent booked his first trip, to Saudi Arabia. Although Changez was told that he would be working as a clerk for a construction company in Jeddah, he was instead assigned to manual labor to construct a high-rise building. He insisted that his broker in Pakistan was not to blame; the fault lay with the crooked company in Saudi Arabia. Because he had already invested in the paperwork and the trip, and because the wages were the same, he agreed to do the work, even though he held advanced degrees. Living in Saudi Arabia also gave him the opportunity to complete the Hajj, which all Muslims must do at least once in their lives if they can afford it. This, combined with the chance to earn money, helped Changez to feel that taking the job was worthwhile. Although he did feel that he had wasted his education, he believed that things would be different for his children.

This began Changez's twenty-year work life of traveling to the Gulf. His longest term was in Saudi Arabia, where he continued to work in construction. Like many Muslim workers from South Asia, he worked on renovations to the Masjid al-Haram complex in Mecca, the holiest site in Islam. This experience led Changez to reinterpret his labor through the Islamic precept of religious duty, or *fard*. He considered this his greatest accomplishment and claimed he would have done the work even without pay. The Saudi government allowed only Muslims to work at the holy sites, and Changez reported that, in contrast to his experiences in other parts of the kingdom and in the rest of the Gulf region, he never experienced any wrongdoing by the companies he worked for. As he explained, going to the Gulf to work on the Masjid al-Haram was part of his fate that settled for him the anxiety of taking work as a construction laborer.

After working in Saudi Arabia for more than five years, Changez returned to Pakistan and continued to take six-month to one-year jobs in construction in Kuwait, the United Arab Emirates, and Qatar. For almost a decade, he toiled on Gulf work sites and, in the process, developed an extensive network of fellow workers. Changez pointed out many employers were reliable and fair, but far too often it was easy for companies to cheat workers. To compare the treatment of foreign workers, he used terms that in Pakistan are associated with class and social differences, such as *biraderi* (patrilineal kinship group) and *zaat* (caste).[25] He belonged to what he considered a noble and dignified background in Pakistan, but in the Gulf, he explained, his status as a worker meant that he, along with other migrant laborers, was at the bottom of society. As much as he persisted with this explanation, he felt that he was failing to capture the entire experience of discrimination against migrants in the Gulf. His description, however, came alive when he talked about migrants' treatment in public spaces such as hospitals:

> Whenever any of the construction workers were injured, they would send us to the hospital only if it was really bad. They would take us to separate parts of the hospital from where the Arabs would go. There was an entire section for foreigners, and this would be even more divided by what country you were from and what you did. This was the reason I couldn't work [in the Gulf] anymore. No matter what how much you worked, you weren't going anywhere. You were still a worker.

Changez hurt his back during his final trip to Dubai. The injury had most likely developed over time through difficult manual labor, and was exacerbated when he was not sent immediately for treatment. Instead, he was told to return to the labor camp and rest until he could work again. After a week of severe back pain, he did go to the hospital, where he experienced discriminatory treatment. After several weeks of intense pain, he decided to return to Pakistan, where he received medical treatment and was told that he would have back problems for the rest of his life. After six months of recovery, he decided he had to make money again. He had an offer to drive a construction truck in the Gulf, but he knew that his poor eyesight might cause a problem.

Soon thereafter, a friend he had made in the Gulf suggested he try to go to the U.S. Although he had thought about this for some time, he believed it would be difficult because of his limited English skills. By then he was in his mid-thirties and felt he had to take the chance or he would never have enough to start a family of his own. He found a broker-travel agent, who booked his trip to the U.S. under a tourist visa. Relying on a social network of family and friends in New York, he quickly found work at a restaurant. Changez worked for more than ten years in Manhattan, until he was finally able to save enough money to buy a two-apartment property in Queens and get married back in Pakistan. In his forties, he entered an arranged marriage with a woman twenty years younger than he was. Initially his wife stayed in Pakistan, and later through the immigration amnesty during the Clinton administration, Changez gained a green card and permanent resident status, which allowed him to bring his wife to New York on an immigrant visa.

Changez was working in downtown Manhattan when the World Trade Center was attacked in 2001. Initially, he decided to take a hiatus from the area until it returned to normalcy. However, the climate throughout New York worsened, and he felt less and less safe traveling on the subway into Manhattan. "There are good and bad people everywhere," he said. "When I started getting threats on the street, it was too much. I had worked and lived on those streets for so many years, and now because of the World Trade Center, we have to pay for it. I could not do this to my family." Although Changez was not directly affected by the U.S. Patriot Act and the threat of detention and deportation, he considered returning to Pakistan with his family, as many in his immediate social circle were beginning to do. After many discussions, he and his wife decided to stay so their children could receive an education. Changez also spent more time at his local mosque, where attendance dropped dramatically after 9/11. It became clear that many in the New York Pakistani community were leaving because of fear of deportation and the climate of racial anxiety that followed 9/11.[26]

Contrary to understandings of the racialized Muslim that imagines Islam as a threat and peril, Islam has become an organized space in which many transnational Muslims can contemplate cultural difference, hierarchy, and social violence. A revitalized Islamic identity is, in many ways, a response to the pressures of diasporic living and the challenges of racial discrimination and social prejudice. Through transnational revivalist movements such as the Tablighi Jamaat, migrants are reclaiming Islam as they construct identities through pedagogies that emphasize ethical and moral reasoning. In the absence of a coherent analysis of a racism that incorporates anti–Islamic sentiments with bodily and cultural essences, revivalist Islam becomes a site to rationalize the racial experiences of migrants in places such as Europe and North America (Metcalf 1996).

Transnational Islam: Encounters with Islamophobia and Racism

Outside Lahore is the small township of Raiwind, which has become well known as the site of former Prime Minister Nawaz Sharif's opulent ranch-style mansion. Along the major road leading from Lahore to Raiwind are newly built housing communities that are popularly referred to as "American-style suburbs" because of the size of the homes and the amenities they contain. Raiwind is also well known—perhaps best known—as the center of the transnational religious movement Tablighi Jamaat, one of whose biggest patrons is Nawaz Sharif.[27] Tablighi Jamaat's religious compound in Raiwind has a madrassa and an eating area, living quarters, and campgrounds for the annual *ijtima*, or assembly, which brings in well over a million attendees. Exact figures are not available, but it has been said that the ijtima is the second-largest gathering of Muslims after the annual Hajj in Saudi Arabia.[28]

Although many of its followers and bases are in Pakistan and elsewhere in South Asia, Tablighi Jamaat is more properly understood as a global social movement, particularly because of its popularity and influence in the migrant communities across the Middle East, Europe, and North America (Masud 2000; Metcalf 1993, 1996; Sikand 2002). It was founded in India in the 1920s by Maulana Muhammad Ilyas in response to growing aggressiveness among ultra-conservative Hindu organizations to convert Muslims by force. "Tabligh" is the act of informing or notifying; "Jamaat" simply means group. Worried that Indian Muslims were falling prey to external influences, Ilyas called for the revitalization of Islam through prayer, support, and social organization. Like other Muslim movements of the time, the Tablighi Jamaat called for the purification of Islamic practice and intentional contact with disparate Muslim communities. Although it is evangelical and missionary in its approach, the

Tablighi Jamaat follows the Islamic doctrine that forbids proselytization to non–Muslims. Instead, its intended audience is Muslim adherents whom, the Tablighi Jamaat argues, must be molded into a religious community. The Tablighi Jamaat, like other revivalists, argues for a return to the *sunnah* of Islam— that is, following the specific words, actions, and deeds of the Prophet. Its basic principles rely on notions of self-transformation, ritual remembrance, repetition, and the sincerity of action. Ilyas envisioned a pedagogy that cultivated proper Islamic subjecthood through the practices of virtuous action and thought that emphasizes embodiment, ritual, and performance.[29] To achieve this ideal of Islamic piety, Tablighis thus perform discursive and bodily practices of their own, but must also preach these ideals to other Muslims (Metcalf 1993).

The goal of individual reform within the movement is to craft a Muslim moral subjectivity that is separate from the material world while simultaneously within it. In other words, the Tablighi Jamaat offers a critique of capitalism that shuns worldly extravagance and opulence while accepting the reality and need to participate in the capitalist world. This critique is not necessarily anticapitalist; instead, it is based in moral perspectives on how to deal legitimately with a materialist world as a practicing Muslim. The Tablighi Jamaat also teaches straightforward techniques to cope with everyday life through the virtues of patience, respect, spiritual elevation, honor, and deference.

The Tablighi Jamaat originated in a context of growing communal riots between Hindus and Muslims and the Khilafat movement's failure to restore the Islamic caliphate in India after the First World War. In this already transnational historical context, Ilyas was concerned with how Muslims encountered other religious, cultural, and social influences. After India and Pakistan were partitioned in 1947, the Tablighi Jamaat began to expand outward into the world where South Asian Muslims were migrating. It initially gained influence in the Gulf and by the 1960s its revivalist program had become global. Countering the idea that orthodox Wahhabism from Saudi Arabia is the only major ideological influence on South Asian Islam, the Tablighi Jamaat has become a major transnational religious movement that has an impact throughout the Middle East, North America, and Europe.

Many of the transnational labor migrants I interviewed had visited the Tablighi Jamaat compound in Raiwind.[30] Because of the movement's loose structure, not all of those I talked to strictly defined themselves as members, although they had joined others on Tablighi missions. Indeed, many of my interviewees joked about the stereotypical appearance of Tablighis, who are bearded and wear *imamas* (a type of turban) and pants pulled up above the ankles. The jokes, however, did not detract from the important role the movement played in their lives. Many viewed their trips to Raiwind and their experiences traveling with the Tablighi Jamaat as a form of religious and spiritual renewal. It affirmed their faith while providing them with a framework for religious action. As one labor migrant said, "Islam is everywhere—when you're eating, when you're working, when you are driving. This is all Islam." Thus, the Tablighi Jamaat offers more than just the ideological construction of an Islamic worldview. It also provides a way to understand social relationships within the Muslim community and a model of religious identity that addresses the hardships of migration and transnationalism. In response to racism and the hierarchized diasporic life that locates migrants as outsiders, the Tablighi Jamaat offers Islam as a way to approach social and cultural conflict through a system based on the promise of practical spiritual resolution. In the absence of a coherent analysis of race and class disparities as they are defined through secular national categories in the transnational experience, the Tablighi Jamaat constructs a religious identity that migrants easily recognize. One important reason the movement has been successful among South Asian Muslims in the Middle East is that it offers a framework for understanding social differences with their Arab co-religionists.

Although this global influence has made the Tablighi Jamaat a hugely successful model of religious revival, it has also made it the target of accusations of ties to terrorism. In the summer of 2001, I visited the Tablighi Jamaat compound in Raiwind to interview attendees and observe the religious activities. During this initial stay, I observed group discussions and lectures in which the central messages followed the basic tenets of Islam and laid out a path to righteous thinking and action. The emphasis was on spreading the word of Islam and its basic beliefs. Indeed, most of those I interacted with performed these ideas in a discursive model of repetition, often quoting from the Quran and hadith in the verbatim style of the lectures. Most of these conversations were in Urdu and classical Arabic; some of the lectures were in English for the few non–South Asians attendees, who mostly were Arabs from Egypt and Palestine and Indonesians.

After these sessions, I was introduced to a number of Pakistani expatriates. Afzal, originally from Gujranwala, an industrial city in Punjab Province, was now living in Berlin, where he ran a gas station. Afzal had earned a doctorate in chemistry at a Pakistani university. He introduced me to Ifthikar, a Pakistani Kashmiri from Mirpur, who lived in London and worked as an accountant.

Ifthikar's family had left Pakistan in the 1950s, and had been brought up in Britain. Both Afzal and Ifthikar were in their mid-thirties and married with several children. They initially engaged me by offering *dawa*, an invitation to Islam, and by rehearsing many of the arguments presented in the lectures and group discussions. After several hours of discussion about Islam, I asked them about their experiences in Europe and the kinds of social problems they faced. Initially, they talked instead about the positive features of living abroad and the strength of the Muslims in their communities. They also asked me about Islam in the U.S. because they were both interested to move there. As I spoke, I deliberately used the English word "racism" to describe discrimination against Muslims in the U.S. I also asked them whether they had encountered racism in Europe, and both matter-of-factly affirmed that there was much racism all over Europe. Afzal, who was more enthusiastic, dismissed racism as a problem outside Islam. The power of Islam, he said, was to lead by example, which can overcome hatred. To make sense of his claim, he recounted this anecdote:

There was one time we went with a Jamaat [religious group] to Frankfurt. Several of us took a van. As was our practice, we would try to pray in every small town that we passed. In one very small town, we were in the middle of *salat* [prayer] when a group of skinheads saw us. We were praying on the street at the bottom of a bridge. The skinheads were standing at the top of the bridge and were yelling at us and spitting. But none of us moved and continued in the motion of our prayers. They came down from the bridge and tried to hit our imam [who was leading the prayer]. He fell down, but he didn't break his *salat*. He immediately went back to praying. They looked at him strangely and didn't know what to do. This way we showed them that you don't have to say anything to teach those who are ignorant about Islam.

According to Afzal, the correct response to racism from the perspective of Islam is to maintain one's belief and practice in a properly cultivated Muslim selfhood. Ifthikar added:

As you know, we don't believe in racism in Islam. There are many races in Islam. In the Quran, it says, "O mankind! We created you from a single [pair] of a male and a female and made you into nations and tribes, that you may know each other (not that you may despise each other). Verily the most honored of you in the sight of Allah is the most righteous of you."[31] This means that we are all different, but we are also the same. When you go to Hajj, you see Muslims from all over the world. This is the glory of Islam.

This oft-cited verse (Quran 49:13) extols diversity and maintains the necessity of social difference; the religious reasoning explains the unity of purpose found in the rationalist spirituality of Islam. For both Afzal and Ifthikar, the correct way to combat racism is to acknowledge difference and coexist under the framework of a universal Muslim subject. As they explained, "Muslims are all equal, but in practicing Islam, we are not, the solution of which is a return to the basics of Islam—most importantly, prayer." Afzal added a coda to his story that punctuated it with the allegorical weight of the miraculous: One of the skinheads apparently had been so impressed by the imam's behavior that he decided to convert to Islam and was now a prominent member of the Muslim community where he lived in Germany. As Afzal explained, this was happening all over Europe. If a racist skinhead could overcome hatred and prejudice, than the correct path of Islam was to teach by example.[32]

Miracles and the glorious possibilities of Islam are thus part of a religious discourse that has become an explanatory system. During my stay in Raiwind, I was told many stories that employed the motif of the miraculous, following a pattern of facing conflict in worldly interaction with those who were not on the right path of Islam, followed by a conclusion with inexplicable and, at times, fantastic action. Migrants are often attracted to such forms of religious reasoning, which give order to affective registers of alienation and abjection through narratives of resolution and redemption. The Tablighi Jamaat thus is not simply a return to a quietist philosophy of spiritual therapy; it is an active framework that has become central to analyzing transnational systems of social hierarchy and stratification that can be answered through a kind of spiritual conflict resolution. Engagement with the politics of the world, then, becomes part of the struggle to maintain Islamic spirituality in the face of the ills of the world.

Conclusion

The consolidation of the South Asian labor diaspora in the global racial system that began during the period of colonial indenture continues into the contemporary period via an economic and political strategy of neoliberalism now practiced across the planet. By creating a formal and an informal labor market, the colonial structural components of the labor contract and recruiting system were pivotal to the mobilization of race and class concepts in the global racial system. As a system that controls and regulates migration through the state apparatus and non-state actors, transnational labor migration has created a contingent class subjected to the selective enforcement of policing, deportation, and criminality. In the current labor migration industry, which imagines Pakistani workers as part of a global Islamic world that extends from the Middle East to Europe and North America, the means to obtain work are both regulated and informal, leading to systems of social stratification and illegality that rely on racialized identities to subdue transnational laborers.

In response to these systems, a diasporic worker consciousness formed that circulates analyses of conditions, context, and hierarchies through networks of affiliation. Although this shared knowledge of labor diaspora reveals important insights into the struggles and conflicts of transnational workers, it does not guarantee solidarity in action and thought. In the absence of a broader critique of a racialized and classed system that makes migrants subject to the instability of capital accumulation, religion is an often overlooked identity from which transnational migrants make sense of their life worlds. By cultivating revitalized Islamic subjectivities as a response to encounters in migrant life, religious reasoning provides explanations of difficult and inexplicable actions.

Further, this religious reasoning is imbued with a moral discourse that provides a template for acceptable conduct and responses to such things as racist behavior. By inverting the terms of racist beliefs and practices into the miracles of religious belief, experiences of racial encounter become elements in allegories of faith and belief. As religious reasoning, such formulations counter racist logics by articulating contrary logics that understand the terms of racism and place them within a rhetoric of Islamic humanism (Devji 2005, 2008). In other words, racism is reinterpreted through the terms of a revivalist Islam that places value in individual subjectivity and the importance of virtuous and pious deeds. Rather than disregarding racist behaviors and practices, such examples of religious reasoning point to productive responses to such actions. This is not an antiracist response based in transforming social structures that are imbued with racism. Instead, it is a direct response to the quotidian life of transnational migrants.

FIVE

Migration, Illegality, and the Security State

The state is not the reality which stands behind the mask of political practice.
It is itself the mask which prevents our seeing political practice as it is.
—Philip Abrams (1988 [1977], 58)

In the world of hyper-capitalism, Dubai is the future. "A hallucinatory pastiche of the big, the bad and the ugly," as Mike Davis (2006, 51) has aptly called it, Dubai is a dream world of urban excess, pleasure-inducing fantasy, and unrestrained free enterprise that runs on inflated oil prices, a manufactured real-estate bubble, a patronage system that begins and ends with the kingdom, and a vast population of foreign service workers, mainly from South Asia, but also from Eastern Europe and Southeast Asia. As an experiment in neoliberal values, Dubai pushes the boundaries of capitalism to its extremes of exploitation, upward distribution, and class privilege. Those who can, live in air-conditioned luxury in sailboat-shaped hotels and on human-made islands in the shape of palm trees, while those who build the hotels and islands are banished to the desert inferno of labor camps beyond the outskirts of the city. The Dubai paradise is a free-for-all of economic engineering and urban fantasy. It is built on the illusion of progress and, quite literally, on the future of a real-estate boom. The belly of the beast is an illicit underworld of dirty money, smuggling, trafficking, and human exploitation. Everything seems new yet empty—the hundreds of identical-looking residential high-rises waiting to be filled; the voraciously expanding free-trade zones; the ever more ostentatious shopping malls that open each year.

Global Futurism and Hidden Workers

In the winter of 2004, during a visit to the labor camps, I came across the deeper meanings of Dubai for migrant workers. Although they are ever present on the streets and at construction sites, laborers are nowhere to be found in the official public and luxury spaces of Dubai. Workers, in fact, are actively excluded from the elite spaces they build. As we entered an industrial area well outside the city, it was easy to miss what are locally referred to as the labor camps. Surrounded by imposing concrete walls to obscure them from the main highway are the dorm-like facilities in which Dubai's migrant workers live. It was not so long ago that these workers were seen walking throughout the city. To sanitize the city for tourist consumption, however, planners relocated the workers to such camps. Now they are bused to work sites, although the transportation is often unreliable.

I was escorted by a Pakistani who had once lived in the camp while working in construction. We sat down to a cup of tea with a group of workers. I was meeting several Pakistanis who had come from Punjab Province and the North-West Frontier Province, what is now called the Khyber-Pakhtunkhwa Province. I had heard that these camps were full of worker unrest that had led to strikes and demonstrations, and I expected the workers to be abuzz with this excitement. Instead, they were subdued and seemed resigned to the battles they waged against their employers. The consensus seemed to be that this was just part of life as an overseas worker in the Gulf.

Not only are wages kept from workers and breached contracts made to seem normal, but the laborers reported a sobering list of corporal punishments that they experienced, including whipping and baton lashing. Suicide rates among workers are difficult to track, but it has been estimated that in 2004 about 100 laborers had killed themselves. Work-related deaths numbered well above 800. Those who survive the grueling work conditions must deal with the soaring temperatures and humidity that put them at great risk for heat exhaustion and heat stroke. When workers are injured, the burden often resides with them to seek care. Compliance with workplace health and safety regulations among employers is rare; enforcement of regulations requiring employers to report health claims is nonexistent.[1]

Some of the workers spoke about these issues candidly, but on the whole, they understood exploitation as one of the risks of traveling abroad. The labor migration system favors the wealthy company owners, as one migrant noted. Trade unions and strikes are illegal in the United Arab Emirates, except in professional occupations, so the construction companies that employ laborers are always at an advantage. Further, there are no independent human-rights, nongovernmental, or labor organizations empowered to oversee labor violations in Dubai. Enforcement of the laws by the government is often a futile demand, with short-lived results. Employers can easily subvert wage agreements by canceling contracts and issuing new ones or by deporting workers for employment violations. Those in technically illegal work relationships—notably, those who entered Dubai on a tourist visa—are often forced to sign agreements that further reduce their rights. Employers promote such relationships because they allow greater control over workers. "For workers, there is no law," one worker said, summing up the experience of labor migrants in the Gulf.

These risks clearly are mobilized according to the workers' status in relationship to the state. As wards of the state, migrant workers hold a legal status that accords them certain contractual guarantees from employers. However, it is up to the government to enforce the regulations, and because trade organizations and demonstrations are illegal, workers have few outlets to bargain collectively with employers and resolve grievances. The government, in fact, promotes a system in which workers are exploitable and does little to protect them, even though labor laws and international standards exist to regulate such basic labor conditions as minimum wages and rights to bargain collectively, to associate, and to strike. This double bind establishes a relationship of migrant illegality in the labor diaspora that acquaints workers with the dilemmas of the legal frameworks of the state, and also creates labor migrants as a class of workers within a rubric of racialization that deems them as expendable in a biopolitical calculation of useful life and death.

As a hub of the South Asian labor diaspora, the Gulf region represents an important node in which the everyday conditions of labor migrants' struggle is made apparent in social formations and exploitation that extend across the globe. For labor migrants, the state, with its policing arms of legal regulation and deportation, is central to the formation of labor diaspora through processes that produce, discipline, and control worker populations.

Migration and the Resurgence of the State

At the end of the twentieth century, social critics were theorizing the shifting role of the state, and its possible demise, via the proliferation of global flows in trade, finance, and labor. The realities of war, empire, and violence at the beginning of the twenty-first century have revitalized the state's strong arm in the form of its military and policing capacities.[2] The state has rearranged power with a vengeance. However, both before the tragedy of 9/11 and after it, the state played a vital role within the transnational migration system as the gatekeeper for national security and shaper of migrant workers. The U.S. state in particular used migration to maintain a system of control rationalized through the rhetoric of security. The War on Terror, which follows precedents in immigration history and the making of modern America (Ngai 2004), exacerbated migrant control, regulation, and discipline to create deportable subjects racialized through notions of illegality and criminality. This framework depends on a complex history of migration patterns and cultural processes at work in producing a labor diaspora within the global racial system.

This chapter situates the state and migration in what George Marcus and Michael Fisher (1986) have called the "world-historical political economy"— that is, it provides a form of critique based on political and economic analysis of global and transnational relationships. By placing the modern state at the center of this analysis, I examine how systems of control and regulation are established beyond the boundaries of a sovereign, single nation-state through a state-sponsored system that produces transnational migration. To evaluate how neoliberal state systems govern transnational migration that send workers from Pakistan into a diasporic world that includes not only the important, regional Gulf hub but also, eventually, such receiving countries as the U.S., I delineate how Pakistani workers have become part of a larger labor diaspora that is perceived as a part of the global migration of Muslims. And, as I argued in the previous chapter, the historical relationship of the state to migration in Pakistan, as a sending country, is pivotal to the construction of transnational workers as an economic and social class. This occurs in terms of the place of labor migrants within the domestic Pakistani economy and within international and regional economies

As part of the global War on Terror, governments across the Muslim world, including those in Pakistan and the Gulf countries, have designed regulatory systems that often target labor migrants through mixed interpretations. They are viewed simultaneously as positive, because their remittances benefit domestic economies, and as negative, as culprits in potential terrorism through their use of unofficial monetary exchange systems. In compliance with the interests of a U.S. security state that seeks to control such flows, these governments use complex technologies of surveillance purportedly designed to prevent terrorism and to combat criminal activities associated with migration, such as the production of false documents, trafficking, and smuggling.

Migrants imagine the state, with its multiple identities and functions, in complex ways. During my fieldwork, I found the exact concepts of the "state" and "government" difficult to locate. One labor migrant, critiquing the idea of the unified state, described the Pakistani government this way: "It's nothing;

it's everything. [It's] everywhere but nowhere." In conversations about the emirate of Dubai, many migrant workers described the state as strict and disciplinary and as "a place where foreign workers don't exist." And many migrants imagined the U.S. government as regulatory; they also recognized that "anything goes, until you get a bad name, and they kick you out." Such descriptions offer a complex assessment of the state as a category of analysis and as an abstraction of multiple intentions and contradictions.

To elaborate these concerns I investigate the relationship between the state and migration in terms of the production of illegality as part of informal and underground economies that often cooperate with formal markets for migrant labor. Beginning in Pakistan, the illicit mechanisms of labor migration blur into a complex economy that simultaneously produces a formal and informal market for labor. The Gulf region also serves as an important hub to naturalize illegality as a prototype to represent migrant workers and the framework to imagine migrants' subjectivity in relationship to the state's legal apparatus. As these frameworks of illegality circulate globally, they distinguish Pakistani workers within a larger labor diaspora, and under the global War on Terror, to demarcate dangerous migrants and potential terrorists. The identification of criminality is itself constructed through broad historical practices of demonizing and racializing migrants. That migrants are constructed through the concept of "illegality" is a direct control of the migration system in which laws and regulations surrounding migrant life construct a selective system of deportability. It is thus through the mobilization of an abstract security state that I trace the specific historical circumstances under which undocumented status and illegality are created and how the concomitant racialization of this illegalized figure is produced.

Illegality and Transnational Migration

Recent scholarship on migration has focused on undocumented migration and the legal role of the state in controlling migration flows. In an insightful review, Nicholas De Genova (2002, 429) explores the implications of these studies via a concept he calls "illegalizations," or "the legal production of migrant 'illegality.'" He regards migrant illegality as a distinct category that is separate from the undocumented migrant produced through the law. As a legal construction of the state, illegality is counterposed with the concept of citizenship. Documentation thus does not always entail legality, and illegality is not synonymous with undocumented status. As De Genova argues, illegality as a political identity frames migration through the terms of selective inclusion and exclusion imposed by conditions of state control and popular representation. In other words, legal migrants can be rendered illegal through the codes and practices that enact social and cultural boundaries. The goal is a process of inclusion through illegalization within the global economy and the selective enforcement of state controls of deportability (De Genova 2002, 440). In this framework, workers are accepted into informal global labor migration markets that also deem them dispensable in times of crisis and thus disposable through deportation.

"Illegality" as a category, much like "citizenship," entails a set of practices instituted through the law and enforced by the state policing. In practical terms, however, the relationship between the law and the state can be inconsistent, because it depends on implementing strategies and tactics in a particular political and historical context. State control regulates migrant illegality through the selective use of the concept of "deportability." The construction of "illegality" and "deportability" is based on a set of criteria that creates notions of the illegal migrant based on multiple logics that cross the terrain of politics, economics, and culture. For example, the citizens of many nation-states regard migration as a threat to their welfare, even when migrant labor is used to produce a fresh workforce or to create a reserve army of labor. Yet both the worker and the state draw such distinctions among migrant laborers; thus, the social status of migrant workers becomes important to the state as a mechanism to exert economic and social control over such labor. This is accomplished not only through direct policing but also through the creation of statuses that are self-policed. Illegality then becomes a mode of subjectivity that creates its own set of practices and processes.

Illegality as it is constructed through legal and judicial practice emanates from a number of arenas of social life. As a state of being and subjectivity from which everyday life is negotiated, migrant illegality connotes not only the noncitizen, but also the foreigner, the outsider, and, most often, the immigrant. Migrant illegality thus is concerned not solely with legal status outside proper citizenship; it is also concerned with constructing others in relation to acceptable citizens. For example, citizens can also be viewed as "illegal" when they are identified as having increased potential to commit crimes.[3] De Genova (2002) extends to migrant subjectivity Michel Foucault's important insights into "illegalities" from *Discipline and Punish*:

Delinquency, controlled illegality, is an agent for the illegality of the dominant groups. . . . Arms trafficking, the illegal sale of alcohol in prohibition countries, or more recently drug trafficking show a similar functioning of this "useful delinquency": the existence of a legal prohibition creates around it a field of illegal practices, which one manages to supervise, while extracting from it an illicit profit from elements, themselves illegal, but rendered manipulable by their organization in delinquency. This organization is an instrument for administering and exploiting illegalities. (Foucault 1979, 279–80).

In my usage, "illegality" is not only an actual state of legal status but also a condition of political subjectivity that places migrants outside the law. Thus, human trafficking as illicit trade in labor migrants becomes a useful and essential component of state-regulated labor migration. The illegality of labor flows is an industry that is sanctioned by the state and exploited in the production of capital. Thus, controlling the illegality that is reflected in the unlawful practices and informal regulations of governments allows the nation-state to manipulate the labor of migrants. For the field of migration studies, this shifts attention from the documentation of immigrants to the status accorded to such documentation by the state (De Genova 2002, 422–23). As Foucault (1979, 280) continues, the organization of delinquency "is also an instrument for the illegality with which the very exercise of power surrounds itself." For the state, power is extended through the use of illegality and the productivity associated with it. Hence, the state enhances techniques of power constructed politically through illegalities as extra-state practices that demonstrate sovereign-like capacities, continuing the logic of the legal production of illegality and widening the power of the state.

Illegality above all is a political identity and subjectivity that is produced through the state and iterated as a social construct that establishes a moral public sphere of regulation. The Pakistani migrant is associated with illegality through a social process that places this labor diaspora within the global racial system. As a process of racialization within the U.S. empire, this system emerged in the imagining of Pakistan as a social and political space. Even before they leave Pakistan, labor migrants are often represented in relation to trafficking in humans, drugs, and terror. They carry this imagined representation with them as they stream into the Middle East, where they are rendered as subjects of exploitation, and to Europe and America, where they are seen as dangerous and threatening Muslims.

Producing Illegality: From Pakistan to the Diaspora

The failure of formal markets around the world to completely regulate surplus capital creates the illusion of a primary free market that is paramount and legitimate. Underground markets that proliferate in these circumstances are then perceived as a failure to enforce regulation within this formal market, which, in turn, is predicated on the idea that complete dominance of a state-sanctioned singular market is possible. In reality, a dual formal and informal market exists throughout the global economy, a situation that is critical to construct labor migrants via social categories that define them as illegal and as participating in illicit worlds. In this way, illegality—both existing and imagined—becomes a global racial typology.

Indeed, because multiple markets exist, participation in these markets raises questions about culpability and intention. In Pakistan, tacit awareness of the system that informalizes the status of labor migrants is conceptualized through the cultural mechanisms of class and access to resources and through the flows of the labor diaspora. A Pakistani state official in charge of overseas migration expressed it this way: "Many of our Pakistanis get jobs in places like the Gulf, Hong Kong, Indonesia, and then they wait until something else turns up. They even go to places like Sri Lanka until they can find a job or a flight somewhere else. Most of them become illegal, but they are just trying to get jobs and make money, mostly with the idea that they must go to the U.S."[4] This bureaucratic rationalization identifies migrant workers' intention to gain access to resources through work. Although the official's statements map a labor-supply system in which migrants negotiate the global service economy in a climb toward better jobs and life chances, they also weave threads of illegality into the narrative by raising the issue of the underground economy. This mapping is not accidental. Indeed, each of the locations the official mentioned is both a well-known site of formal labor migration and part of the informal market in which workers face harsh and difficult conditions, and from which Pakistanis are frequently deported for engaging in illegal activity.

From the official's perspective, illegality is a regular condition of the migration industry; it is simply a risk of entering the labor diaspora. Because working-class migrants fall in and out of legal status, illegality is constructed as an inevitable obstacle to work and make money, and to pursue greater access to resources and capital. The official continued:

For [Pakistanis who are in Pakistan], there are many bad aspects to this. Because we cannot provide for our own people here, they go to other places to find jobs. The problem with this is that Pakistanis are everywhere, and they make us look bad. They drive taxis, they work construction, whatever they can find. A lot of our engineers are waiters. I went to the U.S. once to visit my brother in Miami. I loved it there. But I knew that everybody was looking at me suspiciously, not because they were afraid of me, but because they might be thinking that I wasn't supposed to be there. That's what happens, and we have to pay for it.

For the official, a middle-aged Punjabi, the ability to travel to the U.S. as a tourist marked his class difference from labor migrants, who travel out of necessity. In this example, the official filtered the anxiety that surrounds issues of legal status through transnational concepts that ascribe legality to nationality. Further, ascribing legality to nationality and citizenship creates a distinction between patriotic middle-class Pakistanis (the category with which the official clearly aligned himself) and transnational working-class migrants who, perhaps, do not hold such clear national allegiances. This construction of transnational illegality thus disturbs the proper class performance of middle-class Pakistanis who have access to the pleasures of tourism by collapsing them into a uniform construction of the potentially threatening migrants. The official's analysis of his personal experience traveling in the U.S. reveals an affective response to a complex gaze that could mean many things but that he tied to being viewed as out of place and to being imputed the status of illegality that working-class Pakistanis carry in the U.S. and across the diaspora.

Such mixed feelings are a significant component in the public debate in Pakistan about transnational migration. They express both concern about the brain drain that has sent Pakistan's educated professional class into the diaspora and hope that those migrants will bring progress to Pakistan by remitting capital. They also express mixed feelings about members of the transnational working class who are simultaneously seen as hardworking and as embodying the social construction of illegality that has come to define Pakistan as a nation. This false metonymy defines Pakistanis as outside legal parameters of normal and acceptable behavior defined in terms of model citizenship practices that are then part of an interpretive social structure of racialization in the diaspora. Although the official was critical of such rationalizations of illegality, his framing of class difference and access to proper forms of respectability also revealed that he is complicit in them.

Illegality is associated with labor migrants in Pakistan partly because of the ambivalence in how legal migration is defined and practiced there. The current emigration codes of Pakistan are drawn from the Indian Emigration Act of 1837, which was framed by the British. Many of the protections instituted in that code were designed to facilitate labor migration. Although the Pakistani Emigration Act was updated in 1979, it is generally used as the last resort in state mediation of labor problems. The rights of labor migrants are invoked only when specific complaints are lodged—and, more important, when the state regards a case as reasonably significant. The major target of regulation and policing under the act is not labor migration but local counterfeiting, drug trafficking, and smuggling. An official with Pakistan's Bureau of Emigration in Islamabad put it this way:

> Our job [as bureaucrats] is to make sure everything goes smoothly. In many cases of grievance, there is not much we can do. Our people [Pakistanis] who leave from here are happy with their jobs, and their contracts are satisfactory. But in the end, there are many things that we cannot control, especially in the host country. There [in the host country] it is the job of our missions to represent what we have tried to do here.[5]

Because they know that labor migration provides income, state officials are pragmatic in addressing grievances and cases of poor treatment. Most bureaucrats in Pakistan, like this official, express ambivalence when asked what the state should do to intervene in the well-known and widespread mistreatment of migrant workers. Such resignation is evident not only in regard to the problems of labor migrants but also in discussions of poverty alleviation and economic development, even though such programs usually address a different demographic population.

For the Pakistani state, the production of labor migrants can run counter to the interests of receiving countries. While the Pakistani government views exporting workers as a boon to the domestic economy, for example, the U.S. government views the same phenomenon in terms of containment. The U.S. has a keen interest in Pakistan as a front-line ally not only in the active War on Terror, but also in developing strategies to contain what American intelligence agencies view as security threats. In early 2001, I interviewed the U.S. consul-general in Pakistan. He noted that U.S. policy toward South Asian labor migration tended to view Indian visa seekers in terms of brain drain (those who migrate in pursuit of professional employment), whereas it views Pakistan in terms of "brawn drain" (those who seek visas less for jobs than to reunify families). This distinction not only perpetuates class distinctions; it adds gender to the construction of transnational migration, in terms of feminization and masculinization, and creates different criteria for, and attitudes toward, Indians and Pakistanis who seek legal avenues for migration.[6]

The ascription of illegality to transnational Pakistanis depends on a complicated structure of social relationships and political economies. With its turbulent and often unpredictable political scene and national economy, Pakistan is often considered an opaque market and has become widely known for commonplace, corrupt practices such as kickbacks, bribes, cronyism, and nepotism that are part of everyday life. When the government turned labor recruiting over to private employment agencies in the 1980s, counterfeiting operations sprang up to provide forged passports and visas for prospective migrants. In addition, during the U.S. proxy war against the Soviet Union in Afghanistan in 1980–89, Pakistan had a thriving aboveground black market in arms, drugs, cash, and goods from across the region (Coll 2004; Rashid 2001). This black market became a commonplace feature throughout Pakistan. After the Soviet Union was defeated, and despite the efforts by the Pakistani government to curb the illicit economy in the 1990s, counterfeiting and forgery proliferated. Government officials in Pakistan are often complicit in this practice through bribery and corruption.[7]

The privatized labor-recruiting system is also part of the biopolitical project to link traveling bodies to state-regulated systems of control via documentation in the form of passports, identity cards, visas, as well as employment records and labor contracts. But because it is located outside the direct control of the state, and because of the ambivalence associated with labor migration in Pakistan, private industry often blurs categories of legality and illegality while simultaneously connecting them to state documentation. Thus, for example, one can go to a legal contracting agency to obtain work abroad and unknowingly enter into illegal activities. Conversely, one can also go to an illegal agency (one with an expired license or no license and thus not supervised by the state) and obtain a legal work contract. Thus, legal and illegal migrant recruiting both mirror the structures of the state, making it difficult to identify illicit agents and brokers who deceive migrants into entering complex human smuggling rackets.

This kind of illegality falls into a gray area. It does not strictly meet the robust definition of human trafficking or smuggling in the United Nations Protocol to Prevent, Suppress, and Punish Trafficking in Persons.[8] Nonetheless, the U.S. State Department has placed Pakistan on its watch list as a source, transit point, and destination country for trafficking. Women and girls are sent to Pakistan for forced commercial sex work, and Pakistani boys and men are trafficked to Europe (Italy, Spain, Greece, Cyprus, and the Scandinavian countries); South East Asia (Indonesia, Hong Kong, Malaysia, Singapore, and South Korea); and the Middle East.[9] Curiously, the State Department's report on Pakistan did not discuss a prime destination: North America (Canada and the United States). The State Department's placement of Pakistan on the trafficking watch list is part and parcel of a logic that recognizes patterns of travel and migration by South Asians that concurrently constructs migrants through concepts of illegality that identify them as potential terrorists who must be kept under surveillance.

Labor migrants learn through trial and error who within the vast network of employment brokers is legitimate and who is not. It can be hard to tell the difference. And sometimes migrants disregard agents' official status altogether in favor of calculating the risk of entering an illegal transaction. Many labor migrants know that deception often occurs in the host country as well. Even laborers with legally obtained contracts and documentation complain about receiving their wages late or not receiving them at all while working in the Gulf.

Throughout my fieldwork, I came across labor migrants who described travel agencies that posed as licensed labor agencies supplying travel documents. In fact, some travel agencies that booked airline tickets for migrants actually were legitimate labor brokers. One interviewee said, "A friend of mine told me about this agent . . . in Lahore who would make a ticket for me to [go to] America. When I met the agent and told him I wanted to go to America, he said first go to the Gulf, and then we will make papers for you to go to Canada. Once you get there, we will find a way for you to go to New York."[10] After he had worked on contract in the Gulf for a year, the agent sent him papers to travel to Canada. It was only then that he realized the documents were forged. He was afraid of the consequences of using the documents, so he stayed in Dubai, then returned to Pakistan. A longtime labor migrant who had worked on both legal and illegal labor contracts in many Middle Eastern countries, including Saudi Arabia, Qatar, Kuwait, Libya, and the United Arab Emirates, said that it hardly mattered to him whether his contract was real as long as he was paid for his work. "Sometimes when you go to these countries, it doesn't matter how you get there," he said. "I did it both ways [legal and illegal], and there were good and bad results. . . . It was the same with fake papers."[11]

Labor migrants often take out high-interest loans with moneylenders or borrow money from relatives and friends in order to work abroad. Most labor migrants accrue large debts. Forged documents to prime locations (such as the U.S.) can cost tens of thousands on the black market. The fees to obtain contracted guest work in the Gulf can be nearly half that. Migrant workers thus make complex financial calculations that balance the accrual of debt against the potential of illicit networks and formal networks to place them in better-paying jobs. Once migrant workers secure the networks they need to assemble resources to travel, they often follow the migration patterns that bring them the highest rate of return. Thus, labor migrants can transform their class status through migration. Salim, a middle-aged bachelor who had traveled to the U.S. several times on tourist and business visas, explained that his desire was to make money abroad and ultimately return to Pakistan:

> My entire family is here, but I can make lots of money in the U.S. in a short period of time. After six months, a year, however long it takes, and then I come back to Pakistan and live comfortably. I can have every wish fulfilled here. After all, this is my country, and this is where I will feel the happiest. I have a nice house, several cars, and I also have servants. With the money I make abroad, I was also able to buy another property that I rent out to a family.

He had no interest in settling in the U.S., where he always felt out of place. While traveling to New York, Los Angeles, and Chicago for work, he had acquired a great deal of experience. Although Salim did not hold a college degree, through social networks of friends and business partners he had gradually acquired the skills that allowed him to keep traveling. Fluency in English, in fact, enabled him to make his initial trips to the U.S. Salim made his first visit to New York in the 1980s. He booked his trip through a travel agency run by a family member that helped him obtain a tourist visa. He stayed in the U.S. for seven years, waiting tables and driving a delivery truck. When he returned to Pakistan, he used the money he had saved to start an import–export business. Although he continued to use his family travel agent, he explained, his status changed when he returned to Pakistan, and he was eligible for a business visa. Throughout the 1990s, he was able to travel back and forth between the U.S. and Pakistan, largely because he could prove that intended ultimately to return to Pakistan and because he arranged for different business partners in the U.S. to sponsor his visits.[12]

Worker Solidarity: Exploitation and Illegality

I was conducting fieldwork in Lahore in late May 2001 when some 1,000 Indian and Pakistani workers took to the streets of Dubai to demand payment of back wages. These workers (all of whom were men), and their relatives back home in

Pakistan and India who relied on their remittances, had not seen any wages for four months. The Bartawi Group, a large construction company in the United Arab Emirates that employed more than 5,000 South Asian contract workers, illegally withheld payment of their wages, claiming cash-flow problems. For three days, laborers halted work at the construction site demanding either that their delinquent wages be immediately paid or they be given transportation to their respective embassies to complain. Management refused to negotiate for several days, and on May 22, the workers decided to mount a public demonstration as they walked to the Ministry of Labor to lodge a formal complaint.

By marching in the May heat through modern downtown Dubai, with its high-rise office buildings and five-star hotels (most of which were built by South Asian laborers), the workers were risking not only their jobs but also imprisonment and deportation since public demonstrations and strikes are illegal in the United Arab Emirates, as they are in most of the Gulf region. Finally, the company, perhaps embarrassed by the commotion or prodded by a government concerned about the emirate's image as a friendly tourist economy, sent buses to transport the workers to the ministry. However, they were suspicious of where the buses would actually take them, since workers are often carted off to jails and into deportation cells, so they continued their demonstration on foot. When they reached the ministry, they were informed that the company had decided to pay them two months' worth of wages immediately and the remaining two months' worth that they were owed by the end of the month.[13] Illegally withholding wages from migrant workers is a common point of grievance among workers and a tactic exercised by employers throughout the Gulf to alleviate their own liquidity problems or, more nefariously, to defraud migrants of their labor.

Dubai has entered a post-oil economy that depends on capital accumulation via a finite amount of foreign investment and speculation in real estate. In the 1980s and early 1990s, before speculation boomed, construction companies operated with low revenue margins, often paying workers four to six months after projects were completed.[14] When demand began to exceed supply in the 2000s, profit margins increased exponentially, eliminating the cash-flow problems, but employers continued to use the tactic of delaying wage payment to reinvest profits in new projects and to move capital around to leverage assets. The result of nonpayment by employers is the dramatic upward distribution of resources acquired from exploited migrant workers.

Within this political economy, which depends on exploiting foreign workers to build tourist, financial, and business centers, employers thus craft a social experience of illegality that is different from those discussed so far. Employers' deceptive and exploitative practices are regimented by the state, which also intentionally neglects labor protection. Thus, it is not so much the law that structures migrant illegality as it is the use of exploitative practices through consistent and transparent subversion of the law. Human-rights organizations have documented how contract labor systems in the Gulf make transnational labor migrants susceptible to harsh, often illegal work conditions through the use of such excessive measures as imprisonment, corporal punishment, docking of pay, and illegal withholding of wages and official documents such as passports and work visas. Racially segregated, substandard workers' housing is common in the Gulf, with labor camps often in remote and hard-to-reach locations outside cities.[15]

Within this context, workers around the world have crafted strategies and tactics to struggle against exploitation that often are based in politics of their home countries. In the first decade of the twenty-first century, strikes and demonstrations by migrant workers have grown rapidly throughout the Gulf region; they have, in fact, become a commonplace feature of labor interactions with the state and employers. Despite bans on trade unions and strikes in most of the countries of the Gulf, worker protests are receiving increasing attention, particularly the construction industry in Dubai and Abu Dhabi (Davidson 2008, 2009). Because political parties are often stifled, or are illegal, and few nongovernmental organizations address the problems foreign workers in the Gulf face, legitimate advocates beyond the workers themselves rarely exist.

Few labor histories have comprehensively examined worker unrest in the Gulf. Recent work by Robert Vitalis (2007) on the history of oil companies and the U.S.–Saudi relationship, however, does much to establish the roots of labor conflict and organization in the mid-twentieth century. Major strikes throughout the 2000s have mobilized tens of thousands of workers demanding better treatment, work conditions, and wages. In the United Arab Emirates, for example, recent collective labor action has included protests, organization, work stoppages, public demonstrations, and strikes, often in response to employers' systematic failure to pay wages, improve work conditions, and stop abuse. In turn, workers have been threatened with confiscation of passports, restrictions on movement, and deportation to quash dissent (Keane and McGeehan 2008).

The illegalization of labor migrants through such practices in which the state is complicit serves to discipline workers into the quotidian struggles of migrant illegality. For South Asian labor migrants, working in the Gulf becomes an apprenticeship in normalizing the subordination and exploitation found in labor markets throughout the diaspora. In the U.S. War on Terror, illegality is constructed through the selective policing and deportation of Pakistani and Muslim migrants. The use of legal and extralegal violence by sovereign states is based on the racialization of migrant illegality in terms of criminality and the imagined possibility of future terrorist activity.

Post—9/11 Deportability: Illegality, Criminality, and the Terrorist Potential

The history of the South Asian diaspora in the U.S. begins with small groups of Punjabi migrants that began to arrive on the West Coast at the end of the nineteenth century (Jensen 1988). Larger populations did not arrive until the Immigration and Naturalization Act was passed in 1965. Post-1965 immigration from South Asia is often characterized as comprising an educated middle class drawn mostly to work in professional occupations. In the late 1980s and 1990s, this population began to diversify through the issuing of family-reunification visas. Family reunification, now a priority in U.S. immigration law, was designed to allow professional-class migrants to bring their families to live with them in the U.S. (Prashad 2000). One of the repercussions of this policy has been the formation of a Pakistani American immigrant working class.

The tragic events of 9/11 launched a new era of control and policing in U.S. immigration. The War on Terror campaign significantly changed the composition of Pakistani, South Asian, and Muslim communities in the U.S. through the normalization of racial violence and state-managed forms of policing that subsequently led these groups to engage in mass return migration to avoid deportation. Yet the foundation of these racialized practices predates 9/11: Racial violence against Arabs, Muslims, and South Asians increased significantly in the past several decades (Gualtieri 2009; Hagopian 2004; Maira 2009). The expansion of the War on Terror across the globe, and the racialization of Muslims within the global racial system, in fact, combines historical strains of religion, foreign policy, Orientalism, and systematic oppression. This is seen most clearly in the wars in Iraq and Afghanistan, the domestic U.S. war on immigration, and the state's widespread use of force and violence to police communities of color and deport immigrants of color (Rana and Rosas 2006).

The USA PATRIOT Act, passed immediately after 9/11, gave direct power to the U.S. Attorney-General to detain and prosecute aliens. As legal scholars have argued (Chang 2002; Cole 2003), the justification for giving this broad latitude in detention and deportation is grounded in a history of demonizing presumed national enemies of the U.S. state. The broad anti-terrorism legislation enacted in 1996, along with stringent regulations in immigrant policy, were direct precursors of the Patriot Act and its criminalization of immigrants (Cole and Dempsey 2002). These policies were put into place to uphold a law-and-order society based on concepts of self-protection and security. But behind the U.S. security state's mask of certainty is a xenophobia that has fueled anti-immigrant racism against Pakistanis and other Muslim immigrants by creating generalized profiles of immigrants of color. This shift in the security apparatus thus reinforced a demonization of Muslim labor migrants that was already present.

The crisis connecting terror and immigration in the U.S. since 9/11 has led to new forms of control and policing by the state. In the case of Pakistanis, the state's immigrant-management techniques are based in discourses of illegality and criminality and strategies of deportability. One strategy of control is the use of detention and deportation in which immigrants are held until the government decides that they either have no important information or are not potentially dangerous. Once the determination that no potential threat exists, detainees are deported through forced or voluntarily means. The detention and deportation regime relies on selectively enforcing immigration laws among suspect immigrant populations. Thus, it is not probable cause but the guilt by association with certain ideas, people, or organizations that guides the logic behind who becomes a suspect.

This awareness of state discourses of illegality and proper citizenship is evident in migrant narratives. As one Pakistani immigrant in New York told me in 2002:

> Before I came to the United States, I knew living here would be hard. . . . I don't want my children to grow up in the U.S. I want them to live and be happy in Pakistan. But I know that this is not possible. The U.S. has different possibilities for us, so we do what we can to give our children a better life than what we had. And we suffer through it here because we are seen as foreigners.[16]

When migrants frame overseas work in terms of the opportunity for work and, simultaneously, for a better life, they come to understand the condition in which "foreign" and "alien" is imagined through state and popular forms of racism as "threatening."

The criminalization of the Pakistani immigrant, along with other Muslims, thus is part of a historical pattern of demonizing immigrant groups in the U.S.

For many U.S. immigrant communities, the War on Terror fits into a larger history of anti-immigrant sentiment in which they are viewed as outsiders and as foreign aliens. This war on immigration has precedents in U.S. history, but it is also part of a global economy that connects flows of goods and commodities with those of people and workers. Further, the history of detention and deportation as a process of scapegoating has affected a wide variety of religious, ethnic, racial, and political groups (Cole 2003). The process of imagining illegality and criminality, however, has been directed largely toward Pakistani immigrants in the U.S. through popular and state-sanctioned violence.

Conclusion

For many male laborers, navigating the state system of transnational migration controls is part of the process that allows them to keep pursuing economic resources. This struggle over access to capital is controlled and regulated in many ways, yet channels remain that circumvent these boundaries. Thus, what is considered legal and what is considered illegal depends on the interests of the state and the perspectives of migrants.

As I have argued, the state wields power through a variety of legal and illegal practices. The multiple states systems' ambivalence toward labor migration reflects relationships in which labor migration makes economic sense but the mechanisms of movement are arbitrarily controlled. The confusion in states' practices is recognized by labor migrants who point out the similarities between legal and illegal activity. It is tempting to identify migrant illegality as a result of limited regulation and the inadequacy of the state, yet the incoherence in how states behave reveals the deeper layers of their intentions in everyday politics. The power of the state in creating such migrant publics, then, is replicated in neoliberal economies that give private contractors state-like power (Comaroff and Comaroff 2006). Here I call attention not so much to a model of the state as nefarious as to the banality of allowing such practices to continue under the guise of the state. In this sense, criminality and illegality are part of a global landscape of violence wrought by economic disparities in which threats become a feature necessary to the functioning of the security state. In the global economy, the migration of diasporic populations is now a permanent feature. Analyzing diasporic populations in terms of nation and region of origin, religion, class, and gender reveals some of the connections that frame South Asians in relation to migration.

Clearly, the placement of the Pakistani immigrant within the United States takes on greater significance in the context of state-endorsed racism since 9/11. Much of my research shows that the context in which this racism emerged—that is, in which the concepts of migration, illegality, and terrorism were conflated—were well in place before the tragedy took place. Indeed, in the case of Pakistani migrants in the United States, class, nation of origin, religion, and gender are being combined in a racial typology that draws on understandings of Islam, terror, migration, and illegality. Hence, migrants are framed simultaneously through the discourses of home and host countries.

The Pakistani migrant thus becomes the Muslim migrant and, hence, nation and religion are articulated in terms of race. The U.S. state plays a central role in the racial configuration of Muslim as terrorist through the War on Terror and through its exertion of state power through immigration controls and laws such as the Patriot Act. The Pakistani working-class immigrant portrayed in transnational readings of this subjectivity adds to analyses of how this subject is both represented and given an identity.

SIX

The Muslim Body

The sovereign, epitomizing the subject, is the one by whom and for whom the moment, the miraculous *moment*, is the ocean into which the streams of labor disappear.

—Georges Bataille (1991, 241)

New York City changed after 9/11. Tragedy and sorrow were in the air, but so were fear and intimidation. A reign of swiftly spreading domestic terror targeting Muslim Americans, and those who appeared to be Muslim, inaugurated the twenty-first-century racial order. The escalation of hate crimes in the months that followed 9/11 led to routine racial violence for a broad group of South Asians, Arabs, and other Muslims (Ahmad 2002, 2004). Such everyday racism, although not necessarily new, highlighted the Muslim body as a visible object of racial containment, and many Muslim immigrants fled New York in fear of deportation and the safety of their families.

After the initial wave of attacks subsided, I began talking to people who had returned to Pakistan from the United States. For those migrants, fleeing to Canada, the Arab Gulf, or elsewhere in the diaspora—and even returning to Pakistan—became a necessity. Some said they left the U.S. because they feared separation from their families, the humiliation of detention and deportation, and the danger of racial violence. Others explained their departure in less anguished terms: as a response to family problems in Pakistan, to seek the comfort of the home country, or to find better jobs. Migrants hold a complex set of justifications for return migration in the context of perceived danger. Although their accounts were not always articulated in a straightforward manner, many revealed the fear of racism and the potential of being targeted for disciplinary exclusion.[1]

As word of the post–9/11 detention and deportation regime circulated in the narratives of return migrants, the global War on Terror exacerbated fear. Returnees in Pakistan, for example, interpreted the images of torture committed against Iraqi detainees at Abu Ghraib prison in 2004 as a warning of the dangers inherent in the U.S. immigration system and the brutality of the state's policing powers. As one returnee summarized:

> What happened in [the Abu Ghraib] pictures is nothing new. We [Pakistanis] know this from the torture done to people in Pakistan. In the U.S., if you are deported, they used to treat you OK, but after 2001, this is what they do now. You would hear that they would do small things here and there before, but now they want to humiliate people. I have a friend who was deported, and in the prison they would call him "Bin Laden" and "terrorist." . . . It's become difficult for Muslims to go to the U.S.

Thus, many returnees connected torture in the detention and deportation regime with the migration system. Such sentiments are common. Prospective labor migrants increasingly take the risk of violence and torture into account when they assess the possibility of working overseas. These narratives and the calculation of migration risks pivot on biopolitical notions of life and death. As the same interviewee later told me, "I still want to go back to the U.S. Working and living there is what I know best. I love being in Pakistan, but I don't belong here any more, and maybe I don't belong in the U.S., either."[2]

Sovereignty and the Racialized Body

Such narratives provide only a sampling of how the Muslim body as a racial object is excluded from the U.S. body politic. In this chapter, I examine how racial violence and everyday forms of policing produce the racial disciplining and boundary making through which transnational practices of migration are controlled, and which ultimately reinforce the logic of the imperial state. The concepts of racism and sovereign power that are enacted through state and extralegal practices are central to my approach. In the post–9/11 global racial system, xenophobic racism, imperialism, and histories of transnational migration are encapsulated in the process of racializing Muslims and migrants' bodies.

Examining Pakistani returnees within the context of the U.S. deportation and detention regime, I argue, reveals how sovereign power is applied to certain racialized bodies to create affective orders of security, authority, and fear. In particular, I discuss the conditions of violence imposed on Pakistani detainees and those who ultimately were deported. Such racial disciplining is not an exception; it is, rather, part of what Engseng Ho (2004) identifies as the methodology of an imperial state that uses invisibility, dissimulation, and misrepresentation to conceal violence.[3] I also analyze how these technologies of policing are connected to the transnational production of racial affect. In my fieldwork, I tracked forced and voluntary return from the U.S. to Pakistan, which since 2001 has become common.[4] Return migrants' narratives speak to the wider condition of Muslim immigrants who have fled or were forced to leave the U.S., many of whom have chosen to stay permanently in Pakistan and re-enter family and social networks.

What is apparent from reports on post–9/11 detention and deportation is that racial violence is a central aspect of everyday terror. This force is not arbitrary; it is part of a longer history of U.S. government warfare on domestic populations of color (Gilmore 2007; James 2007). The system of selective detention and deportation deploys the Muslim body as a concrete, objective entity to control and regulate, a logic that is central to an expansive racialized terror formation that broadly disciplines migrants into imperial systems of control.

Detainees considered enemy combatants held in the camps of Guantánamo Bay, Cuba; Bagram, Afghanistan; and Abu Ghraib captured much of the media's attention as a spectacle of the torture that is apparently integral to military incarceration.[5] This type of torture—that is, the infliction of extreme bodily pain in conditions of war—references a process of deconstructing the categories of killing and dying to "unmake" the human being (Scarry 1985, 121–22). As scholars point out this kind of controlled violence remains the exclusive domain of the state, including democratic polities such as the U.S. Thus, the humiliating torture carried out at Abu Ghraib was not arbitrary; it represented a step in the development of historical technologies of state-sanctioned violence (McCoy 2006; Rejali 2007). Such violence is also a routine part of policing in the detention and incarceration systems linked to global migration.

Within this scheme of routine violence and carcerality, the Muslim immigrants detained immediately after 9/11 represent a specific class of people who are racialized and normalized as illegal and criminal. To be clear, such violence is not a part of all migration experiences, but it is a part of a class-based racism in which certain migrants are at risk. In this sense, class has taken on a logic that interprets gender, religious, and cultural practices within a racial framework. The post–9/11 deportation and detention of Arab and South Asian immigrants is grounded in a rationale that links those who overstay their visas or enter the U.S. without proper documents to informal, underground markets engaged in illegal transactions. To obtain information about illegal markets, the state's argument goes, the use of torture is permissible. When exceptional violence becomes the rule, torture is naturalized within the migration system, and the migrant's body is placed in systems of biopolitical control.

State, Sovereignty, and the Body after 9/11

In the U.S., the home front for the War on Terror, populations that previously were invisible in the public sphere are made racially legible. For example, Arab Americans, long considered ethnically white in the state-constructed racial classification system (Gualtieri 2001; Naber 2000), are now being subjected to explicit racial classification as "Muslims" (Jamal and Naber 2008). Thus, the concept of race is once again expanding, shifting, and, perhaps more nefariously, returning to old forms of racial dominance. This process of abject racialization is not spontaneous. It has a long history in the relationship between Europe and America and the Islamic world (Little 2002; Mamdani 2004; McAlister 2005; Said 1978, 1993; see also chapter 1).

At the same time, the U.S. War on Terror has dramatically shifted quotidian forms of life by curtailing civil liberties and imposing new types of policing, surveillance, and intelligence gathering on domestic and international populations. As the U.S. invasions of Afghanistan and Iraq expanded into the global War on Terror, the emergent military-driven economy demanded the construction of enemies through the politics of the war machine (Deleuze and Guattari 1983; Hardt and Negri 2000, 2004). This is how "the Muslim" has come to be represented as a foe to national sovereignty and security and as the purveyor of global conflict (Schmitt 1996). In its effort to frame these priorities, the U.S. government intensified the use of deportation and other kinds of forced removal to purge its populace of potential threats and criminals. The specific practice of removing Muslim bodies from the U.S. nation-state has led one scholar to argue that deportations represent a moral economy that is "a constitutive logic of the neoliberal, imperial state" (Maira 2007, 40). Others, echoing critiques of U.S. rhetoric, have called this form of racialized state violence simply "the deportation terror" (Buff 2008).

Anthropologists are increasingly concerned about issues of sovereignty in everyday life (Hansen and Stepputatt 2005, 2006). Following Michel Foucault (1991, 2003, 2007, 2008), Georges Bataille (1991), Carl Schmitt (1996, 2005), and, more recently, Giorgio Agamben (1998, 2005), sovereignty has become an important concept in theorizing the shifts in everyday life in the post–9/11 Age of Terror. Recent approaches to sovereignty that go beyond traditional conceptualizations of state power and the nation-state expand on what political theorists call "state effects" (Mitchell 1999). Broadly understood, state effects involve the workings of state power in various locations where the state is not a direct force but where competing actors vie in different registers of power in what Aihwa Ong has also referred to as "graduated sovereignty" (Ong 1999, 2006). This insight has led to a revitalization of the study of the state in terms of formal sovereignty and of the complicity of the state in informal practices of de facto sovereignty, authority, and violence by state-like actors (Hansen and Stepputat 2006).

The theoretical apparatus of this approach is indebted to Foucault's concepts of biopower, governmentality, and discipline (Foucault 1991, 2003, 2007, 2008). Biopower and the sovereign right to kill are constitutive elements of modern state power. Indeed, the Weberian notion of the state's monopoly on legitimate violence is essential to constructing the rationales of state security. State control of these means of violence shape bodies, subjectivities, populations, and sovereign notions of territory and, ultimately, calculate who lives and who dies (Foucault 2007).

In these approaches, the body is an important site as an abstraction on which to exert multiple forms of modern state power. In the traditional sense, the sovereign is the supreme and ultimate ruler of all domains of life—for that matter, of life itself (Rose 2006). To link biopower and the regulation of life and death to the body, Foucault (2003) importantly turns to the ideas of race and racism—and ultimately, race war—as a history of the nation form. Biopower in this sense is the theater from which race becomes the terrain of a politics of life and death. This interpellation is important in the modern framework that names the threats that must be eliminated to maintain life and sovereign power. The site of such state warfare is the racialized body that represents specific enemies, threats, dangers. For Bataille (1991) and the more contemporary thinker Sara Ahmed (2004, 2006), sovereign power is not only relational; it is connected to the body through an interpretive phenomenology of embodied and affective power. Thus, the sovereign is linked to a number of components, including the state, power, the body, subjects, enemies, emotions, migration, and the domains of everyday life.

The Detention and Deportation Regime

In the wake of 9/11, what appeared in the guise of a new state security system—the revitalization of immigration controls through legal, social, and state-sanctioned forms of policing—was in fact a magnified and expanded version of practices of legal sovereignty that were already in place (e.g., Chang 2002; Cole 2003; Cole and Dempsey 2002). The USA PATRIOT Act of 2001 expanded the use and domains of surveillance in intelligence investigations. These powers targeted a breadth of potential law-breakers—most notably, non-citizens and activists. Drawing from the McCarran–Walter Act of 1952, the Patriot Act also restricts foreign-language speakers from entering the United States based on the threat that they carry ideologically dangerous ideas.

Most immediately preceded by the Illegal Immigration Reform and Immigrant Responsibility Act of 1996, the Patriot Act draws on a historical genealogy of legal regulation. As David Cole (2003) argues, the legal basis of such controls were long in the making, as demonstrated by the construction of the category "enemy alien." The "enemy alien" classification allows perceived threats from suspect populations in the form of ideology, identity, or even opposition to U.S. interests, to be isolated and removed through the force of deportation. The legal history of this category can be traced to a number of laws and events, including the Alien and Sedition Acts of 1798, the Chinese Exclusion Act of 1882, the Palmer Raids that targeted suspected anarchists (most of whom were immigrants) at the beginning of the twentieth century, the internment of Japanese immigrants and Americans during the Second World War, and the infamous red scare led by Senator Joseph McCarthy (Cole 2003, 7–8).

The specific use of detention and deportation in U.S. immigration control has a similarly wide-ranging history. As Daniel Kanstroom (2007) notes, contemporary U.S. deportation law is based in English colonial law and has roots in the fugitive slave laws and forced removal of American Indians exercised in the eighteenth century and nineteenth century. Deportation law takes a two-pronged approach, according to Kanstroom: extended border control and post-entry social control. Extended border control implements the "basic features of sovereign power: the control of territory by the state and the legal distinction between citizens and noncitizens" (Kanstroom 2007, 5). More troubling are the post-entry social controls that derive from what Kanstroom terms an "eternal probation" or "eternal guest" model, in which non-citizens are "harbored subject to the whim of the government and may be deported for any reason" (Kanstroom 2007, 6). In this model, "eternal" is defined based on the relationship of surplus labor reserves to the mechanism of deportation. Used as a form of social control, deportation places immigrants within shifting notions of sovereignty in which they can be discarded during moments of crisis.

Following 9/11, Muslim immigrants became scapegoats in the U.S. pub-

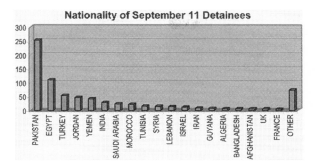

Countries of origin of 9/11 detainees (OIG 2003a, 21).

lic sphere. Simultaneously, the national imaginary employed the categories "Muslim-looking" and "terrorist-looking" to justify state-sanctioned racial violence against a broad spectrum of immigrants of color (Ahmad 2002, 2004). In January 2002, the U.S. Justice Department launched the Absconder Apprehension Initiative, identifying some 300,000 individuals as having violated immigration laws or committed other, minor criminal offenses. Under the initiative, the FBI conducted sweeps of urban Muslim neighborhoods throughout the U.S. that resulted in deportation proceedings for some 5,000 immigrants. In conjunction with the sweeps, the Justice Department launched the National Security Entry–Exit Registration System, also known as Special Registration, in September 2002 to identify suspect immigrants—all of them from Muslim countries and the so-called rogue state North Korea—based on nationality. Approximately 83,310 men considered "foreign visitors" registered with the program, and 13,740 of them were immediately ordered into deportation proceedings. A large portion of these "9/11 detainees" were Pakistani immigrants from the New York area.[6]

In 2003, the *Chicago Tribune* reported that only 2 percent of the unauthorized immigrants in the U.S. had come from the twenty-four predominantly Muslim nations; this group, however, saw a 31.4 percent increase in deportation orders after 2001. Further, 98 percent of the unauthorized immigrants were from all other countries but saw only a 3.4 percent increase in deportation orders.[7] Moreover, the Justice Department did not accurately portray the extent of deportation immediately after 9/11 (see figure above). Oddly, a narrative describing the nationality of the 9/11 detainees mentioned that twenty-nine of them were citizens of Israel, the United Kingdom, and France (Office of the Inspector

General [OIG] 2003a, 21). The embedded assumption is that the detainees were not exclusively from Muslim countries but that they nonetheless could be of Muslim descent, as their nationalities can be be read as "Israeli Arab (or Palestinian)," "British Asian (or Pakistani)," or "French Arab (or Algerian)."

Government statistics obscure not only the extent of deportation but also the demographic impact it has on immigrant populations. For example, many immigrants who leave the U.S. are not reflected in the statistics because they voluntarily return to their home countries. "Voluntary" departure, however, can also stand in for deportation, as detainees may be offered the opportunity to leave after long-term detention and interrogation if they are deemed unable to provide intelligence on criminal, illegal, or terrorist activities. In this sense, voluntary departure thus becomes self-deportation and is not recorded as part of governmental statistics of deportation. The goal of such detentions, in fact, is to coerce detainees into leaving, and into internalizing a logic of criminality, regardless of whether they have committed any crime (Welch 2002). It is partly the fear of long-term detention under Special Registration and of the expanding regime of deportation that has led many Muslim immigrants to seek refuge elsewhere in the diaspora or in their home countries (Nguyen 2005).

The number of return migrants to Pakistan since 9/11 is estimated at well over 100,000, a figure that far exceeds the published statistics on deportation. The effects of this are visible in Brooklyn, which hosts the largest concentrated enclave of Pakistani immigrants in the U.S., most of whom are working-class and working-poor immigrants.[8] Before 2001, the estimated population of "Little Pakistan," an area along Coney Island Avenue in Brooklyn, was reported at 120,000. Return migration and deportation since 2001 has cut that population in half.[9] When I conducted interviews with community activists in the Little Pakistani community in 2008, they made it clear that immigrants continue to feel the repercussions of this dramatic population shift. Legal advocates in Brooklyn report that although applications for legal immigrant status are generally successful, numerous cases and issues remain beyond the scope of activist intervention and that, in turn, continues to drive out-migration from Brooklyn and the United States.[10]

Pakistani immigrants in the U.S. make up a large reserve labor force, and as members of the working classes they are often marginalized.[11] In 2000, more than a quarter of the Pakistani immigrants living in New York City earned less than $20,000 a year, and approximately 28 percent were living below the poverty line. In addition, close to half of the population reports limited proficiency with the English language.[12] Because most of these migrants live in highly concentrated urban enclaves in the U.S., disappearance through deportation and return migration to Pakistan has created entirely new dynamics within the South Asian diaspora.

Carceral Violence and Racial Terror

Since 2001, human-rights organizations have reported on the conditions of racial terror to which detained U.S. immigrants are subjected. In 2004, the American Civil Liberties Union (ACLU) published a series of reports documenting how immigrant detainees were faring after 9/11 in the face of unexplained disappearances, racial profiling, and the separation of families through detention and deportation. The reports' accounts of violations of civil liberties and human rights verify immigrants' claims of procedural malfeasance and abuse. Reports published by the OIG in April 2003 and December 2003 provided further substantiation of such claims, stating:

> The evidence indicates a pattern of abuse by some correctional officers against some September 11 detainees, particularly during the first months after the attacks. Most detainees we interviewed at the [Metropolitan Detention Center] alleged that MDC staff physically abused them. Many also told us that MDC staff verbally abused them with such taunts as "Bin Laden Junior" or with threats such as "you will be here for the next 20–25 years like the Cuban people." Although most correctional officers denied such physical or verbal abuse, the OIG's ongoing investigation of complaints of physical abuse developed significant evidence that it has occurred, particularly during intake and movement of prisoners. (OIG 2003a, 162)

The OIG report describes the incarceration of the 9/11 detainees as unduly harsh and excessively restrictive, providing evidence that a principle of racial containment was in general use by detention staff. This included inadequate access to counsel, the spread of misinformation to detainee families and lawyers, daily twenty-three-hour lockdown, use of heavy restraints, limited recreation, and inadequate notice to detainees of how to file complaints (OIG 2003a, 157–61). The practices, in fact, parallel those used in prisons as solitary confinement, leading a number of human-rights organizations to protest the conditions as inhumane (Meeropol 2005). Further, the "Supplemental Report of Detainee Abuse," released by the OIG in December 2003, concluded:

Based on videotape evidence, detainees' statements, witnesses' observations, and staff members who corroborated some allegations of abuse, . . . some MDC staff members slammed and bounced detainees into the walls at the MDC and inappropriately pressed detainees' heads against walls. We also found that some officers inappropriately twisted and bent detainees' arms, hands, wrists, fingers, and caused them unnecessary physical pain; inappropriately carried or lifted detainees; and raised or pulled detainees' arms in painful ways. In addition, we believe some officers improperly used handcuffs, occasionally stepped on compliant detainees' leg restraint chains, and were needlessly forceful and rough with the detainees—all conduct that violates [Bureau of Prisons] policy. (OIG 2003b, 28)

Thus, the OIG reports document violence that is systematic and, perhaps, an informal part of the U.S. prison system that oversteps official procedures but is used nonetheless. Defying its own policy is precisely what makes the state's policing arm the adjudicator of what constitutes legitimate violence. It is in the domain of informal sovereignty that detention guards gain the leeway to treat detainees with force based on assumptions about immigrants' guilt and relationship to terrorism. Ironically, the terror lies in the violent experience of incarceration, detention, and deportation.

As the OIG reports recount, physical violence was compounded by verbal abuse. Racialized and sexualized epithets used by detention staff included not only "terrorist" and "Bin Laden Junior" but also "motherfucker" and "fucking Muslim." Other abusive phrases recounted by detainees were:

"Whatever you did at the World Trade Center, we will do to you."
"You're never going to be able to see your family again."
"If you don't obey the rules, I'm going to make your life hell."
"You're never going to leave here."
"You're going to die here, just like the people in the World Trade Center died."
(OIG 2003b, 28)

Through a combination of physical and verbal abuse that connects carceral violence to racial terror, the body becomes a site on which to play out sovereign authority. The body as a material and affective register is taunted through anxiety, humiliation, fear, and threats of physical harm directed at the detained and at the families of detainees. It is in this sense that the detainee's body becomes not just a physical entity but also an iterative site that expands to encompass familial and social networks, emotions, silence, and the inexplicable. The detention staff documented by the OIG used psychological, physical, and verbal forms of racial containment that define Muslim detainees as outsiders in the U.S. nation by foregrounding codes of regulatory control that enforce the detainee's body as a foreign body. As Foucault (2003, 249) argues, the power of the state and extralegal forms of control are disciplinary, in making the capacities of the body a site of dominance, and regulatory, in reducing the body to a set of biological processes. The body of the detainee is constructed in a framework of the foreign, illegal migrant who is implicitly criminalized as a racialized Muslim.

Naeem Sheikh, who was picked up in March 2002 and returned to Lahore after a month of detention, described his initial encounter with the FBI and detention staff to the ACLU:

> "He ask me, 'You know Osama bin Laden? You know any terrorist people?' " The agent also asked him if he knew how to pilot a plane—"I said, 'I just know how to drive a taxi' "—and questioned him about his religion. "He said, 'So you are a Muslim?' I said, 'Yes, of course, I'm Muslim.' " (ACLU 2004, 7)

The simple phrases that combine terrorism and Islam in this exchange have become part of the cultural repertoire of responsibility and culpability that is then used against detainees. Detention staff members also made the assumption that they were imposing psychological torture via religious persecution when they initially prohibited Sheikh from praying and denied him halal (Islamically permissable) food. Many other Muslim detainees reported the same conditions. Although Sheikh was later provided special meals, he had to pay for them, further supporting the claim that his religious beliefs marginalize him in an ideological divide that frames him as a racialized Muslim. During his deportation, officials who escorted him to the plane, in a final act of racial humiliation, called him a "terrorist" (ACLU 2004, 7).

The combination of racial and physical abuse seemed incomprehensible to many detainees, as is much racial terror, but the detention staff's rationale is clear: Detainees have violated some law and, by extension, U.S. sovereignty, which requires a disciplinary apparatus to reimpose that sovereignty through physical, verbal, and psychological abuse; immigrants who have overstayed their visas are violating territorial sovereignty, and those who commit criminal offenses, even small ones, are violating social conventions of sovereignty that maintain the rule of law. These circumstances combine a rationale of traditional sovereignty with the imagination of informal networks within the detention and deportation system; this, in turn, permits prison guards to perform extralegal forms of violence and terror as an exercise of sovereign power and as the disciplinary indoctrination of state dominance. Sovereignty thus is not only about the authority of the state but also about the excess of violent policing that purportedly delineates the rule of law and the reinscription of state power. That this violence is acknowledged by state agencies does not undo the violence; instead, such force works to make these acts commonplace and, perhaps, acceptable. It is in this sense that carceral violence is the state of exception that defines the U.S. nation-state, making the prison camp of detention the iconic regime of disciplinary power for migrants as figures of racialized illegality.

Detention as the Disciplinary Camp of Empire

Engseng Ho maintains that the lineage of the current global War on Terror is connected to a history of European imperial expansion through violent military might and the direct authority of colonial administrative structures. Massive social upheaval and oppositional formations in transnational and diasporic migratory populations are a consequence of having imposed this imperial model on Africa, Asia, and the Americas. In the present imperial moment, the United States operates without the intention of colonial occupation, a task that, under neoliberal capitalism, is delegated to "security, military, and colonial functions . . . to private companies, removing them from political oversight" (Ho 2004, 239). Although this model depends on the military might and excessive force of empire, it is through the expansion of free-market principles and the relinquishing of formal colonization that the authority of the U.S. empire continues to flourish. Through invisibility, dissimulation, and misrepresentation, the U.S. has become the custodian of a hidden empire in which sovereign power exerts itself in autonomous zones of economic and social activity through the language of extraterritoriality.[13] Thus, as the U.S. renounces the colonial model, it takes coercive action, from military strikes and espionage to the select dispersion of information to the media and the public, to maintain its authority around the globe.

The presence of excessive force and violence in the U.S. detention and deportation regime reveals the layers of policed sovereignty in which suspect and undesirable immigrant bodies are racialized through classificatory schemes based on national and religious identification. As a framework for racializing Muslims, incarceration reveals a process of criminalization in which detainees are systematically deprived of legal, human, and civil rights (Sheikh 2008). As a site of clearly excessive violence, and in the biopolitical scheme of life and death, the detention and deportation system renders the Muslim detainee's body as not quite human. In this configuration, social death is brought about through sustained violence that concomitantly addresses the value of illegalized immigrant labor. In this necro-political practice of power, death and morbidity represent an intention within the practice of terror during detention and thus become both a figurative and literal possibility for the detainee (Mbembe 2003). Hence, the conditions of the detention cell and the infliction of excessive violence create an embodiment of the "living dead" and the pain of the incarcerated wounded body. The consequences of such exertions produce transnational affective structures of risk and vulnerability through migration systems of forced return, detainee rendition practices, and a global system of deportability.[14]

The immediate power of this kind of imperial control is evident in the testimonials of detainees who describe physical abuse they endured while incarcerated. After he was arrested, Anser Mehmood, a forty-four-year-old Pakistani immigrant who ran a trucking company in New Jersey, was systematically beaten in detention:

> After a night at a holding facility, Mr. Mehmood was taken—in full-body shackles —to the [MDC] in Brooklyn. Upon arrival, he was assaulted by guards while shackled. "They throw me on the wall. My hand was broken at that day. My lip was bleeding. And they terrified me because I was not a criminal. Why they are doing this thing to me? So they repeat the same thing about six or seven times on different walls." (ACLU 2004, 18)

Mehmood also described being placed in "the grave" of solitary confinement, where, he said, officials "never served me any paper. They never visit me any time—for four months and six days" (ACLU 2004, 19). Abuse in detention imagined as death serves not only as a metaphorical description of his bodily condition but also as a description of being denied the right to habeas corpus, literally, the inherent requirement to present the body, or evidence linking the accused under the suspicion of a crime, to a public court of law. Another detainee, Khurram Altaf, also described the isolation of detention and its displacement of social relations: "Without family, life is nothing . . . I'm like a dead person."[15]

Detention and deportation are thus the punitive measures that inflict death not only as a corporal finality but also as a graduated consequence imposed through legal and extralegal policing. What is constructed through the excessive violence of detention is, on the one hand, a domain of graduated sovereignty in which multiple actors are acting on the bodies of immigrants, and, on the other, an affective bare life in which the probability of death is a way to impose invisibility and imperial tutelage. In Agamben's sense, this is the camp par excellence in which death is multiplied for the living homo sacer (Agamben 1998, 2005), a narrative to be retold and calculated in rationales for migration.

But as Agamben's critics have noted, bare life is more complicated than initially theorized (see, e.g., Comaroff 2007; Ong 2006). Bare life is not just the stripping of legal being and rights; it is located in a complex of sovereign power that is simultaneously enforced, contested, and illicit. It is in this formulation of state power and sovereignty that the state has the power to detain and deport; that prison guards are able to enact extralegal violence; and that human-rights advocates can make claims in response to these social controls and reports of violent excess. This circuit of affective violence in the detention and deportation complex disciplines the migrant body into imperial frames of power and dominance with the intention of containing and restricting diasporic movement and possibility. As an example of this restriction, I turn to a narrative of diaspora, post–9/11 forced removal, and the contradictions of return migration.

The Muslim Body in Diaspora

On December 19, 2001, Noor Husain Raza was picked up and taken to an Immigration and Naturalization Service center in Newark. In 1979 he fled Pakistan to avoid political persecution because of his involvement in trade-union activism. Initially he went to the United Arab Emirates, where he worked as an engineer for the Dubai Police Department for a little more than a decade. Later he came to the U.S. in 1992 on a visitor's visa and applied for political asylum based on his forced exile from Pakistan. His initial petition was denied, but he filed to have his case reopened, and in 2001 his application was still pending. He had been working as a baggage handler at Newark International Airport since 1993.

Because of his job at the airport and his immigrant background, Raza was immediately suspected of involvement in the 9/11 attacks. After he was arrested in Newark for immigration violations, he was taken to the county jail in Paterson and soon moved into the general population. He was sixty-one and suffered from several physical ailments, including a heart condition for which prison guards refused to let him see the prison doctor. Because his asylum status was inconclusive, he was kept in in jail for a month, and then was forced to sign a document without reading it, most likely of voluntary deportation. He was sent initially to Karachi, then made his way to Lahore. ACLU interviewers reported:

> His arrest and deportation have been a "tragedy" for him, he said, "I'm not a terrorist. My record is neat and clean. I protect their security and integrity of the United States for 10 years in the Newark Airport." Asked if he would return to the United States if he could, he says yes. "The man who doesn't like dictatorship," he said, "will always ask for freedom." Still he asks how this could have happened to him "when the United States—President Bush—says there is justice, peace and human rights protection, and we are just fighting against the terror . . . not against the religion of Islam." (ACLU 2004, 11)

Raza's return to Pakistan, like that of many other migrants, marked a turning point filled with great challenges and conflicting outcomes. From 2002 to 2006, real-estate prices slowly rose in many of Pakistan's urban centers. A number of returnees put their assets to use by investing in property in middle-class neighborhoods and suburbs. The influx of cash stimulated local developers and real-estate sellers to mark up prices based on a perceived need for properties that would allow return migrants seeking to project their new middle-class status. For example, homes in the Defense Housing Area of Lahore, a high-status urban neighborhood, exploded in value. At the same time, people who owned homes there sold or, in many cases, rented or leased the properties and used their massive capital gains to move to more spacious suburbs.

In 2006, a returnee explained to me that his family had moved into a comfortable, large home in a high-status area and was able to employ servants, which was not possible in his cramped quarters in the U.S. Returning to Lahore also brought his family closer to extended family who had remained in Pakistan. The optimism in such comments changed as money ran out for many of these families and the mounting financial crisis in Pakistan brought real-estate values down. By the end of 2006, many returnees had sold the homes and moved their families to more affordable neighborhoods. Those who did not possess this purchasing power when they returned found themselves renting homes in older, denser middle-class and working-class neighborhoods of Lahore. Many returnees who originally left Pakistan because of limited economic opportunities have found themselves in the same situation and returned to reliable regional circuits of labor migration. Some have again taken temporary contracts in the Gulf region and other locations in the labor diaspora with which these migrants are already familiar.

As much as it is an object, the racialized Muslim body is also located in an imagined geography that designates spaces of suspicion across the U.S. landscape in places of work and worship and in particular neighborhoods (Bayoumi 2008). The domestic War on Terror, following patterns of surveillance and infiltration used historically by the U.S. government against communities of color, is targeting immigrant communities with renewed vigor. These racial geographies are related to the Muslim body through a set of profiles that determine identity and map spatial boundaries. For example, small-scale entrepreneurs, independently employed people, and workers in service industries are disproportionately targeted for immigration policing based on visa status and petty criminal violations (cf. Maira 2009; Nguyen 2005; Sheikh 2004, 2007). Further, Special Registration used nationality, age, and gender as specific determinants of suspicion. Based on a racial logic that predates 2001, the Muslim body has become a site of twenty-first-century disciplining of sovereign power. It is in this sense that Ruth Gilmore (2007, 247) argues for a definition of racism as "state-sanctioned and/or extralegal production and exploitation of group vulnerability to premature death." If racism in its most basic form is the enforcement of boundaries and everyday forms of restriction in which life is circumscribed toward death, then this process presents particular hazards for labor migrants as they pursue social and economic resources amid the known risks of violence, harassment, social death, incarceration, deportation, and, at the extreme, extermination.

For return migrants to Pakistan fleeing deportation and detention, the danger of remaining in the U.S. is often articulated through statements that combine Islam with nationality and appearance. Such articulations, I suggest, are formulated in response to forms of racial objectification of the Muslim body that equates phenotypic difference with cultural and social difference. Following the work of Sara Ahmed (2000, 2004) and Linda Alcoff (2001, 2006), in post–9/11 processes of racialization, bodily comportment and adornment are increasingly used as visual signs of racial difference. These assessments are used to classify the body of the racialized Muslim and to discern difference through naturalized conceptions that connect culture and political identity to the idea of phenotypic difference. This idea of the racialized Muslim body is enforced through the production of racial affect to exclude, intimidate, and imperil. Discussing racialization in terms of ethnographic research, then, raises questions about how to contextualize the race concept when race is not necessarily part of everyday conversation, and whether race needs to be part of everyday conversation for racism to exist. Certainly, discrimination based on items of clothing such as the *hijab* and other gender-specific headgear is extensive.[16] But how does clothing specifically become identified with elements of racism generally based in phenotype? And how are these assumptions used in practices of cultural and social dominance that produce racial affect?

To address these issues, I offer two ethnographic vignettes. These examples examine how boundary making through gendered frameworks is enacted through notions of racialized masculinity and patriarchy and the concept of the racialized Muslim. In both accounts, it is women who are made vulnerable in the active practices of racializing Muslims via assumptions about Islamic patriarchy and narratives of the victimization of the imperiled Muslim woman by the dangerous Muslim man (Razack 2008). These encounters are emblematic of the contradictions of everyday scripts through which immigrants are imagined as problematic figures.

A Pakistani return migrant, Altaf, and his wife, Mary, an immigrant from Haiti who worked in a bank in the New York area. They met through mutual friends and soon decided to marry. Altaf worked odd jobs and, at times, as a computer-networking consultant. After they married, Mary converted to Islam and asked to be called Mariam. She slowly adopted religious dress and donned the hijab at work, which, she said, made her more noticeable in the workplace. Before 9/11, she said, she was treated with indifference and mild disregard, but immediately afterward, she dealt with direct comments and rude behavior. Female co-workers whispered that her husband had "made her" cover up and that she was "becoming a terrorist, too." She initially treated such comments as jokes, but eventually she began explaining to her co-workers that her husband had never forced Islam on her and that she was more religious than he was. She had decided to don the veil based on visits to the local mosque and her interactions with other Muslim women. Nonetheless, her racial position in the workplace as black and as a Haitian immigrant began to take shape in relation to her husband's religious and national background as a Muslim and a Pakistani. Altaf explained that the treatment his wife experienced, coupled with the threat of deportation after 9/11, forced them to consider moving to Pakistan:

> Americans see that my wife is black, and they treat her badly, even though she has a good job. It doesn't matter that she is in a bank. People are always saying things indirectly, but you feel it. They would say things because she was an immigrant and dark. They would joke, and she would listen to them at first, and

later it was tough. I knew I might be in trouble because my visa ran out, so I left for Pakistan. I knew they wouldn't just let me go, and so I told my wife I would go back to Pakistan for a while until things settled and I can come back. But she was afraid of being alone, so she came with me.

It was thus through the combination of state enforcement of immigration policy and the practices of everyday forms of racialization that Altaf and Mariam came to understand their place within U.S. racial hierarchies. The result was a feeling that they did not belong.

Although this story of return migration is common, several aspects make it notable in terms of post–9/11 racial thinking and the processes of suspicion, racial translation, and gendered comportment. The suspicion co-workers directed toward Mariam was constructed in relation to Islam and her marriage to Altaf. Her donning of the hijab articulated a religious transformation and a social construction of learnable religious beliefs that amplified this distrust, because Mariam's co-workers translated her Islamic garb and practice into signs of violence and danger—code words for terrorism—that they condemned through verbal taunting and social boundary making. Also, the presence of a phenotypic racism based on a passive anti-black and anti-immigrant sentiment intensified through Mariam's association with Islam and her shift in dress, which marked her as both a racialized black immigrant and a Muslim. Finally, to her co-workers, conversion and the donning of Islamic garb called forth gendered notions of self-oppression. They interpreted her transformation as a social threat, eliciting direct engagement and verbal responses whose intent was to limit Mariam's social position within the workplace to an inferior and subordinate status.

Altaf's and Mariam's return to Pakistan was also fraught with problems. Although they initially wanted to settle in Lahore, their marriage disrupted Altaf's extended family and ultimately led them to separate. Altaf's family's inablity to accept her cultural differences, language barrier, and limited economic opportunities led Mariam to return eventually to the U.S. Altaf traveled to the Gulf to work. He insisted that he would return to the U.S. one day, but not until the situation improved. He continued to feel threatened by detention and deportation, even though he had never been apprehended for a visa violation in the U.S. Altaf's familiarity with the everyday forms of racial restriction that followed 9/11 increased his awareness of the forms of abjection used to differentiate social groups. This was not going to change any time soon, he said, and to succeed in the U.S., one had to learn to deal with it in everyday life.[17]

Amina, a woman in her late twenties, was born and raised in the U.S. In 2000, she married a Pakistani man, Waqas. Although their marriage was not arranged in the strict sense, according to Amina, their union was organized through her family and the mosque they attended in the U.S. The couple initially faced skepticism based on the assumption that they were "marrying for [immigration] papers." They also faced disapproval from Americans with misconceptions about arranged marriage. The couple traveled back and forth from the U.S. to Pakistan but began to attract attention and suspicion after 9/11.

At one point, Amina and Waqas went to the U.S. Consulate in Islamabad to obtain documents for Waqas. Amina described an encounter she had there with personnel whom she described as white, male Americans:

> They looked at me like I was uneducated and didn't know what I was talking about, even though I speak perfect English. But it was also clearly because I wear the veil and my husband was dressed in *shalwar kameez* [traditional dress] and wears an *amama* [Islamic headgear]. They would look at him and think we had a forced marriage. Just because we are doing things the Islamic way, we are discriminated against.

This interaction illustrates a number of points, including, again, the assumption that gender oppression can be interpreted from Islamic dress and cultural practices such as marriage. The consular officials constructed Amina as an imperiled woman, even though she was defiantly feminist in her own right, as she argued to me. Amina and Waqas were nonetheless read as "uncivilized" because she wore the full veil and he wore traditional Pakistani clothing and had a full beard. Bodily comportment and mannerisms also presented Amina as a particular kind of racialized and gendered figure constructed through the stereotype of the domination of Muslim women under Islamic patriarchy. Waqas was seen not only as a conservative Muslim man but also as lacking class status and education because he did not speak English. This inference translated to Amina, as well, who earned a bachelor's degree in accounting in the U.S. and was the primary breadwinner of the couple. To add to her ongoing disruption of stereotypes of the oppressed, veiled Muslim woman, Amina often acted as a translator for her husband. This behavior complicated the consular officials' attempts to force Amina into ready-made categories such as "imperiled woman" (Razack 2008).

The logic that lay under this encounter did not escape Amina or Waqas. Instead, it left them confounded at the presumed moral authority of those who had judged them. Their perception of injustice reinforced their Islamic practices of renewal and piety. As they explained, their religious beliefs remained their source of refuge when confronting racism. This response to the production of racial affect, although not entirely liberating, allowed them to cope with the seemingly vexing assumptions about the religious and social comportment that they embody. In the end, Amina and Waqas became disillusioned and gave up on returning to the U.S. They settled instead in the United Arab Emirates.[18]

Donning traditional and Islamic garb created a state of racialized subjectivity that related to both Amina's and Waqas's clothing. As a form of comportment that evokes the concept of the racial uniform,[19] in the Du Boisian sense of a racialized subjectivity,[20] Amina contradicted constructed notions of what it means to be a proper American. Although she is a U.S, citizen (and Mariam of the previous vignette held a green card), their wearing of Islamic dress was seen as non-normative gender comportment in the context of American ideals of femininity; it also constructed them as immigrants in relation to racial whiteness, which, in turn, translated the women into external threats. In this sense, the racial uniform materializes the racialized Muslim body into a post–9/11 framework of racial formation via a complex assortment of visual cues. The combination of the Muslim body and the racial uniform is part of the grammar of post–9/11 racialization that makes "the Muslim" a racial category. Donning a racial uniform means claiming, and being claimed as, part of the figure of the racialized Muslim and thus as an embodied representation of a broad constituency of Muslims who differ in race, ethnicity, nationality, and social and cultural background.

Conclusion

The placement of the Pakistani immigrant within the complex political economies of migration to the U.S. has taken on greater complexity in the face of state-endorsed racism since 9/11. In addition to exerting state power through immigration control and legal statutes such as the Patriot Act, the U.S. state plays a central role in this racial configuration of the Muslim as a terrorist in its representations of the multiple Wars on Terror. The necro-politics of migration dictates that certain workers must disregard their bodies in the gamble for greater life chances. Labor migrants represent an extreme of this tenuous existence in the current global economy while they are left unprotected by global capitalism and manipulated by forms of labor migration that attribute such negative moral values to them that their disappearance seems unremarkable.

Through sovereign violence and the reinscription of state power, immigrants' bodies are removed from the national body through the detention and deportation regime to substantiate the security state and simultaneously reclaim sovereign notions of the boundaries of the nation-state. Under informal forms of sovereignty, the migrant body faces multiple enactments of state power that, although contradictory, seek to discipline and regulate migration. The consolidation of state-sanctioned racism against Muslim immigrants is part of a history of racial terror and technologies of violence used to subordinate racialized groups in the U.S. and across the globe. The goal of states' terror formation is to instill a sense of security in the nation while identifying potential threats and dangers to sovereignty. This is how the themes of detention and deportation that persist in return migration evoke a sense of violence, racialization, criminalization, illegality, deportability, and death.

In the end, state technologies of violence reify sovereign power through multiple registers of formal and informal violence that function to eliminate and purge bodies deemed illicit from the territorial boundaries of the nation. This has serious consequences for patterns of migration and labor diaspora within the global economy. Through multiple registers of sovereign power, racism and violence have become a means to make unwanted labor disappear.

Return migration to Pakistan has also had contradictory results and solidified particular ideas about the control and power of the U.S. imperial state. Through racialized extensions of the body that identify comportment, clothing, and other cultural markers, social boundaries are established through everyday forms of racism. For returnees to Pakistan, the disruptions to their lives continue in the encounters with U.S. state power that dictate their further movements and migration in the diaspora. Yet the longing for the possibilities America is perceived to offer continues, and, I imagine, will persist.

Racial Feelings in the Post–9/11 World

In the opening scene of the film *Man Push Cart* (2005), written and directed by Ramin Bahrani, a pushcart vendor named Ahmad (played by Ahmad Razvi) starts his workday. The first seven minutes of the film have minimal dialogue but are full of activity, with the camera focused on Ahmad conducting the daily rituals of the immigrant service class. In the early-morning hours, he arrives at a busy warehouse to find his pushcart. After loading the cart with goods to sell throughout the day, he drags it through the yellow cab–filled streets of Manhattan, a scene depicted several times in the film, making his way to Midtown to sell coffee, donuts, and bagels. With much effort, the breathless Ahmad slowly pushes his cart to a stop at a red light. From a van passing by, he hears an older desi singing a beautiful couplet from a Mohammad Rafi tune: "*Mujhe dard-e-dil ka pata na tha, mujhe aap kis liye mil gaye* (I didn't know of this pain of the heart, for what reason did I find you?)." The desi asks Ahmad if he is OK. He says yes, and they both move on.

Ahmad exemplifies the downward mobility of the immigrant working class. He was once a rock star in Pakistan but now toils as a pushcart vendor to pay his debts. He hustles to make money; after he turns in his pushcart, he takes to the streets of New York to sell pirated pornographic DVDs to working class men of color. Not only does he suffer from the economic obligations of migration; he also has to prove himself within his familial and social network. He is a single father who must earn enough money to reclaim his son from his in-laws, who refuse to give the child up until Ahmad earns enough money to support him. As the pressure to make money rises, Ahmad's emotions begin to take a toll. In an act of blind compassion, he takes in an abandoned kitten, which becomes a symbol of his immigrant condition and his slowly unraveling social bonds. He carefully feeds the sick kitten milk and wipes away its vomit; in the end, though, Ahmad must dig a grave for the newborn. Each day seems to bring new failure; like Sisyphus, he must start every morning by rolling out his pushcart and earn the money to finally redeem himself. In addition to the obvious parallels to Greek tragedy, the film sets Ahmad in a Kafkaesque world in which migrants are trapped by difficult work conditions, exploitative economic relationships, loneliness, racism, and the social marginalization that surrounds them.

Early in the film, Ahmad meets Mohammad, a suit-wearing fellow desi who recognizes Ahmad as a famous rock star in his native Pakistan. Unable to understand why Ahmad is toiling as a pushcart vendor, Mohammad befriends him and hires him to do temporary work finishing his comfortable apartment. Mohammad takes Ahmad to parties and tells his friends that Ahmad is the "Bono of Lahore" (neglecting to mention that he is a pushcart vendor). When Ahmad desperately asks Mohammad for a loan, he learns how shallow their friendship is. Thus, through his former celebrity Ahmad becomes the victim of another cultural meaning of "fallen" status: the metaphor of invisibility and the shallow bonds that connect the immigrant working class to the desi middle class and elite.

The affective ethos of Man Push Cart—one of a deliberate pathos—is evident in the disturbingly banal main character. It is also present in the auditory soundscape of city sounds from Ahmad's everyday life. Ahmad, like many immigrants, is a victim of economic migrancy—a life world that replaces patriarchal and heteronormative familial and kin relationships with fast friendships, social networks of necessity, and fictive kin. This disruption of heteronormativity is part of male migrancy, a disruption that is doubled, and perhaps tripled, for queer migrants who do not fit into established patterns of patriarchal families in their home countries and are cast out. This is one of the enduring messages of Man Push Cart: Families are disrupted, reconfigured, and reimagined through migration. Disrupting stereotypes of Muslim patriarchy and masculinity, Ahmad gives up his life as a rock star and his home, to move to New York to marry the woman he loves and begin a new life as a pushcart vendor. When she dies, Ahmad is left as a single male immigrant who must sacrifice himself for his son and others. His in-laws blame him for taking their daughter away from them, and in return take his son away from him. Ahmad has only his fellow workers and his crew of male desis. As Ahmad is stripped of his family and humanity, he transfers his affection to a kitten that cannot survive. But he must, and he does, continue.

Losing family is a common aspect of immigrant life. The matter-of-fact melancholy of the migrant expresses how loss and mourning are constituted as part of the experience of movement and feeling out of place (Ahmed 2004; Cheng 2001; Eng and Kazanjian 2003). In Bahrami's astounding follow-up

Ahmad dragging his pushcart through Manhattan after the morning shift
in *Man Push Cart* (directed by Ramin Bahrani).

film, *Chop Shop* (2007), immigrant melancholy is expanded to include vulnerable children and teens caught in the lower tiers of the service economy in New York City. Ahmad Razvi returns as the character Ahmad, a bit older and wiser and working as a mechanic at an auto-body shop in Queens. The notion of nuclear family is again disrupted in the form of a brother–sister pair who are forced to work in the unexpected and unacknowledged netherworlds of the American economy.

The melancholy of immigrant life is crafted in a number of other affective registers throughout *Man Push Cart*. In a scene set in a pool hall, the brutality of racism emerges through a retelling of how a desi friend named Atif has been jumped by three Latino assailants (described in the film with the racial epithet "spics"). Atif is stabbed in the stomach and called "terrorist." He survives the attack without justice—only a physical scar and a story to tell. Although the film depicts a world of male immigrants who are noticeably Pakistani, and occasionally Arab, it is not easy to assign the tag "Muslim" here. It is in the violence in which a character is called "terrorist" that the racialization of Muslim and the place of the immigrants in the service economy is made clear.

Man Push Cart intentionally disrupts the idea of a cohesive racialized Muslim and instead places the complexity of immigrant life at the center of the narrative. This serves not to deny the figure of the racialized Muslim but to expand the possibility of reading race through multiple permutations of the race concept. Racism is in the stories of physical violence and everyday experience; it is built into the political economy of the city that makes the immigrant working class vulnerable by excluding them from the rights and resources of security, comfort, and acceptability. Exclusion is also found in the hierarchies of the competitive immigrant working class of color that pits them against one another, leaving each to combat isolation, alienation, and solitude.

Comparative Race Futures

Labor migration is an integral part of the global racial system that historically has combined conceptions of race, class, gender, religion, and sexuality to maintain subordinated subject populations. To workers in the global economy, this system offers a limited set of life chances and opportunities that keep the engines of world capitalism chugging along. The global racial system constructs immigrant workers and Muslims not only as an economic underclass, but also as a cultural underclass framed in the terms of "civilization" and the hierarchy that serves it. The threads of post–9/11 racial formation that transform class and gender via the concept of race reconstruct the figure of the Muslim within historical and conceptual frameworks that have been in place at least since the European conquest of the Americas.

The incorporation of labor migration into the global racial system follows colonial, postcolonial, and imperial trajectories that maintain hierarchies through a racial logic. Glossed as "globalization," transnational work is codified through the systemic categories of race, gender and sexuality, class, religion, ethnicity, and nationality to perpetuate dominance, subordination, and the upward distribution of resources acquired through dispossession. Through the construction of a racialized figure of "the Muslim," panics and moral regulation, imperial spectacles, the informalizing of labor migration, discourses of illegality and criminality, and the transference of racial violence and exclusion onto Muslim bodies, the Pakistani migrant is constructed as an object of terror, illegality, and criminality that must be policed in the War on Terror. Terrifying Muslims is a project of control and security that expands the U.S. racial formation and regimes of racial terror and violence while simultaneously creating the Muslim migrant as a potential terrorist. This serves several purposes that need to be carefully untangled. The figure of the Muslim is as complicated as the figure of the migrant, another constantly expanding category of racism.

Ruth Gilmore (2007) has described racism as the predisposition to premature death through the restrictions and boundaries of everyday life. Through regulation and discipline, bodies are made into racial things that are produced, controlled, and disappeared. The question of life chances is tethered to premature death in the structures of possibility and impossibility that make globalization a complex system of accumulation and dispossession. Transnational workers take this risk and convert in into the challenge of possibility. The price is an overwhelming process of racialization that constrains them as bodies, ideas, systems, and objects. In my examples, I have demonstrated how this happens to Pakistani labor migrants in the global arena, in which religion becomes a focal point of their racial vulnerability as workers. The dangers read into their subjecthood are of terrorism, illegality, and criminality, concepts that overlap global workers with the racialized figure of the Muslim. As a rationale for boundary making and regulation, manufacturing enemies in the name of security and containment and policing them serves the purposes of U.S. state formation and American empire. It is part of the machinery of war and the state's monopoly on violence. In a gesture toward the history in which the racialized figure of the Muslim was created, the global War on Terror constructs an enemy in vulnerable populations such as easily disposable and expendable transnational workers who can be isolated through everyday practices of terror prevention.

Bringing to light the many ways in which the global economy works to make people and things into objects of circulation and consumption is a major task of this book. This process is not a mere abstraction; it consists of a set of material effects produced by the inequalities of global capitalism that are present in everyday lives. By placing working-class migration in the foreground of the global racial system, my intention is to expose how labor migrants are made illegal in the global economy and the connection to the reign of racial terror and violence that is at the heart of the imperial War on Terror. Employing an intersectional and relational approach, a hallmark of comparative race and gender studies that has much to offer the future studies of race, I argue that racism is not merely a functionalist relationship of actions and practices but a vast repository of techniques, strategies, logics, and tactics. Generations of scholars have toiled to expose the systemic basis of oppressions such as racism, while others have dismissed this work as misguided. Now more than ever, as an expanding racism propels its victims toward premature death, it has become urgent for studies of race to uncover the overlooked, the understated, and the taken for granted.

If there is an underlying explanation for the system that racializes transnational workers, it is the unequal distribution of resources that forces populations across the globe in pursuit of economic opportunity. Such systems are always based on the exploitation and easy abandonment of a workforce that is temporary and unprotected by labor laws. In the end, the immediate solution is to craft protections for transnational workers that recognize their contributions and respect their lives. Many human-rights and labor-rights activists and organizers have been at work to make such connections visible across the globe.

A recent example is the hard work of the New Orleans Workers' Center for Racial Justice (NOWCRJ), which has taken on a case for Indian workers who were brought to the U.S. by the Signal Corporation. Working through Dewan Consultants, a migration labor agency in India, Signal hired scores of workers to rebuild New Orleans after Hurricanes Katrina and Rita in 2005. Dewan charged workers exorbitant fees (more than $20,000 each) to obtain H-2B visas, which permitted temporary and seasonal nonagricultural work. Workers were further promised green cards, permanent resident status, and eventual reunification with their families through sponsorship to the U.S. Many of the workers had taken out hefty loans and sold their homes and belongings to pay for the chance to achieve the American dream. When they arrived in the U.S., however, the workers quickly learned about the false and illegal premises under which they were brought. Signal reneged on its original promises and began a campaign of illegal policing and violence by its own private security force that used threats of deportation, a common trick in illegal recruiting in the unregulated global economy. Some of the workers had labored in the Persian Gulf and had seen these practices before. They immediately organized to demand more humane treatment; Signal responded by sending armed guards to arrest the organizers. The workers organized a series of walkouts and a hunger strike that lasted more than three weeks. The victory they won through these actions brought widespread media attention and the intervention of congressional leaders, who asked the U.S. Justice Department and immigration officials to look into the accusations of fraud. Signal ultimately blamed the Indian recruiters and a subcontractor, thus escaping direct blame by taking advantage of weak international regulations and U.S. laws concerning H-2B workers.[1]

The story of Signal's malfeasance is not novel or exceptional. In fact, such incidents are pervasive in the world of labor migration. The NOWCRJ alone has documented scores of cases of worker abuse in post–Hurricane Katrina New Orleans. Instead of hiring local African American working class laborers, for instance, companies outsourced the work to immigrant and domestic laborers of color from Asian and Latin American countries and from American Indian reservations. These workers were chosen because of their assumed docility and legal and socioeconomic vulnerability; they were thus easy to manage using the colonial strategy of divide and rule.[2] That such transnational labor practices generate such a milieu of fear, exorbitant debt, and threats of deportation is a commentary on the expansion of capitalism and the global racial system under globalization. The system targets people who are susceptible to exploitation in networks of labor migration, including those who have become used to exploitative work conditions in places like the Persian Gulf. As Svati Shah (2008) argues, the exploitation by corporations of male workers in New Orleans after Katrina has much in common with the illegal trafficking of women to the U.S. by organized crime networks.[3] By acting in a way that takes advantage of people who are economically vulnerable and legally dependent, these corporations maximize profits with impunity.

As global patterns of worker exploitation expand, labor migrants are creating their own movements to protest these conditions. The global justice movement, which is growing by the day, is struggling to reconcile the many contradictions of the global economy that exploit footloose labor in the global racial system. Grassroots organizers are leading the way not only in undoing economic injustice, but also in exposing racism for what it is: a system of modern violence, terror, and exploitation. Through their tireless work, the collaborations of such labor organizers with migrant workers are crafting new ways to imagine a just world. Despite the absence of a definitive resolution to the problems of racism and exploitation, the future remains hopeful in their hands.

Introduction

1 Salman Masood, "Two Pakistani Contractors are Taken Hostage in Iraq," *New York Times*, July 27, 2004.

2 Although I followed these events while in Pakistan that summer on regional news channels, much of the information was chronicled in the *New York Times*: see ibid.; Jeffrey Gettleman, "Iraq Group Issues Threat to Behead a Missing Marine," June 28, 2004; Khalid al-Ansary and Ian Fisher, "Seventy Are Killed by Car Bomber in an Iraqi City," July 29, 2004; David Rohde and Salman Masood, "In Pakistan, Turning Grief into New Political Muscle," July 30, 2004; Ian Fisher and Somini Sengupta, "Iraqis Postpone Conference as Kidnappings Increase," July 30, 2004; Ian Fisher, "Insurgents Fire Rockets at Two Baghdad Hotels," July 3, 2004; Somini Sengupta, "Five GIs Killed in Attack; Philippines Bars Iraq Trip," July 9, 2004; Seth Mydans, "Looking Out for the Many, in Saving the One," August 1, 2004; Sabrina Taverse, "Twelve Hostages From Nepal Are Executed in Iraq, a Militant Group Claims," September 1, 2004.

3 Throughout this book, I refer to transnational migrants as a semi-permanent workforce that travels to numerous locations and engages in multiple patterns of migration (e.g., chain, step, seasonal, radial/circular). The term "international migrant," by contrast, is often used to describe those who migrate in one direction. I emphasize the transnational aspect of the migration experience to point to the often liminal state of labor migrants in relation to nation, race, and legality, to name a few of the central concepts that shape their subjectivity.

4 For example, throughout the 1980s, the U.S. government promoted so-called jihad in Afghanistan to defeat the Soviet Union. The mujahideen, trained by the U.S. and Pakistan, were later abandoned by their U.S. and Saudi sponsors to divide up the remains of war-torn Afghanistan (Devji 2005; Rashid 2001).

5 In *Society Must Be Defended* (2004), Foucault describes biopolitics as the primacy of race war in the development of state power. He argues, "Racism first develops with colonization, or in other words with colonizing genocide. . . . War is about two things: it is not simply a matter of destroying a political adversary, but of destroying the enemy race, of destroying that [sort] of biological threat that those people over there represent to our race" (Foucault 2004, 257).

6 This is also the point of many of the fine essays in Hagopian 2004. The geographic notion of the Middle East is a key component of how U.S. foreign policy has been framed for the past half-century. Countries of the Muslim world not explicitly defined as part of the Middle East, such as Pakistan, now have a pivotal role in the War on Terror that links them to a broader "Muslim" area. Iran and Indonesia are similarly imagined in regional and foreign policy. This geography requires a critical rethinking of Middle Eastern and South Asian area studies and ethnic studies. In an important issue of the *Journal of Asian American Studies*, edited by Sunaina Maira (June 2006), the place of Arab Americans is usefully thought through in the field of Asian American studies.

7 As Karim H. Karim (2000) argues, the concept of Islamic peril and threat is centuries old and is constantly reimagined.

8 Some of the important works that investigate U.S.-based migration and South Asian diasporas directly relevant to this approach are Ewing 2008a; Gopinath 2005b; Kumar 2000, 2002; Leonard 1992, 2007; Maira 2002, 2009; Mathew 2005; Prashad 2000, 2001. On general approaches and European-based South Asian diasporas, see Brown 2006; Ewing 2008b; Werbner 1990, 2002, 2003.

9 This category includes Arab Americans, South Asian Americans, Iranian Americans, and Southeast Asian Americans, to name a few. The point is that they are collapsed racially according to phenotypic and cultural traits. The category is also expansive in that it goes beyond religion to include those who are mistaken for Muslims and beyond the strict concept of biological racism to include black, Latina/o, and white Muslims.

10 Sunaina Maira (2007, 42) also makes this point in an excellent analysis of the Hayat case in Lodi, California, in which a father and son of Pakistani origin were falsely charged with terrorist activity and prosecuted based on the logic of preventive detention.

11 This does not mean that women are not part of these streams of migration. It is based more on the fact that I studied flows of workers to the Middle East, and then to other locations, that started in Pakistan and that were largely contractually designated for men. The Pakistani state is very careful about contracting women workers because of the possibility of exploitation and trafficking. Pakistani women have been recruited for contracted transnational labor in the Middle East since the late 1990s mostly to work in professional occupations such as medicine, finance and banking, and information technology. These categories offer fewer jobs than do occupations that call for male labor migration from Pakistan. This gender difference in contracted employment is complex and substantial, and it alters the terms of social assignment and the possibility of divisions of labor within the diaspora. It is in this sense that class differences create a particular performance of masculinity through diasporic labor.

12 Referred to as the Arab Gulf states, and officially as the Gulf Cooperation Council, they include Bahrain, Kuwait, Oman, Qatar, Saudi Arabia, and the United Arab Emirates.

13 For fictional descriptions of the complex changes created by the oil economy of Gulf countries, see Munif 1987, 1993a, 1993b. Kanafani 1997 also captures the dilemmas of labor migration for Palestinians in the Gulf.

14 For an analysis of the complex organizing that took place in Karachi in this period, see Ali 2005.

15 *Dubai chalo* translates as "Let's go to Dubai," a popular reference to the largely working-class migration to Gulf countries since the 1970s. Although these migrations continue, professional-class overseas Pakistanis have been more frequently referred to since the 1990s. This group also spans the globe, with the U.S. regarded as the ideal destination. *Amrikan* translates as "American."

16 For an example in the New York taxi industry, see Mathew 2005.

17 As Timothy Mitchell (1991) observes, the state produces its effects in multiple fields through a reified and disembodied appearance through state and non-state actors.

18 Begona Aretxaga (2003) uses the term "maddening state" to describe the Kafkaesque modalities of the state's political and bureaucratic structures that take on a psychoanalytic character.

19 I conducted my fieldwork during extended stays in Lahore in 2000–2001 and New York in 2001–2003. I also made intermittent visits, lasting from a few weeks to a few months, to Lahore, New York, and Dubai between 1998 and 2006. I conducted more than one hundred interviews, approximately twenty of them with state officials, and the rest with labor migrants. I have changed all of the names of the labor migrants I interviewed to protect their identities. The interviews were conducted in Urdu, Punjabi, and English. All translations are mine.

Chapter 1. Islam and Racism

1 Sherene Razack (2008, 5) argues that the "casting out" of Muslims from the North American body politic through the global War on Terror is grounded in three allegorical figures: the dangerous Muslim man, the imperiled Muslim woman, and the civilized European. The civilized European is a figure of white supremacy that encompasses a number of referents. By exploring race thinking and the legal and social functions of the concept of the camp to banish Muslims through the technologies of the police state, such as surveillance, detention and deportation, incarceration, and torture, Razack offers an important analytical framework to examine imperial governance in the post–9/11 context. As she notes, the expansion of the twenty-first-century notion of empire and the colonial logic of the threat of notions

of premodern Muslim terrorist men is tethered to technologies of gender rendered into sexual torture and racial terror for captive detainees and, more broadly, the figure of the racialized Muslim.

2 Although not discrete, the concepts of anti–Muslim racism and Islamophobia outline how modern racism has incorporated Muslims and Islam as a singular population. I maintain the distinction between Islamophobia and anti–Muslim racism also to name forms of prejudice that are lodged against Islam as a religion rather than against Muslims as a people, although the two are often entangled.

3 At various historical moments, Islam, Judaism, and Christianity have stood in opposition to one another in different ways, but in the genealogy I trace, I examine Islam and Judaism as they stand in opposition to Christianity. On the contemporary role of Islamophobia and anti–Semitism in Europe, see Bunzl 2005; Silverstein 2004, 2005. For an analysis of sexuality and sexual desire in the encounter between the Middle East and the West see Massad 2007.

4 Of course, this begs the question of whether racism existed without a conception of race. Rather than entertain that complex question, I maintain that the logic of current forms of Islamophobia can be traced to the history of race in the European and American context. Benjamin Isaac's recent controversial monograph (Isaac 2004) does much to trace the concept of racism to the age of classical antiquity. Significantly, this book follows the logic of many historians of racism who trace the concept of racism (and not race) to a hatred of Jews that is often classified through the problematic category "anti–Semitism" (see, e.g., Bunzl 2005). Bunzl elaborates on the contemporary political dimensions within Europe in Bunzl 2007. Although he is correct to call the concepts of Islamophobia and anti-Semitism modern, his historical analysis of the long durée of the race concept and racism remains problematic. In particular, the term "anti–Semitism" as an argument of racial particularity disavows racisms that may be historically shared or overlapping, as I argue is the case of the Muslim and the Jew—two identities once racially understood as Semitic. On the political valences of the term "anti–Semitism," see also Anidjar 2003, xiii, 2008; Butler 2003, 101–27; Cockburn and St. Clair 2003.

5 For example, Howard Winant (2000, 172) defines race as "a concept that signifies and symbolizes sociopolitical conflict and interests in reference to different types of human bodies." Leith Mullings (2005, 684) has also offered a definition of racism as

> a relational concept. It is a set of practices, structures, beliefs, and representations that transforms certain forms of perceived differences, generally regarded as indelible and unchangeable, into inequality. It works through modes of dispossession, which have included subordination, stigmatization, exploitation, exclusion, various forms of physical violence, and sometimes genocide. Racism is maintained and perpetuated by both coercion and consent and is

rationalized through paradigms of both biology and culture. It is, to varying degrees at specific temporal and spatial points, interwoven with other forms of inequality, particularly class, gender, sexuality, and nationality.

6 Talal Asad critiques the notion of religion as a transhistorical essence made common in the anthropological frameworks of Clifford Geertz. Religion in the anthropological imagination, Asad argues, must be thought of as contingent and dynamic, as opposed to a Eurocentric conception that defines religion as bounded and universal. To undo this essentialism of universality, religious symbols must be thought of as intimately linked to social life, and thus the concept of religion must change alongside social practice (Asad 1993, 53). To study the concept of religion, it must be framed in terms of a historically specific construction and examined as it changes over time. This influential critique has led to important theoretical and conceptual shifts in ethnographic practice for scholars of religion and modernity. Yet a question lingers as to the place of the race concept in relation to religion.

7 Karen Leonard (2003, 56–61) points to two specific arenas of scholarly research on Islam and race: (1) African American Islam and the role of race, culture, and class; and (2) the recent racialization of Muslims. This leaves a great deal open in terms of how religion—specifically, Islam—is racialized. Much of Leonard's summary of the literature relies on scholarship that imputes polar notions of race that place South Asian Americans and Arab Americans between black and white. This mode of analysis is clearly due to the gap in thinking through the history of race and racism as they relate to Islam and Muslims.

8 Examples of the terrorist and the immigrant as archetypal figures are widely discussed in Silverstein 2005; Werbner 2005.

9 The landmark Runnymeade Trust report "Islamophobia: A Challenge for Us All," published in 1997, is credited with institutionalizing the concept of "Islamophobia" in British discourse by conflating it with discrimination against Islam and religion and Muslims as a group. Although I am critical of this approach because it does not effectively define anti–Muslim racism, this was the culmination of important antiracist work in the U.K. and across Europe that was far ahead of the U.S. The report's use of "Islamophobia" to gloss a number of forms of systematic oppression as a singular concept also clearly mirrors the development of the term anti–Semitism. The report is available online at http://www.runnymedetrust.org/publications/17/74.html (accessed October 10, 2009).

10 In the context of the so-called Danish cartoon controversy of 2006, in which Danish and other European newspapers published a series of caricatures of the Prophet Muhammad that many Muslims deemed offensive, the argument has been made that the term "Islamophobia" confuses religious hatred with religious criticism. While I have reservations about this point, I think it is important to make clear that my argument is not about Islamic theology. It is about the formal and

informal forms of discrimination committed against practitioners and those believed to be practitioners of Islam. In other words, I argue that it is as a social group, not as a religious group, that Muslims are racialized.

11 For an example of this debate, see Stolcke 1995; Visweswaran 1998. On the relationship between race talk and culture talk in relation to the Muslim, see Mamdani 2001. Although the relationship varies widely, culture talk according to Stolcke (1995) encompasses race and racism as a subset of cultural artifacts, whereas Visweswaran (1998) cautions that such an approach minimizes the power of the race concept to organize through cultural means. It is thus that race talk is euphemistically conceived as culture in the broad sense. On the persistence of race in cultural and political economy, see Harrison 1995, 2008. See also the intervention into the study of racism in anthropology in Mullings 2005.

12 For example, Steven Vertovec (2002, 23–24) defines "Islamophobia" in the context of Britain as a form of cultural essentialism and xenophobia that is demonstrated through the vilification of Islam, as well as in institutional discrimination against Muslims. Tariq Modood (1997, 4) provides a more forceful definition:

> The contemporary prejudice against Muslim immigrants is based on an anxiety about (what are perceived to be) features of values and practices derived from Islam. . . . For the Islamophobia in question is more like anti-semitism than anti–Judaism. It is more a form of racism than a form of religious intolerance though it may perhaps be best described as a form of cultural racism, in recognition of the fact that the target group, the Muslims, are identified in terms of their non–European descent, in terms of their not being white, and in terms of their perceived culture, and that the prejudice against each of these aspects interacts with and reinforces the prejudice against the others.

13 For more on this shift in the context of U.S. politics, see Omi and Winant 1994, 95–136.

14 Interestingly, Tariq Ramadan initially shied away from connecting Islamophobia and racism. His argument for an assimilationist politics for Muslims in the West rests on the idea of including Muslims' difference within Western nations through alliance building and incorporation. As he explains, "I have consciously decided not to deal specifically with the problems of political security faced by European and American States, or with Islamophobia or social discrimination—not because I think these problems are secondary but because my thinking is based on a higher level" (Ramadan 2004, 6). In more recent writing, he has extended this argument of inclusionary politics and refers to discrimination and structural racism as connected to a process of "culturalizing" and "Islamizing" (Ramadan 2009, 75–76).

15 In anthropological thought, culture is based in colonial hierarchies that defined it in terms of civilization and the imputed categories of superiority and inferiority.

This reified use of culture often cloaks racial ideologies of separation and biological notions of purity that ultimately are threatened by the possibility of miscegenation. It is in this sense that the anthropological use of ethnology as a form of racialized knowledge production is centrally complicit in constructing the ideological edifice of racial difference and hierarchy.

16 It is important to note that "Moor" referred to North African Muslims, denoting an identity based on religious difference, although many Moors traced their origins to Arab roots based in a particular land-based identity. The term "Morisco" is related to "Moor" in that it identifies a convert to Christianity from Islam (L. P. Harvey 2005, 2–10). The term "Moor" thus is a religious appellation whose meaning shifted over time to include racial connotations of skin color supposedly connected to a brownish or darker hue (moreno). Thus, throughout this section, I use "Moor" and "Muslim" interchangeably to refer to the imagined conflation of the two by Catholic Spain, other Europeans, and the explorers.

17 Although he concedes a widespread othering of Muslims in Spain after 1499, L. P. Harvey (2005, 6–12) argues that it is impossible to determine whether this was racist, given the broad range of skin colors they displayed. Nonetheless, he, like many other scholars, does point out that the term "Moor" was often associated with dark complexions and darkness. Harvey's reading relies on a definition of race that is based in phenotypic difference that views blackness as inferior (cf. Gomez 2005, 29; Menocal 2002, 271–72). The problem with this definition is that it reifies phenotypic descriptions of black and white when racial essentialism is far more complex.

18 On the ongoing dilemma between Christian Spain and its Muslim past, present, and future, see also Aidi 2003, 2006.

19 Jasbir Puar and Amit Rai (2002) describe this as the triangulation of the monster, terrorist, and fag in the post–9/11 racial formation, a genealogy of gender and sexuality that has a precedent in the founding logic of the race concept. Also see Massad 2007.

20 See Andrea Kalin and Bill Duke, dirs., Prince among Slaves (documentary, Unity Productions Foundation, 2007).

21 For an elaboration of this religious complexity in early South Asian immigrant communities in the U.S., see Jensen 1988. The early scholarly literature on South Asian Americans often used the term "Hindu" while acknowledging its discrepancy. Vijay Prashad (2000) offers a different history that proposes the term "desi" as an inclusive identity.

22 Without doubt, the goal of the Arab American and South Asian American communities in these battles was to be assigned legally to the category of whiteness to procure the right to citizenship. For critical readings of these strategies, see Gualtieri 2001; Visweswaran 1997.

23 In addition to Auschwitz, other camps used similar terms that tied the Jew to the Muslim. At Buchenwald, for example, Jewish prisoners were called "*müder Scheich* (tired sheiks)," and at the women's camp Ravensbrück they were called "*Muselweiber* (Muslim women)," See Agamben 1999, 44.

24 Gil Anidjar elaborates the place of Arabs as an ethnic group and of Jews as a religious group within this racial economy of the enemy. In his argument, race, religion, and ethnicity are central to understand how these two categories emerged as political identities and, ultimately, the history of the concept of the political. One might contend that the Muslim is an extension of this argument of a racial–religious continuum in relation to Anidjar's historical object of study, Europe, as well as in the U.S. (Anidjar 2003, 2008).

Chapter 2. Racial Panic

1 Stanley Cohen (1972, 9) described moral panics in terms of fear and anxiety surrounding youth culture:

> Societies appear to be subject, every now and then, to periods of moral panic. A condition, episode, person or group of persons emerges to become defined as a threat to societal values and interests; its nature is presented in a stylised and stereotypical fashion by the mass media; the moral barricades are manned by editors, bishops, politicians and other right-thinking people; socially accredited experts pronounce their diagnoses and solutions; ways of coping are evolved or (more often) resorted to; the condition then disappears, submerges or deteriorates and becomes more visible. Sometimes the panic is passed over and forgotten, but at other times it has more serious and long-term repercussions and it might produce changes in legal and social policy or even in the way in which the societies conceive themselves.

The panics Cohen refers to involve a mixture of legal and illegal activities such as drug use, student militancy, political demonstrations, hooliganism, and all sorts of crime. More recently, the concept of moral panic has been used in the British press to describe the effects of pedophilia, sex scandals in the church, sex work, and, of course, immigration. Moral panics involve a process whereby social anxieties and fear are organized in a fashion that becomes known as rational and logical. As Cohen describes, moral panics are part of the rationality that becomes the explanation of events.

2 Following Cohen's insights, Stuart Hall and his colleagues at the Birmingham Center for Contemporary Cultural Studies began thinking about how racial explanations were implicated in the concept of moral panics to explain the racist backlash sweeping Britain (Hall et al. 1978). They argued that, under conditions of economic

and political crisis, moral panics over black criminality are alleviated by the state's intervention via police action and the creation of an ideological superstructure to justify authoritarian measures. Central to the configuration of black criminality is the concept of a law-and-order society (Centre for Contemporary Cultural Studies 1982). This is to say that in moments of crisis, upholding the rule of law becomes the means through which the practices of the state apparatus are legitimized through the arm of the police. Ideas about race are mobilized in moral panics as a result of a directly or indirectly perceived threat. The rule of law then becomes a selective enforcement on particular racial groups that are assigned this level of threat. The entire edifice of the law relies on the universality of its subjects, yet racial difference assigns various relationships of these subjects to state power. This is achieved through the ideological work of racist common sense. In Paul Gilroy's examples, the visual imagery of panic combines criminality and illegality with the racial signifier of blackness: "The cavalcade of lawless images—stowaways, drifters, pimps and drug dealers . . . extends into the present in the forms of muggers, illegal immigrants, black extremists and criminal Rastafarians (dreads). The black folk-devil has acquired greater power with each subsequent permutation" (Gilroy 1982, 145). At the time, blackness in the U.K. was the predominant political identification for people of color; in "Police and Thieves," Gilroy discusses Afro-Caribbeans as criminals and Asians as illegal immigrants. Both are racialized pictures of criminality that are reconstituted in moments of crisis.

3 See http://www.fbi.gov/pressrel/pressre102/122902press.htm. Accessed October 2009.

4 Neil A. Lewis, "FBI Issues Alert for Five Illegal Immigrants Uncovered in Terrorist Investigation," New York Times, December 30, 2002.

5 Associated Press, "Pakistani Says FBI Mug Shot Is a Case of Stolen Identity," in New York Times, January 2, 2003.

6 Agence France-Presse, "FBI Admits Tip on Illegal Immigrants in Terror Probe Was False," in The News, (Lahore), January 8, 2003.

7 Muhammad Badar Alam, "Fallible Bureau of Investigation," The News, (Lahore), January 12, 2003.

8 Migrants often travel abroad through travel agents who are unofficial brokers for overseas laborers. They possess access to networks of social affiliation that can provide jobs for clients who do not have official work visas. Ashgar made clear that he was in contact with a number of brokers and agents throughout his travels. I discuss this system more thoroughly in chapters 4 and 5.

9 The Federal Investigation Agency is Pakistan's equivalent to the American FBI.

10 Interview, Badar Alam, February 25, 2006.

11 The Immigration Act of 1917 (39 Stat. 874) specifically identifies Asia and the Pacific Islands as Afghanistan, Arabia, Borneo, Celebes, Ceylon (Sri Lanka), India,

Indochina, Java, the Malay Peninsula, New Guinea, Siam (Thailand), Sumatra, and parts of Russian Turkestan and Siberia.

12 Rather than accepting the historical narrative of Kaiser Wilhelm's declaration of threats from the East, specifically from Japan, in 1895, Gary Okihiro (1994) traces the yellow peril as far back as the fifth century B.C. Okihiro argues that Hippocrates and Aristotle, among others, imagined "the Asian" as a threat through the conflict between the Greeks and Persians.

13 Tom Zeller, "Terror Diaspora," New York Times, March 3, 2002.

14 The use of the term "enemy combatant" is telling in this regard because it represents figures who are outside both the rule of law of nation-states (in this example, the U.S.) and international law.

15 As an example, see Thomas Friedman "The Two Domes of Belgium," New York Times, January 27, 2002.

16 See, e.g., "Khalid Sheikh Mohammed," available online at http://www.global security.org/military/world/para/ksm.htm (accessed December 2009).

17 The CIA, which has long been suspected of waterboarding, a form of torture that creates the sensation of drowning, admitted to using this illegal torture technique on three detainees, including Khalid Sheikh Mohammed, in secret offshore detention prisons referred to as "black sites": see Jane Mayer, "The Black Sites: A Rare Look Inside the CIA's Secret Interrogation Program," New Yorker, August 13, 2007.

18 Marc Santora, "A Boyhood on the Mean Streets of a Wealthy Emirate," New York Times, March 3, 2003.

19 See, e.g., James Risen, "The Suspect: Tied to Many Plots, an Elusive Figure Who Came to U.S. Attention Late," New York Times, March 2, 2003.

20 This kind of reasoning is rampant in the U.S. military, where a cross-section of Muslim Americans—from South Asian to Arab, Southeast Asian, and converts— joined the armed forces in a show of patriotism. The most controversial case of suspected espionage tied to religious belief and racism is that of Captain James Joseph Yee, a Muslim military chaplain who was charged with colluding with detainees considered enemy combatants at the Guantánamo Bay detention facility. The suspicions were clearly based on hearsay and innuendo, as demonstrated by the fact that he was later brought up on charges of adultery that were eventually dropped (see Yee and Molloy 2005).

21 Mohammed is thought to have more than fifty aliases, including Ashraf Refaat Nabith Henin, Khalid Adbul Wadood, Salem Ali, Fahd bin Adballah bin Khalid, Abdulrahman A. A. Alghamdi, Mukhtar the Baluchi, Hashim Abdulrahman, Hashim Ahmed, and Khalid al-Shaykh al-Ballushi. Intelligence briefings also have used several transliterations of Mohammed's name, including Khalid Sheikh Mohammed, Khalid Shaikh Muhammed, Khalid Shaykh Mohammad, Khaled Shaikh Mohammad, and Khalid Shaykh Muhammed.

22 On the targeting of queer immigrants of color, see also Audre Lorde Project 2004.

Chapter 3. Imperial Targets

1 Interview, Lahore, July 17, 2004.

2 On the connection of these categories of identity, see Naber 2000, 2002, 2006; Volpp 2002. Following the practices of feminist and queer activists, Nadine Naber (2008, 8) suggests "SWANA (Southwest Asian and North African)" as an alternative to "Arab American" and "Middle Eastern," which include non–Arab groups such as Iranians and are organized through shared geography and similar historical relationships to U.S. imperialism. "AMSA (Arab, Muslim, and South Asian Americans)" has also been proposed (Maira and Shihade 2006, 124).

3 The visible demographic of South Asians in the U.S., most of whom are Indian in origin, are from the professional, educated classes drawn to the American service economy after immigration laws shifted in 1965 to specifically attract technically skilled migrants. When family reunification became an immigration priority in the 1990s, this population, which had been largely middle class, began to change in character to include larger demographics from the lower-middle and working classes (Mathew 2005, 119; Prashad 2000). In the case of Pakistan, gender roles, differences in education, and access to resources meant that working-class migrants initially were mostly men. Since the 1980s, many of these working-class men have sponsored the immigration of their extended families or maintained their transnational family relationships through seasonal migration. In the latter kinship arrangement, family members are divided between home and host country, and sometimes scattered in multiple countries. The transnational migrants work for extended periods of time, then return to their families during vacations or at seasonal intervals in Pakistan. I elaborate on these coordinates of transnationalism in the chapters that follow.

4 "Arab" itself is a complex and contested category that encompasses ethnic, religious, linguistic, and national diversity. The term is most often connected to linguistic and cultural similarity and the nationalist movements that imagined a pan–Arab identity; "Arab" in this sense is a political category formed during the Cold War. As Nadine Naber (2008, 5) makes clear, "Although U.S. popular cultural representations often conflate the categories 'Arab' and 'Muslim,' not all Arabs are Muslims and not all Muslims are Arabs."

5 For more on the rivalry between British and Russian colonial powers and the formation of the so-called New Great Game in Central Asia between multinational interests and the American imperial war in Afghanistan, see Rashid 2001, 2002, 2008.

6 This cross-border region historically occupied by the Pashtun ethnic group was dubbed "AfPak" by the White House strategist Richard Holbrooke in 2008.

7 Although such categories of naming can be used positively for unification, they can also be used to dominate and control through the maintenance of societal structures

of power (Brown 1995). This should not prevent these terms from being used in liberation struggles, even though such naming is a part of a contingent politics of liberal multiculturalism that can often subdue radical possibility (Prashad 2006).

8 These are at least some of the themes in post–9/11 films. A number of others, employed in the war and action genres, perpetuate the image of Islam as violent or corrupt or both. Far too often, the logic is simplistic and undermines the complex intentions of the filmmakers: see, e.g., *Body of Lies* (Ridley Scott, Warner Bros., 2008), *The Kingdom* (Peter Berg, Universal Pictures, 2007), *Lions for Lambs* (Robert Redford, Andell Entertainment, 2007), and *Rendition* (Gavin Hood, Anonymous Content, 2007).

9 Numerous postcolonial feminists have thoroughly critiqued the logic of these rescue narratives (see, e.g., Grewal 1996; Mohanty 1991; Shohat 2006; Spivak 1988).

10 In an unusual glossary of terms for the HBO miniseries *Generation Kill*, which aired in 2008, "haji" is defined as

> an Iraqi of Arab or Muslim of any ethnicity: from the Arabic "Haji," which is the honorific term for anyone who has made the trip to Mecca, the Haj: most Americans [?] who use the term Haji are probably not referring to that pilgrimage but to the once popular children's cartoon Johnny Quest in which the white boy hero's turban-wearing sidekick was named Haji: not necessarily a pejorative term, Haji may be used as an adjective to describe anything Middle Eastern, e.g. Iraq's customary flat bread is referred to as "Haji Bread" or "Haji tortillas." (Available online at http://www.hbo.com/generation-kill# generation-kill/inside/index.html [accessed August 23, 2010])

Here, the term "haji" is racialized by associating it with a popular-culture cartoon image of heroic white supremacy. The definition also racially reinscribes "Americans" as non–Arab, non–Muslim, and non–Middle Eastern. Within the context of the show's dialogue, "Haji" is clearly a racial epithet.

11 Robert Kaplan (2005, 100), using deliberately racialist (and ethnologically flawed) reasoning, argues that the widespread use of "Indian Country" in the U.S. military's armed conflicts in Latin America, the Philippines, Vietnam, and the Middle East was an extension of a genealogy that connects Mongols to indigenous people globally.

12 For a similar intersectional reading see the work of Jasbir K. Puar. On the Abu Ghraib photographs, see Puar 2005; on the visual culture of television and film, see Puar and Rai 2002, 2004.

13 For a cogent analysis of portrayals of Arabs and Muslims in film after 9/11, see Shaheen 2008.

14 Although the show failed to gain a sustained viewership, it was consistently nominated for television awards. It enjoyed a second season as *Sleeper Cell—American Terror* (2006).

15 Scholars have pointed to the important connections between anticolonial struggles and the African diaspora to argue that, in these linkages, African Americans developed opposition to American foreign policy. For the Nation of Islam, this appeared as an anti–American critique of the Cold War (Von Eschen 1997, 174), and for African American Muslims, this anti-imperial resistance led to transnational exchanges with Arab Muslims through a rejection of American nationalism (Curtis 2007). Contemporary American Islam is also fraught with clashes and conflicts between and within immigrant Islam, as represented demographically by South Asian Americans and Arab Americans, and African American Islam, which challenges the possibility of a unified Muslim American *umma*, or community of believers (Jackson 2005).

16 Even the name Darwyn al-Sayyid clearly represents the contrived intentions of the writers of the show to create a character as a cultural intermediary of reformed Islam. "Darwyn," of course, is a reference to the founder of modern evolutionary thought; the surname "al-Sayyid" is a title often given to Muslims who are direct descendants of the Prophet Muhammad.

17 There is a growing literature on the relationship of Arab Americans to whiteness (see, e.g., Gualtieri 2001; Moore 1995; Naber 2000; Orfalea 2006; Samhan 1999).

18 Ethan Rieff and Cyrus Voris, the creators of the show, are well aware of these historical and political continuities. In fact, they have lauded them as the strength of the series. Although Clark Johnson, who directed the opening episodes of *Sleeper Cell*'s two seasons, claims to have leftist views, Rieff is politically conservative, a position both creators claim brings balance to the show ("Commentary," *Sleeper Cell*, DVD, 2006). They argue that they present terrorism in all of its complexity, in contrast to relying on the stock stereotype of the Arab villain of American action films. Although this is doubtful, the show clearly aims to produce new Arab *and* Muslim villains as a range of multicultural and multiracial stereotypes. For documentation of the Arab stock character in film, see Shaheen 2001, 2008. See also Sut Jhally, *Reel Bad Arabs* (documentary, 2006), which is based on Shaheen 2001. Rieff and Voris also argue that they draw from archival material to create their fictionalized accounts. Kamran Pasha, of Pakistani origin, is a writer and consultant for the show.

19 For example, in the Showtime series *The L Word*, Latinas are played by the mixed-race actors Sarah Shahi, who is of Iranian and Spanish descent (she plays an Arab women in the second season of *Sleeper Cell*), and Janina Gavankar, who is of Indian and Dutch descent. This broad notion of Islamic terrorists as brown-skinned is perpetuated in the casting of male actors. For example, Kal Penn played Ahmed Amar in the sixth season of *24* (2007); Ajay Naidu played Rakim Ali in an episode of *The West Wing* titled "Isaac and Ishmael" (2001); and Naveen Andrews portrayed the Iraqi torture agent Sayid Jarrah on *Lost* (2004–2010). That the actors are non–Muslim is less important in the casting rationales being employed than that they have a "terrorist look."

20 For example, in addition to playing Sikh and Hindu Indian characters, the actor Ajay Mehta has played cabbies in several American movies, including *People I Know* (2002), *Spider-Man* (2002), and in *Serendipity* (2001) his credits are described as "Pakistani cab driver"—perhaps the unspoken metonymic meaning of a cabbie's nationality.

21 It is important to note that Jack Shaheen was a consultant on *Syriana*. For his view of the film, see Jack G. Shaheen, "Arabs and Muslims in Hollywood's 'Munich' and 'Syriana,' " *Washington Report on Middle East Affairs*, March 2006.

22 See, e.g., A. O. Scott, "Clooney and a Maze of Collusion," *New York Times*, November 23, 2005.

23 In an insightful analysis, Kathryn Joyce (2009) describes this as an anti-state, pro-reproduction movement that promotes a notion of "biblical patriarchy" and the vision of a Christian nation.

24 See Human Rights Watch, " 'We Are Not the Enemy': Hate Crimes against Arabs, Muslims, and Those Perceived to Be Arab or Muslim after September 11," report no. 14 (6-G), November 2002.

Chapter 4. Labor Diaspora

1 I never saw women enter the office, although the director eventually did proudly show me lists of contracts he obtained for women to work in the accounting and health-care fields. All of these contracts were for professional labor, not for unskilled or care work such as domestic labor. When I asked about this division of women's labor, the director stated that spaces such as labor agencies are no place for women. I was further told that this was a consequence of Pakistan's "traditional" society. This was not the case at all labor agencies I visited. On a number of occasions, I saw women (with male chaperones) waiting to be interviewed for transnational contracts, mostly for secretarial, accounting, health-care, and technology jobs in the Gulf and Southeast Asia.

As I discuss later, the government of Pakistan controls such gendered labor carefully. This does not mean, however, that labor pools for care work do not exist. Such controls often informalize such work, making labor migrants more vulnerable to exploitation. See, e.g., Shah 2007, which makes this argument in terms of sex work and construction work in the informal economy of Mumbai.

2 Representing the Pakistani diaspora as diverse is clearly important to the government of Pakistan, as well. For example, in its yearbook for 2004–2005, the Overseas Pakistanis Division of the Ministry of Labor, Manpower, and Overseas Pakistanis estimated that in 2004, the population of Pakistanis living in the U.S. (including students) had reached about 600,000 and that more than twice that number were in the U.S. without documentation (i.e., they had overstayed their visas or otherwise fallen out of legal status). The division also estimated that about

1.9 million Pakistanis were living and working in the Gulf region. However, the official figures are most likely underestimates because migrants without official passports from Pakistan or children born to Pakistanis outside the country who are not eligible for citizenship in the Gulf states are not counted. This is particularly true for refugees who escaped war-torn Afghanistan and the harsh conditions of the Khyber-Pakhtunkhwa Province (formerly North-West Frontier Province) in Pakistan. Thus, the total population of Pakistanis in the Gulf could be as high as 4 million to 6 million.

In 2005, the Bureau of Emigration, another branch of the Ministry of Labor, reported that 156,000 contract workers had been sent to the Gulf in 2004, whereas only 150 had been sent to the U.S. These figures highlight the fact that a large number of emigrants to the U.S. do not pass through the administrative structures of the government and contracting agencies, which mostly serve the Middle East.

3 Interview, Lahore, January 17, 2001. I attended this labor agency between January and February 2001.

4 In Pakistan, for example, this dual British and American imperial formation as a colonial, postcolonial, and neocolonial relationship is apparent in state formation in the arenas of the military, education, and popular culture, to name a few. For example, in the early years of its development, the Pakistani military received substantial training and resources from the British. The U.S. started providing training and resources in the 1950s (Cohen 1998; Rizvi 2000; Siddiqa 2007).

5 This is true in both India and China (Look Lai 1993). It was also an important factor in the movement of labor to the Americas (Jensen 1988; Takaki 1989). Later in these migrations, women entered the diaspora, largely through the informal markets of smuggling and trafficking. On the debates in India that connect class to gender and women to morality, see, e.g., Kale 1998, 167–71. On Chinese women in the U.S., see Cheng 1984. For a comprehensive analysis of race and gender in U.S. labor history, see Glenn 2002. Evelyn Glenn relates the formal and informal movement of women in the nineteenth century and their migration to the concepts of work and labor.

6 For evidence of this early history in the twentieth century, see Bald 2006, 2007; Leonard 1992.

7 Although I rely heavily on the work of Hamza Alavi for a theory of class in South Asia, this theory does not adequately account for the factors that drive transnational migration. Particularly useful is Alavi's argument that new urban classes were created in the shift from colonial to postcolonial societies through partition and industrialization in places such as Pakistan that culminated in conflicts over resource distribution (Alavi 1973, 1983, 1989).

8 My ethnographic fieldwork focuses on the narratives of migrants from the Punjab Province of Pakistan. Punjabis represent a large contingent of contemporary labor migration from Pakistan, largely due to the effects of the Green Revolution that

dramatically transformed agricultural production in the country, and in South Asia generally, in the mid-1960s. The social and economic upheaval created by agricultural change led to an enormous surplus in labor reserves. For another example of a major migration flow from Pakistan, of the Pashtun ethnic group to the Indian Ocean region, see Nichols 2008.

9 The Asian Development Bank published the figures for 1980 to 1993 in 1996 (Bagchi 1999, 3221).

10 State Bank of Pakistan, *Annual Report*, 1999–2000, 136; State Bank of Pakistan, *Annual Report*, 2007–2008, 5, both available online at http://www.sbp.org.pk/reports/annual/index.htm (accessed December 1, 2009).

11 This shift also had much to do with the need for a state intelligentsia who could provide quantitative data that would fulfill the requirements of structural-adjustment programs and ensure the continuance of foreign loans to Pakistan.

12 The history of the Pakistan in the postcolonial condition has taken an increasingly economic character because of the state's control of multinational investment and its role in mediating the interests of the propertied classes. This is so "because the state in the postcolonial society directly appropriates a very large part of the economic surplus and deploys it in bureaucratically directed economic activity in the name of promoting economic development" (Alavi 1973, 148).

13 The Pakistani Bureau of Emigration oversees the control of migration through two subagencies: the public-sector Protector of Emigrants, and the private-sector Overseas Employment Corporation. These agencies are responsible for licensing recruiting agents and for protecting the legal welfare of labor migrants.

14 Jagdish Bhagwati's argument in favor of a brain-drain tax received some attention in the late 1970s in United Nations circles but was quickly set aside (see Bhagwati 1998).

15 Government of Pakistan, *Survey of Pakistan*, 1999–2000. The fourth province, Balochistan, does not send a significant number of migrants to the Gulf, according to these figures. However, Balochis have a presence throughout the Gulf and abroad that is not captured in government statistics on work contracts.

16 In other circumstances, such as the mobilization of youth by the Karachi-based Muhajir Qaumi Movement, fun is tethered to militancy to bring together practices of political violence, religious nationalism, and the performance of masculine physicality (Verkaaik 2004).

17 This includes racing souped-up cars, performing motorcycle tricks, partying, and a general culture of boasting. These feats are widespread in Pakistan; they are also visible in the diaspora, particularly around sports events and Independence Day parades.

18 Pakistan has a fairly low demographic of detected HIV and AIDS cases. In 2007, it was estimated at 96,000 in a total population of 165 million, a prevalence of .1 percent, according to the Joint United Nations Programme on HIV/AIDS, "Pakistan

Profile," available online at http://www.unaids.org/en/CountryResponses/Coun tries/pakistan.asp (accessed December 1, 2009). S. A. Shah, O. A. Khan, S. Kristen- sen, and S. H. Vermund (1999) conducted a study in 1996–98 in Sindh Province that identified a total of seventy-nine cases; 61 percent to 86 percent of the reported cases were migrant workers. Despite the small size of this sample, it has become widely accepted that HIV was brought to Pakistan by migrant workers in the 1990s, where it reached epidemic proportions in specific locations mainly via intravenous drug users and, less so, via sex work and homosexual contact (see, e.g., Rai et al. 2007). Much of what is believed about HIV and AIDS in Pakistan is thus based on anecdotal evidence, and labor migrants in small towns are often stigmatized as spreading HIV.

19 See, e.g., Ashfaq Yusufzai, "Pakistan Battles HIV/AIDS Taboo," BBC News, May 9, 2007, available online at http://news.bbc.co.uk/2/hi/south_asia/6539437.stm (ac- cessed Decemeber 1, 2009); "Pakistan: Workers with HIV Deported from Gulf States," Integrated Regional Information Networks news service, December 18, 2008, available online at http://www.irinnews.org/Report.aspx?ReportId=82015 (accessed December 1, 2009).

20 Interview, Islamabad, November 15, 2000.

21 Interview, Lahore, January 20, 2005.

22 Interview, Lahore, December 27, 2000.

23 Interview, Gujranwala, May 23, 2001.

24 Interview, Lahore, November 7, 2000.

25 "Biraderi" is a common category used to ascertain formal kinds of kinship differ- ence; it is often used to advance social interest. In the context of Pakistan, this notion of caste refers to ancestral background that differentiates ethnicity, reli- gious sect, kinship group, and feudal categories that establish a hierarchical divi- sion of labor.

26 Interviews, New York, March 2003.

27 A wide spectrum of Pakistani politicians, celebrities, and sports stars are adherents of the Tablighi Jamaat, including the singer Junaid Jamshed and the cricket players Shahid Afridi, Saeed Anwar, and Mohammed Yousuf. Yousuf, a former Christian, embraced Islam through the influence of the Tablighi Jamaat on Pakistan's na- tional cricket team.

28 As a point of controversy, the Tablighi Jamaat is often criticized for this comparison because of the sacred nature of the Hajj and its position as a major pillar of Islam.

29 Charles Hirschkind (2006) and Saba Mahmood (2004) examine similar move- ments in Egypt and the emphasis on virtue as a disciplining apparatus of Muslim subjectivity.

30 It is important to note that both men's and women's groups are active in the Tablighi Jamaat. The Jamaats, or groups, are most often divided by gender; they travel to offer *dawa* on this basis. My encounters at the Tablighi Jamaat compound

were entirely with men. In Raiwind, the Ladies Ijtima is located in a separate building, with an independent set of speakers and sessions for women similar to those in the men's section.

31 *The Quran: Text, Translation and Commentary*, translated by Abdullah Yusuf Ali, New York: Tahrike Tarsile Qu'ran, 1987.

32 Interviews, Raiwind, May 5, 2001.

Chapter 5. Migration, Illegality, and the Security State

1 The figures for suicide and death among workers were compiled by the embassies of India, Pakistan, and Bangladesh and do not account for specific causes of death or injury. They are from Human Rights Watch, "Building Towers, Cheating Workers: Summary and Recommendations," November 2006, 40–47, available online at http://www.hrw.org/en/reports/2006/11/11/building-towers-cheating-workers (accessed July 17, 2009).

2 For example, the work of Arjun Appadurai has been pivotal to the study of these global changes. For his theory of globalization and the diminishing role of the state, see Appadurai 1996. For his more recent, general analysis of global violence, inequality, and the centrality of the state in addressing these issues, see Appadurai 2006.

3 For examples of this relationship of policing, criminality, and immigration, see Gilroy 1987; Hall et al., 1978.

4 Interview with male bureaucrat in his mid-fifties, Lahore, April 25, 2001.

5 Interview, Bureau of Emigration, Islamabad, April 16, 2001.

6 This relationship of the U.S. to Pakistan through the state control of migration is further revealed in the intelligence gathering under way by U.S. officials, primarily the FBI and CIA, in collaboration with the Pakistani government. Such forms of state control have far-reaching effects throughout the Pakistani labor diaspora. The three major areas of interest and control are human trafficking, drug enforcement, and terrorism. Although this set of ethnographic interviews predated 9/11, and were thus conducted in the context of the shift from the Clinton administration to the Bush administration, this kind of intelligence increased massively in this period. At the beginning of the transition, the Bush administration dramatically increased resources for task forces pursing these areas; this took on greater significance in the aftermath of 9/11 and the context of Pakistan's strategic position in the War on Terror and the U.S. military campaigns in Afghanistan.

7 This system was described to me in February 2001 by a former officer of the Federal Investigation Agency who worked in the Immigration Wing of the Lahore International Airport. He explained that this was a highly lucrative industry that proliferated through bribes paid to officials to provide documents and facilitate the passage of prospective migrants. Underpaid officials are easily swayed by these

incentives, which greatly boosts their income. The official was later transferred to Karachi to work in customs, a far more lucrative posting.

8 This document is available online at http://www2.ohchr.org/english/law/protocol traffic.htm (accessed August 7, 2009).

9 U.S. State Department, "Trafficking in Persons," report, 2004), available online at http://www.state.gov/documents/organization/2004/34158.pdf (accessed August 7, 2009).

10 Interview, Lahore, May 5, 2001.

11 Interview, Lahore, November 28, 2000.

12 Interviews, Lahore, April 2001, July 2004; interviews, New York, January 2004.

13 "Unpaid Construction Workers Take Complaints to Ministry," *Gulf News*, May 23, 2001; "Dubai Labourers Protest over Delay in Salary," *News* (Lahore), May 23, 2001; "Company Settles Wages with Protesting Workers," *Gulf News*, May 28, 2001.

14 Human Rights Watch, "Building Towers, Cheating Workers," 30.

15 Ibid., idem, "Bad Dreams: Exploitation and Abuse of Migrant Workers in Saudi Arabia." report, July 2004, available online at http://www.hrw.org/en/reports/2004/07/13/bad-dreams-0 (accessed August 7, 2009); idem, " 'The Island of Happiness': Exploitation of Migrant Workers on Saadiyat Island, Abu Dhabi," report, May 2009, available online at http://www.hrw.org/en/reports/2009/05/18/island-happiness (accessed August 7, 2009).

16 Interview, thirty-four-year-old Punjabi man, New York, October 25, 2002.

Chapter 6. The Muslim Body

1 In this sense, I follow the work of Sara Ahmed (2004, 2006) on racial affect as intensified emotions that mediate social relations of exclusion and the circulation of an embodied sense of disciplinary power.

2 Interview, forty-year-old man, Lahore, February 15, 2006.

3 Mark Dow (2004) argues that the use of secrecy and excessive force in detention after 9/11 are an extension of longstanding biases and mistreatment of immigrant detainees that in many ways normalized the abuse of Arab, South Asian, and Muslim immigrants.

4 From 2003 to 2008, I interviewed Pakistanis in Brooklyn and recently returned migrants in Pakistan to gather information about the conditions in, and their reasons for, fleeing the U.S.

5 This argument is made by director Errol Morris in *Standard Operating Procedure* (documentary, Participant Productions, 2008), on Abu Ghraib, and director Alex Gibney, *Taxi to the Dark Side* (documentary, Jigsaw Productions, 2007), on Bagram and Guantánamo Bay.

6 See OIG 2003a; Cam Simpson et al., "Immigration Crackdown Shatters Muslims' Lives," *Chicago Tribune*, November 16, 2003. Although these are the specific num-

bers released from these particular programs, the total number of those detained and deported under a similar logic is uncertain.

7 Simpson et al., "Immigration Crackdown Shatters Muslims' Lives."

8 Asian American Federation of New York, "Census Profile: New York City's Pakistani American Population," December 2004, available online at http://www.aafny.org/cic/briefs/Pakistani.pdf (accessed April 21, 2010).

9 The large disparity reflects the different sources of reporting; the lower figure comes from U.S. government officials and the Pakistani Consulate in New York. These numbers are a combination of those deported and those estimated to have returned to Pakistan: see Daniela Gerson, "For Some, Harder Times since 9/11," *New York Sun*, October 1, 2003; Tatsha Robertson, "Deportation Surge Leaves Void in Brooklyn's Little Pakistan," *Boston Globe*, August 14, 2005. The higher number is from community activists working in the Pakistani immigrant community: see Andrea Elliot, "In Brooklyn, 9/11 Damage Continues," *New York Times*, June 7, 2003.

10 Interview, New York, May 14, 2008. In addition, in November 2009, the landmark case *Turkmen v. Ashcroft*, a class-action civil-rights lawsuit headed by the lawyers at the Center for Constitutional Rights on behalf of the Muslim, Arab, and South Asian immigrants rounded up in raids after 9/11, settled their claims of abuse at the Metropolitan Detention Center in Brooklyn against the U.S. government for $1.26 million. The plaintiffs included Muslims from Egypt, Pakistan, and Turkey and a Hindu man born in India: see http://ccrjustice.org/ourcases/current-cases/turkmen-v.-ashcroft. Although this case signaled an important shift in the judiciary's response to the use of state-sanctioned force after 9/11, such racial violence is much broader in scope and is interwoven in complex ways with state interests and local actors.

11 On the class demographics of immigrants in the Special Registration process, see Asian American Legal Defense and Education Fund, "Special Registration: Discrimination and Xenophobia as Government Policy," report, January 2004, available online at http://www.aaldef.org/article.php?article_id=133 (accessed February 4, 2009).

12 Asian American Federation of New York, "Census Profile."

13 Ho (2004, 230) is careful to acknowledge the U.S. colonialism of overseas occupations in relation to the conquest of the Southwest and the genocide of Native Americans.

14 Extraordinary rendition began under the Clinton administration and was used far more significantly during the Bush administration's War on Terror campaign. Jane Mayer (2008) describes this secret program, its relationship to torture methods used in interrogation, and the attempts to circumvent legal practices and rights in great detail. The system of rendition took on particular importance in the relationship between the U.S. and Pakistan. Some 400 to 800 people were transferred into U.S. custody between late 2001 and 2005 in Pakistan's partner role in the War on

Terror. Former Pakistani President Pervez Musharraf acknowledged 369 detainee transfers and describes them in relation to the arrests of a number of high-profile terrorist suspects (Musharraf 2006). Human Rights Watch regards a number of these detainees as "disappeared" and "ghost prisoners": see Human Rights Watch, "Ghost Prisoner: Two Years in Secret CIA Detention," report, February 26, 2007, available online at http://www.hrw.org/en/reports/2007/02/26/ghost-prisoner (accessed January 15, 2009).

15 Quoted in David Rohde, "U.S.-Deported Pakistanis: Outcastes in 2 Lands," *New York Times*, January 20, 2003, A9.

16 For example, Louise Cainkar (2009) reports that, after 9/11 in metropolitan Chicago, women who wore the hijab were more vulnerable to attacks than were Arab and Muslim men. She usefully calls this "cultural sniping" and uses it as an example of how women's bodies become specific targets over ideological issues.

17 Interviews, Lahore, January 2006.

18 Interviews, Lahore, January–February 2006.

19 On Robert Park and colleagues' concept of the "racial uniform" as part of a racialized body in relation to social distance, assimilation, and accommodation, see Yu 2001. Rather than strictly dismissing this approach as victimizing, I invert these terms to understand the racial uniform as imposed in relation to racialized notions of Islam and the Muslim body.

20 See Du Bois 1993 (1903). For a dialectical argument regarding Du Bois's racial veil, see Winant 2004, 25–38.

Conclusion

1 Damien Ramos and Robert Caldwell, "Indian Shipyard Workers Accuse Their Employer of Human Trafficking and Forced Labor," New Orleans Independent Media Center, March 11, 2008, available online at http://neworleans.indymedia.org/news/2008/03/12261.php. For more information, see http://www.nowcrj.org.

2 "And Injustice for All: Workers' Lives in the Reconstruction of New Orleans," available online at http://www.nowcrj.org/publications/reports (accessed May 31, 2009).

3 Svati Shah, "Mississippi Mutiny Challenges Anti-Trafficking Law," *Samar*, May 13, 2008, available online at http://www.samarmagazine.org/archive/article.php?id=259 (accessed May 31, 2009).

Abella, Manolo I. 1987. "Asian Labour Mobility: New Dimensions and Implications for Development." *Pakistan Development Review* 26, no. 3: 363–77.

Abraham, Nabeel. 2004. "Anti–Arab Racism and Violence in the United States." *Not Quite American? The Shaping of Arab and Muslim Identity in the United States*, ed. Yvonne Y. Haddad. Waco: Baylor University Press.

Abrams, Phillip. 1988 (1977). "Notes on the Difficulty of Studying the State." *Journal of Historical Sociology* 1, no. 1: 58–89.

Addleton, Jonathon S. 1992. *Undermining the Centre: The Gulf Migration and Pakistan.* Karachi: Oxford University Press.

Agamben, Giorgio. 1998. *Homo Sacer: Sovereign Power and Bare Life.* Stanford: Stanford University Press.

———. 1999. *Remnants of Auschwitz: The Witness and the Archive.* New York: Zone.

———. 2005. *State of Exception.* Chicago: University of Chicago Press.

Ahmad, Eqbal. 2001. *Terrorism: Theirs and Ours.* New York: Seven Stories.

Ahmad, Muneer I. 2002. "Homeland Insecurities: Racial Violence the Day after September 11." *Social Text* 20, no. 3: 101–15.

———. 2004. "A Rage Shared by Law: Post–September 11 Racial Violence as Crimes of Passion." *California Law Review* 92, no. 5: 1259–330.

Ahmed, Sara. 2000. *Strange Encounters: Embodied Others in Postcoloniality.* London: Routledge.

———. 2004. *The Cultural Politics of Emotion.* New York: Routledge.

———. 2006. *Queer Phenomenology: Orientations, Objects, Others.* Durham: Duke University Press.

Aidi, Hishaam. 2002. "Jihadis in the Hood: Race, Urban Islam, and the War on Terror." *Middle East Report* 224: 36–43.

———. 2003. "Let Us Be Moors: Islam, Race and 'Connected Histories.' " *Middle East Report* 229: 42–53.

———. 2006. "The Interference of al-Andalus: Spain, Islam, and the West." *Social Text* 24, no. 2: 67–88.

Alavi, Hamza. 1973. "The State in Postcolonial Societies: Pakistan and Bangladesh." *Imperialism and Revolution in South Asia*, ed. Kathleen Gough and Hari P. Sharma. New York: Monthly Review.

——. 1983. "Class and State." *Pakistan: The Roots of Dictatorship*, ed. Hassan Gardezi and Jamil Rashid. London: Zed.

——. 1989. "Formation of the Social Structure of South Asia under the Impact of Colonialism." *South Asia: Sociology of "Developing Societies,"* ed. Hamza Alavi and John Harriss. New York: Monthly Review.

Alcoff, Linda. 2001. "Toward a Phenomenology of Racial Embodiment." *Race*, ed. Robert Bernasconi. Malden, Mass.: Blackwell.

——. 2006. *Visible Identities: Race, Gender, and the Self*. New York: Oxford University Press.

Ali, Amjad. 2001. *Labour Legislation and Trade Unions in India and Pakistan*. Karachi: Oxford University Press.

Ali, Kamran Asdar. 2005. "The Strength of the Street Meets the Strength of the State: The 1972 Labor Struggle in Karachi." *International Journal of Middle East Studies* 37: 83–107.

Ali, Tariq. 2002. *The Clash of Fundamentalisms: Crusades, Jihads, and Modernity*. New York: Verso.

——. 2008. *The Duel: Pakistan on the Flight Path of American Power*. New York: Scribner.

American Civil Liberties Union. 2004. "America's Disappeared: Seeking International Justice for Immigrants Detained after September 11." Report, January.

Anidjar, Gil. 2003. *The Jew, the Arab: A History of the Enemy*. Stanford: Stanford University Press.

——. 2004. "Terror Right." *New Centennial Review* 3, no. 3: 35–69.

——. 2008. *Semites: Race, Religion, Literature*. Stanford: Stanford University Press.

Appadurai, Arjun. 1996. *Modernity at Large: Cultural Dimensions of Globalization*. Minneapolis: University of Minnesota Press.

——. 2006. *Fear of Small Numbers: An Essay on the Geography of Anger*. Durham: Duke University Press.

Arendt, Hannah. 1968. *The Origins of Totalitarianism*. New York: Harcourt Brace Jovanovich.

Aretxaga, Begona. 2003. "Maddening States." *Annual Review of Anthropology* 32: 393–410.

Arif, G. M., and Mohammad Irfan. 1997. "Population Mobility across the Pakistani Border: Fifty Years Experience." *Pakistan Development Review* 36, no. 4: 989–1009.

Asad, Talal. 1993. *Genealogies of Religion: Discipline and Reasons of Power in Christianity and Islam*. Baltimore: John Hopkins University Press.

——. 2007. *On Suicide Bombing*. New York: Columbia University Press.

Audre Lorde Project. "Communities at a Crossroads: U.S. Right-Wing Policies and Lesbian, Gay, Bisexual, Two Spirit and Transgender Immigrants of Color in New York City." Report, December 2004.

Azam, Farooq-i. 1995. "Emigration Dynamics in Pakistan." *International Migration* 33, nos. 3–4: 729–56.

Badiou, Alain. 2005. *Being and Event*. London: Continuum.

Bagchi, Amiya Kumar. 1999. "Globalisation, Liberalisation, and Vulnerability: India and Third World." *Economic and Political Weekly* 34, no. 45 (November 6): 3219–30.

Bald, Vivek. 2006. "Overlapping Diasporas, Multiracial Lives: South Asian Muslims in U.S. Communities of Color, 1880–1950." *Souls* 8, no. 4: 3–18.

——. 2007. "'Lost' in the City: Spaces and Stories of South Asian New York, 1917–1965." *South Asian Popular Culture* 5, no. 1: 59–76.

Barbora, Sanjay, Susan Thieme, Karin Astrid Siegmann, Vineetha Menon, and Ganesh Gurung. 2008. "Migration Matters in South Asia: Commonalities and Critiques." *Economic and Political Weekly* 43(24): 57–65.

Bataille, Georges. 1991. *The Accursed Share: An Essay on General Economy*, vols. 2–3. New York: Zone.

Bayoumi, Moustafa. 2006. "Racing Religion." *New Centennial Review* 6, no. 2: 267–93.

——. 2008. *How Does It Feel to Be a Problem? Being Young and Arab in America*. New York: Penguin.

Bhagwati, Jagdish. 1998. *Writings on International Economics*. Delhi: Oxford University Press.

Bose, Sugata. 2006. *A Hundred Horizons: The Indian Ocean in the Age of Global Empire*. Cambridge: Harvard University Press.

Brown, Judith M. 2006. *Global South Asians: Introducing the Modern Diaspora*. Cambridge: Cambridge University Press.

Brown, Wendy. 1995. *States of Injury: Power and Freedom in Late Modernity*. Princeton: Princeton University Press.

Buff, Rachel Ida. 2008. "The Deportation Terror." *American Quarterly* 60, no. 3: 523–51.

Bunzl, Matti. 2005. "Between Anti–Semitism and Islamophobia: Some Thoughts on the New Europe." *American Ethnologist* 32, no. 4: 499–508.

——. 2007. *Anti–Semitism and Islamophobia: Hatreds Old and New in Europe*. Chicago: Prickly Paradigm.

Butler, Judith. 2003. *Precarious Life: The Powers of Mourning and Violence*. London: Verso.

——. 2009. *Frames of War: When Is Life Grievable?* New York: Verso.

Cainkar, Louise. 2009. *Homeland Insecurity: The Arab American and Muslim American Experience after 9/11*. New York: Russell Sage Foundation.

Carter, Marina. 1995. *Servants, Sirdars, and Settlers: Indians in Mauritius, 1834–1874*. Delhi: Oxford University Press.

Centre for Contemporary Cultural Studies, ed. 1982. *The Empire Strikes Back: Race and Racism in '70s Britain*. London: Hutchinson.

Chakrabarty, Dipesh. 1989. *Rethinking Working-Class History: Bengal, 1890–1940*. Princeton: Princeton University Press.

Chang, Nancy. 2002. *Silencing Political Dissent*. New York: Seven Stories.

Cheng, Anne. 2001. *The Melancholy of Race*. New York: Oxford University Press.

Cheng, Lucie. 1984. "Free, Indentured, Enslaved: Chinese Prostitutes in Nineteenth-

Century America." *Labor Immigration under Capitalism: Asian Workers in the United States before World War II*, ed. Lucie Cheng and Edna Bonacich. Berkeley: University of California Press.

Chow, Rey. 2006. *The Age of the World Target: Self-referentiality in War, Theory, and Comparative Work*. Durham: Duke University Press.

Cockburn, Alexander, and Jeffrey St. Clair. 2003. *The Politics of Anti–Semitism*. Oakland, Calif.: AK Press.

Cohen, Stanley. 1972. *Folk Devils and Moral Panics: The Creation of Mods and Rockers*. London: MacGibbon and Kee.

Cohen, Stephen P. 1998. *The Pakistan Army*. Karachi: Oxford University Press.

Cole, David. 2003. *Enemy Aliens: Double Standards and Constitutional Freedoms in the War on Terrorism*. New York: New Press.

Cole, David, and James X. Dempsey. 2002. *Terrorism and the Constitution: Sacrificing Civil Liberties in the Name of National Security*, 2d ed. New York: New Press.

Coll, Steve. 2004. *Ghost Wars: The Secret History of the CIA, Afghanistan, and Bin Laden, from the Soviet Invasion to September 10, 2001*. New York: Penguin.

Collins, John. 2002. "Terrorism." *Collateral Language: A User's Guide to America's New War*, ed. John Collins and Ross Glover. New York: New York University Press.

Comaroff, Jean. 2007. "Beyond Bare Life: AIDS, (Bio)Politics, and the Neoliberal Order." *Public Culture* 19, no. 1: 197–219.

Comaroff, Jean, and John L. Comaroff. 2006. *Law and Disorder in the Postcolony*. Chicago: University of Chicago Press.

Corrigan, Philip. 1994. "Undoing the Overdone State." *Canadian Journal of Sociology* 19, no. 2: 249–55.

———. 2002. "Some Further Notes on the Difficulty of Studying the State: England and the First Empire, 1975 Onwards." *Journal of Historical Sociology* 15, no. 1: 121–65.

Corrigan, Philip, and Derek Sayer. 1985. *The Great Arch: English State Formation as Cultural Revolution*. Cambridge: Blackwell.

Curtis IV, Edward E. 2007. "Islamism and Its African American Muslim Critics: Black Muslims in the Era of the Arab Cold War." *American Quarterly* 59, no. 3: 683–710.

———. 2009. *Muslims in America*. New York: Oxford University Press.

Dannin, Robert. 2002. *Black Pilgrimage to Islam*. New York: Oxford University Press.

Das Gupta, Monisha. 2006. *Unruly Immigrants: Rights, Activism, and Transnational South Asian Politics in the United States*. Durham: Duke University Press.

Davidson, Christopher M. 2008. *Dubai: The Vulnerability of Success*. New York: Columbia University Press.

———. 2009. *Abu Dhabi Oil and Beyond*. New York: Columbia University Press.

Davis, Mike. 2006. "Fear and Money in Dubai." *New Left Review* 41 (September–October): 47–70.

———. 2007. *Planet of Slums*. New York: Verso.

De Genova, Nicholas. 2002. "Migrant 'Illegality' and Deportability in Everyday Life." *Annual Review of Anthropology* 31: 419–47.

——. 2005. *Working the Boundaries: Race, Space, and "Illegality" in Mexican Chicago*. Durham: Duke University Press.

Deleuze, Gilles, and Felix Guattari. 1983. *Anti-Oedipus: Capitalism and Schizophrenia*. Minneapolis: University of Minnesota Press.

Devji, Faisal. 2005. *Landscapes of the Jihad: Militancy, Morality, Modernity*. Ithaca: Cornell University Press.

——. 2008. *The Terrorist in Search of Humanity: Militant Islam and Global Politics*. New York: Columbia University Press.

Diouf, Sylviane A. 1998. *Servants of Allah: African Muslims Enslaved in the Americas*. New York: New York University Press.

Donnan, Hastings, and Pnina Werbner, eds. 1991. *Economy and Culture in Pakistan: Migrants and Cities in a Muslim Society*. London: Macmillan.

Dow, Mark. 2004. *American Gulag: Inside U.S. Immigration Prisons*. Berkeley: Univeristy of California Press.

Drinnon, Richard. 1990. *Facing West: The Metaphysics of Indian-Hating and Empire-Building*. New York: Schocken.

Du Bois, W. E. B. 1993 (1903). *The Souls of Black Folk*. New York: Alfred A. Knopf.

Duggan, Lisa. 1995. "Sex Panics." *Sex Wars: Sexual Dissent and Political Culture*, ed. Lisa Duggan and Nan D. Hunter. New York: Routledge.

——. 2003. *The Twilight of Equality? Neoliberalism, Cultural Politics, and the Attack on Democracy*. Boston: Beacon Press.

Dunbar-Ortiz, Roxanne. 2003. "The Grid of History: Cowboys and Indians." *Monthly Review* 55, no. 3: 83–92.

——. 2004. "Indian Country," October 11, available online at http://www.counterpunch .org/ortiz10122004.html.

Eng, David L., and David Kazanjian. 2003. *Loss: The Politics of Mourning*. Berkeley: University of California Press.

Espiritu, Yen Le. 1992. *Asian American Panethnicity: Bridging Institutions and Identities*. Philadelphia: Temple University Press.

Ewing, Katherine Pratt. 2008a. *Being and Belonging: Muslims in the United States since 9/11*. New York: Russell Sage Foundation.

——. 2008b. *Stolen Honor: Stigmatizing Muslim Men in Berlin*. Stanford: Stanford University Press.

Farquhar, Judith, and Margaret M. Lock. 2007. *Beyond the Body Proper: Reading the Anthropology of Material Life*. Durham: Duke University Press.

Ferguson, James, and Akhil Gupta. 2002. "Spatializing States: Toward an Ethnography of Neoliberal Governmentality." *American Ethnologist* 29, no. 4: 981–1002.

Fernandes, Leela. 1997. "Producing Workers: The Politics of Gender, Class, and Culture in the Calcutta Jute Mills." Philadelphia: University of Pennsylvania Press.

Foucault, Michel. 1979. *Discipline and Punish*. New York: Vintage.

——. 1991. *The Foucault Effect: Studies in Governmentality*. Chicago: University of Chicago Press.

——. 2003. *"Society Must Be Defended": Lectures at the College de France, 1975–1976*. New York: Palgrave Macmillan.

——. 2007. *Security, Territory, Population: Lectures at the College de France, 1977–1978*. New York: Palgrave Macmillan.

——. 2008. *The Birth of Biopolitics: Lectures at the College de France, 1978–79*. New York: Palgrave Macmillan.

Fredrickson, George M. 2002. *Racism: A Short History*. Princeton: Princeton University Press.

Gardezi, Hassan N. 1995. *The Political Economy of International Labour Migration*. Montreal: Black Rose.

Ghosh, Amitav. 1989. "The Diaspora in Indian Culture." *Public Culture* 2, no. 1: 73–78.

Gilani, Ijaz Shafi. 1985. *Citizens, Slaves, Guest-Workers: The Dynamics of Labour Migration from South Asia*. Islamabad: Institute of Policy Studies.

Gill, Lesley. 2004. *The School of the Americas: Military Training and Political Violence in the Americas*. Durham: Duke University Press.

Gilmore, Ruth W. 2007. *Golden Gulag: Prisons, Surplus, Crisis, and Opposition in Globalizing California*. Berkeley: University of California Press.

Gilroy, Paul. 1982. "Police and Thieves." *The Empire Strikes Back: Race and Racism in '70s Britain*, ed. Centre for Contemporary Cultural Studies. London: Hutchinson.

——. 1987. *"There Ain't No Black in the Union Jack": The Cultural Politics of Race and Nation*. Chicago: University of Chicago Press.

Glenn, Evelyn Nakano. 2002. *Unequal Freedom: How Race and Gender Shaped American Citizenship and Labor*. Cambridge: Harvard University Press.

Glover, William J. 2008. *Making Lahore Modern: Constructing and Imagining a Colonial City*. Minneapolis: University of Minnesota Press.

Goldberg, David Theo. 1993. *Racist Culture: Philosophy and the Politics of Meaning*. Cambridge: Blackwell.

——. 2002. *The Racial State*. Cambridge: Blackwell.

——. 2009. *The Threat of Race: Reflections on Racial Neoliberalism*. Malden, Mass.: Wiley-Blackwell.

Gomez, Michael Angelo. 2005. *Black Crescent: The Experience and Legacy of African Muslims in the Americas*. Cambridge: Cambridge University Press.

Gopinath, Gayatri. 2005a. "Bollywood Spectacles: Queer Diasporic Critique in the Aftermath of 9/11." *Social Text* 23, nos. 3–4: 157–69.

——. 2005b. *Impossible Desires: Queer Diasporas and South Asian Public Cultures*. Durham: Duke University Press.

Grewal, Inderpal. 1996. *Home and Harem: Nation, Gender, Empire, and the Cultures of Travel*. Durham: Duke University Press.

———. 2005. *Transnational America: Feminisms, Diasporas, Neoliberalisms*. Durham: Duke University Press.

Grewal, Inderpal, and Caren Kaplan, eds. 1994. *Scattered Hegemonies: Postmodernity and Transnational Feminist Practices*. Minneapolis: University of Minnesota Press.

Gualtieri, Sarah. 2001. "Becoming 'White': Race, Religion, and the Foundations of Syrian/Lebanese Ethnicity in the United States." *Journal of American Ethnic History* 20, no. 4: 29–58.

———. 2009. *Between Arab and White: Race and Ethnicity in the Early Syrian American Diaspora*. Berkeley: University of California Press.

Hagopian, Elaine C., ed. 2004. *Civil Rights in Peril: The Targeting of Arabs and Muslims*. Chicago: Haymarket.

Hall, Stuart, Chas Critcher, Tony Jefferson, John Clarke, and Brian Roberts, eds. 1978. *Policing the Crisis: "Mugging," the State, and Law and Order*. London: Macmillan.

Haney López, Ian. 1996. *White by Law: The Legal Construction of Race*. New York: New York University Press.

Hansen, Thomas Blom. 2001a. "Bridging the Gulf: Global Horizons, Mobility and Local Identity among Muslims in Mumbai." *Community, Empire, and Migration: South Asians in Diaspora*, ed. Crispin Bates. New York: Palgrave.

———. 2001b. *Wages of Violence: Naming and Identity in Postcolonial Bombay*. Princeton: Princeton University Press.

Hansen, Thomas Blom, and Finn Stepputat. 2005. *Sovereign Bodies: Citizens, Migrants, and States in the Postcolonial World*. Princeton: Princeton University Press.

———. 2006. "Sovereignty Revisited." *Annual Review of Anthropology* 35: 295–315.

Hardt, Michael, and Antonio Negri. 2000. *Empire*. Cambridge: Harvard University Press.

———. 2004. *Multitude: War and Democracy in the Age of Empire*. New York: Penguin.

Harrison, Faye V. 1995. "The Persistent Power of 'Race' in the Cultural and Political Economy of Racism." *Annual Review of Anthropology* 24: 47–74.

———. 2008. *Outsider Within: Reworking Anthropology in the Global Age*. Urbana: University of Illinois Press.

Harvey, David. 2003. *The New Imperialism*. Oxford: Oxford University Press.

———. 2005. *A Brief History of Neoliberalism*. Oxford: Oxford University Press.

Harvey, L. P. 1990. *Islamic Spain, 1250 to 1500*. Chicago: University of Chicago Press.

———. 2005. *Muslims in Spain, 1500 to 1614*. Chicago: University of Chicago Press.

Hing, Bill Ong. 1993. *Making and Remaking of Asian America through Immigration Policy, 1850–1990*. Stanford: Stanford University Press.

———. 2006. *Deporting Our Souls: Values, Morality, and Immigration Policy*. Cambridge: Cambridge University Press.

Hirschkind, Charles. 2006. *The Ethical Soundscape: Cassette Sermons and Islamic Counterpublics*, New York: Columbia University Press.

Ho, Engseng. 2004. "Empire through Diasporic Eyes: The View from the Other Boat." *Society for Comparative Study of Society and History* 46, no. 2: 210–46.

Hodgen, Margaret T. 1964. *Early Anthropology in the Sixteenth and Seventeenth Centuries.* Philadelphia: University of Pennsylvania Press.

Hoodbhoy, Pervez, ed. 1998. *Education and the State: Fifty Years of Pakistan.* Karachi: Oxford University Press.

Inda, Jonathan X., and Renato Rosaldo. 2008. *The Anthropology of Globalization: A Reader,* 2d ed. Malden, Mass.: Blackwell.

Irfan, Mohammad. 1986. "Migration and Development in Pakistan: Some Selected Issues." *Pakistan Development Review* 25, no. 4: 743–55.

Isaac, Benjamin H. 2004. *The Invention of Racism in Classical Antiquity.* Princeton: Princeton University Press.

Jackson, Sherman A. 2005. *Islam and the Blackamerican: Looking toward the Third Resurrection.* Oxford: Oxford University Press.

Jamal, Amaney A., and Nadine C. Naber. 2008. *Race and Arab Americans before and after 9/11: From Invisible Citizens to Visible Subjects.* Syracuse: Syracuse University Press.

James, Joy. 2007. *Warfare in the American Homeland: Policing and Prison in a Penal Democracy.* Durham: Duke University Press.

Jensen, Joan M. 1988. *Passage from India: Asian Indian Immigrants in North America.* New Haven: Yale University Press.

Joseph, Lawrence. 1988. *Curriculum Vitae.* Pittsburgh: University of Pittsburgh Press.

Joyce, Kathryn. 2009. *Quiverfull: Inside the Christian Patriarchy Movement.* Boston: Beacon Press.

Jung, Moon-Ho. 2006. *Coolies and Cane: Race, Labor, and Sugar in the Age of Emancipation.* Baltimore: Johns Hopkins University Press.

Kale, Madhavi. 1998. *Fragments of Empire: Capital, Slavery, and Indian Indentured Labor Migration in the British Caribbean.* Philadelphia: University of Pennsylvania Press.

Kalra, Virinder S. 2009. *Pakistani Diasporas: Culture, Conflict, and Change.* Karachi: Oxford University Press.

Kanafani, Ghassan. 1991. *Men in the Sun and Other Palestinian Stories.* Cairo: American University in Cairo Press.

Kanstroom, Dan. 2007. *Deportation Nation: Outsiders in American History.* Cambridge: Harvard University Press.

Kaplan, Amy. 2002. *The Anarchy of Empire in the Making of U.S. Culture.* Cambridge: Harvard University Press.

Kaplan, Amy, and Donald E. Pease. 1993. *Cultures of United States Imperialism.* Durham: Duke University Press.

Kaplan, Caren, Norma Alarcon, and Minoo Moallem. 1999. *Between Woman and Nation: Nationalisms, Transnational Feminisms, and the State.* Durham: Duke University Press.

Kaplan, Robert D. 2005. *Imperial Grunts: The American Military on the Ground.* New York: Random House.

Karim, Karim H. 2000. *Islamic Peril: Media and Global Violence.* Montreal: Black Rose.

Kazi, Shahnaz. 1989. "Domestic Impact of Overseas Migration: Pakistan." *To the Gulf and Back: Studies on the Economic Impact of Asian Labour Migration*, ed. Rashid Amjad. New Delhi: International Labour Organisation.

——. 1999. "Gender Inequalities and Development in Pakistan." *Fifty Years of Pakistan's Economy: Traditional Topics and Contemporary Concerns*, ed. Shahrukh Rafi Khan. Karachi: Oxford University Press.

Keane, David, and Nicholas McGeehan. 2008. "Enforcing Migrant Workers' Rights in the United Arab Emirates." *International Journal of Minority and Group Rights* 15: 81–115.

Kumar, Amitava. 2000. *Passport Photos*. Berkeley: University of California Press.

——. 2002. *Bombay–London–New York*. New York: Routledge.

Lal, Brij V. 1983. *Girmitiyas: The Origins of the Fiji Indians*. Canberra: Journal of Pacific History.

Laqueur, Walter. 2001. *A History of Terrorism*. New Brunswick: Transaction.

Lee, Robert G. 1999. *Orientals: Asian Americans in Popular Culture*. Philadelphia: Temple University Press.

Lefebvre, Alain. 1999. *Kinship, Honour, and Money in Rural Pakistan: Subsistence Economy and the Effects of International Migration*. Surrey: Curzon.

Leonard, Karen Isaksen. 1992. *Making Ethnic Choices: California's Punjabi Mexican Americans*. Philadelphia: Temple University Press.

——. 2003. *Muslims in the United States: The State of Research*. New York: Russell Sage Foundation.

——. 2007. *Locating Home: India's Hyderabadis Abroad*. Stanford: Stanford University Press.

Little, Douglas. 2002. *American Orientalism: The United States and the Middle East since 1945*. Chapel Hill: University of North Carolina Press.

Look Lai, Walton. 1993. *Indentured Labor, Caribbean Sugar: Chinese and Indian Migrants to the British West Indies, 1838–1918*. Baltimore: John Hopkins University Press.

Lowe, Lisa. 1991. *Critical Terrains: French and British Orientalisms*. Ithaca: Cornell University Press.

——. 1996. *Immigrant Acts: On Asian American Cultural Politics*. Durham: Duke University Press.

Luibheid, Eithne. 2002. *Entry Denied: Controlling Sexuality at the Border*. Minneapolis: University of Minnesota Press.

Magdoff, Harry. 1969. *The Age of Imperialism: The Economics of U.S. Foreign Policy*. New York: Monthly Review.

——. 2003. *Imperialism without Colonies*. New York: Monthly Review.

Mahmood, Saba. 2004. *Politics of Piety: The Islamic Revival and the Feminist Subject*. Princeton: Princeton University Press.

Maira, Sunaina. 2002. *Desis in the House: Indian American Youth Culture in New York City*. Philadelphia: Temple University Press.

——. 2007. "Deporting Radicals, Deporting La Migra: The Hayat Case in Lodi." *Cutural Dynamics* 19, no. 1: 39–66.

——. 2008a. "Belly Dancing: Arab-Face, Orientalist Feminism, and U.S. Empire." *American Quarterly* 60, no. 2: 317–45.

——. 2008b. "Flexible Citizenship/Flexible Empire: South Asian Muslim Youth in Post–9/11 America." *American Quarterly* 60, no. 3: 697–720.

——. 2009. *Missing: Youth, Citizenship, and Empire after 9/11.* Durham: Duke University Press.

Maira, Sunaina, and Magid Shihade. 2006. "Meeting Asian/Arab American Studies: Thinking Race, Empire, and Zionism in the U.S." *Journal of Asian American Studies* 9, no. 2: 117–40.

Majid, Anouar. 2004. *Freedom and Orthodoxy: Islam and Difference in the Post–Andalusian Age.* Stanford: Stanford University Press.

——. 2009. *We Are All Moors: Ending Centuries of Crusades against Muslims and Other Minorities.* Minneapolis: University of Minnesota Press.

Mamdani, Mahmood. 2001. *When Victims Become Killers: Colonialism, Nativism, and the Genocide in Rwanda.* Princeton: Princeton University Press.

——. 2004. *Good Muslim, Bad Muslim: America, the Cold War, and the Roots of Terror.* New York: Pantheon.

Manalansan IV, Martin F. 2005. "Race, Violence, and Neoliberal Spatial Politics in the Global City." *Social Text* 84–85, nos. 3–4: 141–55.

——. 2006. "Queer Intersections: Sexuality and Gender in Migration Studies." *International Migration Review* 40, no. 1: 224–49.

Marcus, George E., and Micheal M. J. Fischer. 1986. *Anthropology as Cultural Critique: An Experimental Moment in the Human Sciences.* Chicago: University of Chicago Press.

Marr, Timothy. 2006. *The Cultural Roots of American Islamicism.* Cambridge: Cambridge University Press.

Massad, Joseph. 2007. *Desiring Arabs.* Chicago: University of Chicago Press.

Masud, Muhammad Khalid, ed. 2000. *Travelers in Faith: Studies of Tablighi Jamaat as a Transnational Islamic Movement for Faith Renewal.* Boston: Brill.

Matar, Nabil I. 1999. *Turks, Moors, and Englishmen in the Age of Discovery.* New York: Columbia University Press.

Mathew, Biju. 2005. *Taxi! Cabs and Capitalism in New York City.* New York: New Press.

Mayer, Jane. 2008. *Dark Side: The Inside Story of How the War on Terror Turned into a War on American Ideals.* New York: Doubleday.

Mbembe, Achille. 2003. "Necropolitics." *Public Culture* 15: 11–40.

McAlister, Melani. 2005. *Epic Encounters: Culture, Media, and U.S. Interests in the Middle East since 1945.* Berkeley: University of California Press.

McCoy, Alfred W. 2006. *A Question of Torture: CIA Interrogation, from the Cold War to the War on Terror.* New York: Henry Holt.

Meeropol, Rachel, ed. 2005. *America's Disappeared: Detainees, Secret Imprisonment, and the "War on Terror."* New York: Seven Stories.

Mehta, Uday Singh. 1999. *Liberalism and Empire: A Study in Nineteenth Century British Liberal Thought.* Chicago: University of Chicago Press.

Menocal, Maria Rosa. 2002. *The Ornament of the World: How Muslims, Jews, and Christians Created a Culture of Tolerance in Medieval Spain.* Boston: Little, Brown.

Metcalf, Barbara D. 1993. "Living Hadith in Tablighi Jama'at." *Journal of Asian Studies* 52, no. 3: 584–608.

Metcalf, Barbara D., ed. 1996. *Making Muslim Space in North America and Europe.* Berkeley: University of California Press.

Metcalf, Thomas R. 2007. *Imperial Connections: India in the Indian Ocean Arena, 1860–1920.* Berkeley: University of California Press.

Mishra, Sudesh. 2005. "Time and Girmit." *Social Text* 23, no. 1: 15–36.

Mishra, Vijay. 1996. "The Diasporic Imaginary: Theorizing the Indian Diaspora." *Textual Practice* 10, no. 3: 421–47.

——. 2006. *Literature of the Indian Diaspora: Theorizing the Diasporic Imaginary.* New York: Routledge.

Mitchell, Timothy. 1991. "The Limits of the State: Beyond Statist Approaches and Their Critics." *American Political Science Review* 85, no. 1: 77–96.

——. 1999. "Society, Economy, and State Effects." *State/Culture: State Formation after the Cultural Turn,* ed. George Steinmetz. Ithaca: Cornell University Press.

——. 2002. *Rule of Experts: Egypt, Techno-politics, Modernity.* Berkeley: University of California Press.

Moallem, Minoo. 2005. *Between Warrior Brother and Veiled Sister: Islamic Fundamentalism and the Politics of Patriarchy in Iran.* Berkeley: University of California Press.

Modood, Tariq. 1997. "Introduction: The Politics of Multiculturalism in the New Europe." *The Politics of Multiculturalism in the New Europe: Racism, Identity and Community,* ed. Tariq Modood and Pnina Werbner. London: Zed.

Mohanty, Chandra Talpade. 1991. "Under Western Eyes: Feminist Scholarship and Colonial Discourses." *Third World Women and the Politics of Feminism,* ed. Chandra Talpade Mohanty, Ann Russo, and Lourdes Torres. Bloomington: Indiana University Press.

Moore, Kathleen M. 1995. *Al-Mughtaribun: American Law and the Transformation of Muslim Life in the United States.* Albany: State University of New York Press.

Mufti, Aamir. 2007. *Enlightenment in the Colony: The Jewish Question and the Crisis of Postcolonial Culture.* Princeton: Princeton University Press.

Mullings, Leith. 2005. "Interrogating Racism: Toward an Antiracist Anthropology." *Annual Review of Anthropology* 34: 667–93.

Munif, Abdelrahman. 1987. *Cities of Salt: A Novel.* New York: Random House.

——. 1993. *The Trench.* New York: Vintage.

———. 1993. *Variations on Night and Day*. New York: Pantheon.

Musharraf, Pervez. 2006. *In the Line of Fire: A Memoir*. New York: Free Press.

Naber, Nadine C. 2000. "Ambiguous Insiders: An Investigation of Arab American Invisibility." *Ethnic and Racial Studies* 23, no. 1: 37–61.

———. 2002. " 'So Our History Doesn't Become Your Future': The Local and Global Politics of Coalition Building Post September 11th." *Journal of Asian American Studies* 5, no. 3: 217–42.

———. 2006. "The Rules of Forced Engagement: Race, Gender, and the Culture of Fear among Arab Immigrants in San Francisco Post–9/11." *Cultural Dynamics* 18, no. 3: 269–92.

———. 2008. "Introduction: Arab Americans and U.S. Racial Formations." *Race and Arab Americans before and after 9/11: From Invisible Citizens to Visible Subjects*, ed. Amaney A. Jamal and Nadine C. Naber. Syracuse: Syracuse University Press.

Napoleoni, Loretta. 2005. *Terror Incorporated: Tracing the Dollars behind the Terror Networks*. New York: Seven Stories.

National Commission on Terrorist Attacks upon the United States. 2004. *The 9/11 Commission Report: Final Report of the National Commission on Terrorist Attacks upon the United States*. New York: W. W. Norton.

Nichols, Robert. 2008. *A History of Pashtun Migration, 1775–2006*. Karachi: Oxford University Press.

Ngai, Mae M. 2004. *Impossible Subjects: Illegal Aliens and the Making of Modern America*. Princeton: Princeton University Press.

Nguyen, Tram. 2005. *We Are All Suspects Now: Untold Stories from Immigrant Communities after 9/11*. Boston: Beacon.

Nordstrom, Carolyn. 2007. *Global Outlaws: Crime, Money, and Power in the Contemporary World*. Berkeley: University of California Press.

Northrup, David. 1995. *Indentured Labor in the Age of Imperialism, 1834–1922*. Cambridge: Cambridge University Press.

Office of the Inspector General, U.S. Department of Justice. 2003a. "The September 11 Detainees: A Review of the Treatment of Aliens Held on Immigration Charges in Connection with the Investigation of the September 11 Attacks." Report, April.

———. 2003b. "Supplemental Report on September 11 Detainees' Allegations of Abuse at the Metropolitan Detention Center in Brooklyn, New York." Report, December.

Okihiro, Gary. 1994. *Margins and Mainstreams: Asians in American History and Culture*. Seattle: University of Washington Press.

Omi, Michael, and Howard Winant. 1994. *Racial Formation in the United States: From the 1960s to the 1990s*. New York: Routledge.

Ong, Aihwa. 1999. *Flexible Citizenship: The Cultural Logics of Transnationality*. Durham: Duke University Press.

———. 2006. *Neoliberalism as Exception: Mutations in Citizenship and Sovereignty*. Durham: Duke University Press.

Ong, Aihwa, and Stephen J. Collier. 2005. *Global Assemblages: Technology, Politics, and Ethics as Anthropological Problems*. Malden, Mass.: Blackwell.

Orfalea, Gregory. 2006. *The Arab Americans: A History*. Northampton, Mass.: Olive Branch.

Papanek, Gustav F. 1967. *Pakistan's Development: Social Goals and Private Incentives*. Cambridge: Harvard University Press.

Pasha, Mustapha Kamal. 1998. *Colonial Political Economy: Recruitment and Underdevelopment in the Punjab*. Karachi: Oxford University Press.

Persaud, Randolph B. 2001. "Racial Assumptions in Global Labor Recruitment and Supply." *Alternatives* 26, no. 4: 377–99.

Peutz, Nathalie. 2006. "Embarking on an Anthropology of Removal." *Current Anthropology* 47, no. 2: 217–41.

——. 2007. "Out-laws: Deportees, Desire, and 'The Law.'" *International Migration* 45, no. 3: 182–91.

Prakash, Gyan. 1990. *Bonded Histories: Genealogies of Labor Servitude in Colonial India*. Cambridge: Cambridge University Press.

Prashad, Vijay. 2000. *The Karma of Brown Folk*. Minneapolis: University of Minnesota Press.

——. 2001. *Everybody Was Kung Fu Fighting: Afro-Asian Connections and the Myth of Cultural Purity*. Boston: Beacon.

——. 2005. "How the Hindus Became Jews: American Racism after 9/11." *South Atlantic Quarterly* 104, no. 3: 583–606.

——. 2006. "Ethnic Studies Inside Out." *Journal of Asian American Studies* 9, no. 2: 157–76.

Puar, Jasbir K. 2005. "On Torture: Abu Ghraib." *Radical History Review* 93 (Fall): 13–38.

——. 2007. *Terrorist Assemblages: Homonationalism in Queer Times*. Durham: Duke University Press.

Puar, Jasbir K., and Amit S. Rai. 2002. "Monster, Terrorist, Fag: The War on Terrorism and the Production of Docile Patriots." *Social Text* 20, no. 3: 117–48.

——. 2004. "The Remaking of a Model Minority: Perverse Projectiles under the Specter of (Counter)Terrorism." *Social Text* 22, no. 3: 75–104.

Puri, Harish K. 1983. *Ghadar Movement: Ideology, Organisation, and Strategy*. Amritsar: Guru Nanak Dev University.

Rai, Mohammad A., Haider J. Warraich, Syed H. Ali, and Vivek R. Nerurkar. 2007. "HIV/AIDS in Pakistan: The Battle Begins." *Retrovirology* 4: 22–25.

Ramadan, Tariq. 2004. *Western Muslims and the Future of Islam*. Oxford: Oxford University Press.

——. 2009. *What I Believe*. New York: Oxford University Press.

Ramdin, Ron. 2000. *Arising from Bondage: A History of the Indo-Caribbean People*. New York: New York University Press.

Rana, Junaid, and Gilberto Rosas. 2006. "Managing Crisis: Post–9/11 Policing and Empire." *Cultural Dynamics* 18, no. 3: 219–34.

Rashid, Ahmed. 2001. *Taliban: Militant Islam, Oil, and Fundamentalism in Central Asia*. New Haven: Yale University Press.

——. 2002. *Jihad: The Rise of Militant Islam in Central Asia*. New Haven: Yale University Press.

——. 2008. *Descent into Chaos: The U.S. and the Failure of Nation Building in Pakistan, Afghanistan, and Central Asia*. New York: Viking.

Razack, Sherene. 2008. *Casting Out: The Eviction of Muslims from Western Law and Politics*. Toronto: University of Toronto Press.

Reddy, Chandan. 2005. "Asian Diasporas, Neoliberalism, and Family: Reviewing the Case for Homosexual Asylum in the Context of Family Rights." *Social Text* 84–85, nos. 3–4: 101–19.

Reis, João José. 1993. *Slave Rebellion in Brazil: The Muslim Uprising of 1835 in Bahia*. Baltimore: Johns Hopkins University Press.

Rejali, Darius M. 2007. *Torture and Democracy*. Princeton: Princeton University Press.

Retort and Iain A. Boal. 2005. *Afflicted Powers: Capital and Spectacle in a New Age of War*. London: Verso.

Rizvi, Hasan Askari. 2000. *Military, State, and Society in Pakistan*. New York: St. Martin's Press.

Roediger, David R. 2008. *How Race Survived U.S. History: From Settlement and Slavery to the Obama Phenomenon*. London: Verso.

Rogin, Michael. 1993. " 'Make My Day!' Spectacle as Amnesia in Imperial Politics (and the Sequel)." *Cultures of United States Imperialism*, ed. Amy Kaplan and Donald E. Pease. Durham: Duke University Press.

Rony, Fatimah Tobing. 1996. *The Third Eye: Race, Cinema, and Ethnographic Spectacle*. Durham: Duke University Press.

Rose, Nikolas. 2006. *The Politics of Life Itself: Biomedicine, Power, and Subjectivity in the Twenty-first Century*. Princeton: Princeton University Press.

Rubin, Gayle. 1984. "Thinking Sex: Notes for a Radical Theory of the Politics of Sexuality." *Pleasure and Danger: Exploring Female Sexuality*, ed. Carole S. Vance. Boston: Routledge and Kegan Paul.

Said, Edward W. 1978. *Orientalism*. New York: Vintage.

——. 1993. *Culture and Imperialism*. New York: Vintage.

Salaita, Steven. 2006a. *Anti–Arab Racism in the USA: Where It Comes from and What It Means for Politics Today*. London: Pluto.

——. 2006b. *The Holy Land in Transit: Colonialism and the Quest for Canaan*. Syracuse: Syracuse University Press.

Samhan, Helen Hatab. 1999. "Not Quite White: Race Classification and the Arab–American Experience." *Arabs in America: Building a New Future*, ed. Michael W. Suleiman. Philadelphia: Temple University Press.

Sanders, Edith R. 1969. "The Hamitic Hypothesis: Its Origin and Functions in Time Perspective." *Journal of African History* 10, no. 4: 521–32.

Sassen, Saskia. 1988. *The Mobility of Labor and Capital: A Study in International Investment and Labor Flow*. Cambridge: Cambridge University Press.

———. 1998. *Globalization and Its Discontents: Essays on the New Mobility of People and Money*. New York: New Press.

Scarry, Elaine. 1985. *The Body in Pain: The Making and Unmaking of the World*. New York: Oxford University Press.

Schmitt, Carl. 1996. *The Concept of the Political*. Chicago: University of Chicago Press.

———. 2005. *Political Theology: Four Chapters on the Concept of Sovereignty*. Chicago: University of Chicago Press.

Schueller, Malini Johar. 1998. *U.S. Orientalisms: Race, Nation, and Gender in Literature, 1790–1890*. Ann Arbor: University of Michigan Press.

Scott, James C. 1998. *Seeing Like a State: How Certain Schemes to Improve the Human Condition Have Failed*. New Haven: Yale University Press.

Semmerling, Tim Jon. 2006. *"Evil" Arabs in American Popular Film: Orientalist Fear*. Austin: University of Texas Press.

Shaban, Fuad. 1991. *Islam and Arabs in Early American Thought: Roots of Orientalism in America*. Durham: Acorn.

———. 2005. *For Zion's Sake: The Judeo-Christian Tradition in American Culture*. London: Pluto.

Shah, Nayan. 2001. *Contagious Divides: Epidemics and Race in San Francisco's Chinatown*. Berkeley: University of California Press.

Shah, S. A., O. A. Khan, S. Kristensen, and S. H. Vermund. 1999. "HIV-Infected Workers Deported from the Gulf States: Impact on Southern Pakistan." *International Journal of the Study of AIDS* 10, no. 12: 812–14.

Shah, Svati P. 2006. "The Politics of Red Light Visibility in Mumbai." *Cultural Dynamics* 18, no. 3: 269–92.

———. 2007. "Distinguishing Poverty and Trafficking: Lessons from Field Research in Mumbai." *Georgetown Journal on Poverty, Law, and Policy* 14, no. 3: 441–54.

———. 2008. "South Asian Border Crossings and Sex Work: Revisiting the Question of Migration in Anti-Trafficking Interventions." *Sexuality Research and Social Policy* 5, no. 4: 19–30.

Shaheed, Zafar. 2007. *Labour Movement in Pakistan Organization and Leadership in Karachi in the 1970s*. Karachi: Oxford University Press.

Shaheen, Jack G. 2001. *Reel Bad Arabs: How Hollywood Vilifies a People*. New York: Olive Branch Press.

———. 2008. *Guilty: Hollywood's Verdict on Arabs after 9/11*. Northampton, Mass.: Olive Branch Press.

Shankar, Shalini. 2008. *Desi Land: Teen Culture, Class, and Success in Silicon Valley*. Durham: Duke University Press.

Sharabi, Hisham. 1988. *Neopatriarchy: A Theory of Distorted Change in Arab Society*. New York: Oxford University Press.

Sheikh, Irum. 2004. "Abuse in American Prisons." *Muslim World Journal of Human Rights* 1, no. 1: 1–13.

——. 2007. "Government Spy or a Terrorist: Dilemmas of a Post–9/11 Academic Researcher." *Amerasia* 33, no. 3: 26–40.

——. 2008. "Racialising, Criminalizing, and Silencing 9/11 Deportees." *Keeping out the Other: A Critical Introduction to Immigration Enforcement Today*, ed. David C. Brotherton and Philip Kretsedemas. New York: Columbia University Press.

Shohat, Ella. 2006. *Taboo Memories, Diasporic Voices*. Durham: Duke University Press.

Shohat, Ella, and Robert Stam. 1994. *Unthinking Eurocentrism: Multiculturalism and the Media*. London; New York: Routledge.

Shukla, Sandhya. 2001. "Locations for South Asian Diasporas." *Annual Review of Anthropology* 30, no. 1: 551–72.

Siddiqa, Ayesha. 2007. *Military Inc.: Inside Pakistan's Military Economy*. London: Pluto.

Sikand, Yoginder. 2002. *The Origins and Development of the Tablighi Jama'at (1929–2000): A Cross-Country Comparative Study*. New Delhi: Orient Longman.

Silliman, Stephen W. 2008. "The 'Old West' in the Middle East: U.S. Military Metaphors in Real and Imagined Indian Country." *American Anthropologist* 110, no. 2: 237–47.

Silva, Denise Ferreira da. 2007. *Toward a Global Idea of Race*. Minneapolis: University of Minnesota Press.

Silverstein, Paul A. 2004. *Algeria in France: Transpolitics, Race, and Nation*. Bloomington: Indiana University Press.

——. 2005. "Immigrant Racialization and the New Savage Slot: Race, Migration, and Immigration in the New Europe." *Annual Review of Anthropology* 34: 363–84.

Slotkin, Richard. 1973. *Regeneration through Violence: The Mythology of the American Frontier, 1600–1860*. Middletown: Wesleyan University Press.

——. 1986. *The Fatal Environment: The Myth of the Frontier in the Age of Industrialization, 1800–1890*. Middletown: Wesleyan University Press.

——. 1992. *Gunfighter Nation: The Myth of the Frontier in Twentieth-Century America*. New York: Atheneum.

Smedley, Audrey. 1999. *Race in North America: Origin and Evolution of a Worldview*. Boulder: Westview.

Spivak, Gayatri Chakravorty. 1988. "Can the Subaltern Speak?" *Marxism and the Interpretation of Culture*, ed. Cary Nelson and Lawrence Grossberg. Urbana: University of Illinois Press.

Stalker, Peter. 2000. *Workers without Frontiers: The Impact of Globalization on International Migration*. Boulder: Lynne Rienner.

Stocking, George W. 1987. *Victorian Anthropology*. New York: Free Press.

Stolcke, Verena. 1995. "Talking Culture: New Boundaries, New Rhetorics of Exclusion in Europe." *Current Anthropology* 36: 1–24.

Stoler, Ann Laura. 1995. *Race and the Education of Desire: Foucault's History of Sexuality and the Colonial Order of Things*. Durham: Duke University Press.

——. 2002. *Carnal Knowledge and Imperial Power: Race and the Intimate in Colonial Rule*. Berkeley: University of California Press.

——. 2006. "Imperial Formations and the Opacities of Rule." *Lessons of Empire: Imperial Histories and American Power*, ed. Craig J. Calhoun, Frederick Cooper, and Kevin W. Moore. New York: New Press.

——. 2009. *Along the Archival Grain: Epistemic Anxieties and Colonial Common Sense*. Princeton: Princeton University Press.

Streets, Heather. 2004. *Martial Races: The Military, Race, and Masculinity in British Imperial Culture, 1857–1914*. New York: Palgrave.

Tagg, John. 1988. *The Burden of Representation: Essays on Photographies and Histories*. Amherst: University of Massachusetts Press.

Takaki, Ronald. 1989. *Strangers from a Different Shore: A History of Asian Americans*. New York: Penguin.

Talbot, Ian, and Shinder S. Thandi. 2004. *People on the Move: Punjabi Colonial and Postcolonial Migration*. Karachi: Oxford University Press.

Tchen, John Kuo Wei. 1999. *New York before Chinatown: Orientalism and the Shaping of American Culture, 1776–1882*. Baltimore: John Hopkins University Press.

Thompson, E. P. 1966. *The Making of the English Working Class*. New York: Vintage.

Tinker, Hugh. 1974. *A New System of Slavery: The Export of Indian Labour Overseas, 1830–1920*. New York: Oxford University Press.

——. 1977. *The Banyan Tree: Overseas Emigrants from India, Pakistan, and Bangladesh*. New York: Oxford University Press.

Trouillot, Michel-Rolph. 2001. "The Anthropology of the State in the Age of Globalization: Close Encounters of the Deceptive Kind." *Current Anthropology* 42: 125–38.

Tsing, Anna Lowenhaupt. 2005. *Friction: An Ethnography of Global Connection*. Princeton: Princeton University Press.

Turner, Richard Brent. 2003. *Islam in the African-American Experience*. Bloomington: Indiana University Press.

Verkaaik, Oskar. 2004. *Migrants and Militants: Fun and Urban Violence in Pakistan*. Princeton: Princeton University Press.

Vertovec, Steven. 2002. "Islamophobia and Muslim Recognition in Britain." *Muslims in the West*, ed. Yvonne Y. Haddad. New York: Oxford University Press.

Virilio, Paul. 1989. *War and Cinema: The Logistics of Perception*. London: Verso.

——. 2000. *The Information Bomb*. New York: Verso.

Visweswaran, Kamala. 1997. "Diaspora by Design: Flexible Citizenship and South Asians in U.S. Racial Formations." *Diaspora* 6, no. 1: 5–29.

——. 1998. "Race and the Culture of Anthropology." *American Anthropologist* 100, no. 1: 70–83.

Vitalis, Robert. 2007. *America's Kingdom: Mythmaking on the Saudi Oil Frontier*. Stanford: Stanford University Press.

Volpp, Leti. 2002. "The Citizen and the Terrorist." *University of California, Los Angeles, Law Review* 49: 1575–600.

Von Eschen, Penny M. 1997. *Race against Empire: Black Americans and Anticolonialism, 1937–1957*. Ithaca: Cornell University Press.

Welch, Michael. 2002. *Detained: Immigration Laws and the Expanding INS Jail Complex*. Philadelphia: Temple University Press.

Werbner, Pnina. 1990. *The Migration Process: Capital, Gifts, and Offerings among British Pakistanis*. New York: Berg.

——. 1999. "Global Pathways: Working-Class Cosmopolitans and the Creation of Transnational Ethnic Worlds." *Social Anthropology* 7, no. 1: 17–35.

——. 2002. *Imagined Diasporas among Manchester Muslims: The Public Performance of Pakistani Transnational Identity Politics*. Santa Fe: School of American Research Press.

——. 2003. *Pilgrims of Love: The Anthropology of a Global Sufi Cult*. Bloomington: Indiana University Press.

——. 2005. "Islamophobia: Incitement to Religious Hatred—Legislating for a New Fear?" *Anthropology Today* 21, no. 1: 5–9.

Williams, William A. 1980. *Empire as a Way of Life: An Essay on the Causes and Character of America's Present Predicament, along with a Few Thoughts about an Alternative*. New York: Oxford University Press.

Willoughby, John. 2006. "Ambivalent Anxieties of the South Asian–Gulf Arab Labor Exchange." *Globalization and the Gulf*, ed. John W. Fox, Nada Mourtada-Sabbah, and Mohammed al-Mutawa. New York: Routledge.

Winant, Howard. 2000. "Race and Race Theory." *Annual Review of Sociology* 26: 169–85.

——. 2001. *The World Is a Ghetto: Race and Democracy since World War II*. New York: Basic.

——. 2004. *The New Politics of Race: Globalism, Difference, Justice*. Minneapolis: University of Minnesota Press.

Yee, James, and Aimee Molloy. 2005. *For God and Country: Faith and Patriotism under Fire*. New York: Public Affairs.

Yu, Henry. 2001. *Thinking Orientals: Migration, Contact, and Exoticism in Modern America*. New York: Oxford University Press.

Yun, Lisa. 2008. *The Coolie Speaks: Chinese Indentured Laborers and African Slaves in Cuba*. Philadelphia: Temple University Press.

Zaidi, S. Akbar. 1999. *Issues in Pakistan's Economy*. Karachi: Oxford University Press.

——. 2005. *Issues in Pakistan's Economy*, 2d ed. Karachi: Oxford University Press.

Zulaika, Joseba, and William A. Douglass. 1996. *Terror and Taboo: The Follies, Fables, and Faces of Terrorism*. New York: Routledge.

Haji, 77, 78, 192n10

Hall, Albert P., 81

Hamdani, Michael John, 61

Hamites, 37, 47. *See also* Semitic–Hamitic hypothesis

Heteronormativity, disruption of, 12, 119–20, 175

Hijab, discrimination of, 169, 170, 171, 201n16

Hindoo and Orientalism, 64

Hindus, 42, 44

HIV-positive labor migrants, 119, 196–97n18

Homosexuality as white menace, 63. *See also* Queer domesticity

Homosociality, 119

H-1B visa, 7

H-2B visa, 179

Human trafficking, 144–45

Hurricane Katrina, 179–80

Iberian Inquisition, religious passing during, 33, 36

Illegal immigration and terror, 66

Illegal Immigration Reform and Immigrant Responsibility Act (1996), 158

Illegality: exploitation as causal agent of, 146–48; migrant construction through, 53, 138–40; production of, 141–46; state discourses of, 150; terrorism and, 60–61, 72–73

Immigrant-management techniques, 150–51, 157–59

Immigration Act (1917), 64–65, 189–90n11

Immigration and Naturalization Act (1965), 191n3

Immigration and Naturalization Service (INS), 58, 166

Immigration laws. *See under names of specific laws*

Imperial age of Indian Ocean migrations, 16

Imperial economy, foreign workers in, 4–5

Imperialism. *See* American empire; British empire

Indentured labor and British, 100–102, 105–9

India: as colonial sub-center, 16–17; depot system and, 105; Emigration Act (1837) in, 106–7

Indian Country, 76–78, 192n11

Indian Ocean imperial system, 16–17

Indian subcontinent, conflict in, 75

Indian troops in First World War, 16–17

Informal money-transfer systems, 112–13

Information-technology workers, 7

Inquisition, Iberian, religious passing during, 33, 36

In re Feroz Din (1928), 45

International migrants, 181n3

Interwar labor market, 109

Iraq in First World War, 16–17

Iraq war: abductions during, 1–3; invocation of Indian Country, 77–78. *See also* War on Terror

Islam: African American identification with, 41–42, 193n15; rationalist spirituality of, 131–32; Tablighi Jamaat movement and, 128–30, 132; types of, 121–22. *See also* Muslim, the

Islamic peril, 7, 69, 71; American Orientalism and, 55, 64–65; moral panic and, 50–51; in Muslim racial formation, 72–73; in Terror Diaspora, 66–67

Islamophobia: in British discourse, 185n9, 186n12; conceptual history of, 27–30, 184n2

Israeli-Palestinian conflict in *Sleeper Cell*, 84–85

Japanese American internment, 43

Jews in concentration camps, 46–47, 188n23. *See also* Anti-Semitism; Semitic–Hamitic hypothesis

Jihadist culture, 4, 69

Jim Crow South, violence against Arabs in, 51

Kafeel system, 120–21

Khan, Raja Azad, 2, 3

Khyber-Pakhtunkhwa Province, 117–18, 135, 194–95n2

Kinship structures, 71–72, 197n25

Krishan Nagar (Pakistan), 61–62

Kuwait, citizenship laws in, 68

Labor camps in Dubai, 135

Labor contracts for indentured workers, 105, 106

Labor diaspora: class structure and, 14; colonial indentured labor migration and, 100–102, 105–9; contemporary contract labor migration and, 102–4; mutualism among, 120; in Persian Gulf region, 12–13, 86–87, 104; social networks and, 8, 123–24

Labor markets, transnational: failure of formal market and, 141; gendered control of, 111–12, 115, 182n11, 194n1; during indenture period, 100–102, 105–9; overseas labor agencies and, 98–99, 179

Labor protests: in Brazil, 40; in Persian Gulf region, 109, 147–48; in United States, 179

Labor recruiting system in Pakistan, 116, 144

Labor regulatory systems, 137

Lahore (Pakistan): Defense Housing Area in, 167; Krishan Nagar jewelry industry in, 61–62; Model Town over-

seas labor agency and, 97–98; Raiwind township in, 128

Latinas, Latinos: comparative racialization of, 53; cross-racial casting of, 193n19; racial profiling of, 51; as terrorist suspects, 48

Legal cases involving naturalization rights, 43–45

Limpieza de sangre (blood purification), 35, 36

Little Pakistan (New York City), 160

Madrassas (Islamic schools), in *Syriana*, 88

Malcolm X, 81–82

Man Push Cart, 174–75, 176

Martial races, Indians as, 16–17, 107

Masculinity: in Catholicism, 39; in martial races, 16–17, 107; normalized heterosexuality and, 12, 119–20; patriarchal reconfiguration and, 10–11, 71, 171, 194n1; as site of regulation, 111–12, 115, 182n11

Masjid al-Haram complex (Mecca), 126

McCarran-Walter Act (1952), 158

Mehmood, Anser, 165

Mesopotamia in First World War, 16–17

Metropolitan Detention Center (MDC), 161–62, 200n10

Middle East, 63, 75; abductions in, 1–4; abstracted notion of, 5, 62, 66, 85, 86, 88, 93, 182n6; emigrants from, 19–20, 48, 51–52, 75–79; Haji and, 77, 78, 192n10; HIV-positive migrants in, 119–20; informal banking networks in, 113; oil discovery in, 109; racialized citizens in, 58, 60; as trouble spot, 17. *See also* Persian Gulf region; *and specific countries*

Migrant illegality, 11, 138–42

Migration, 7–8, 13, 124, 175

Pakistan, 6–7, 198n6; South Asian labor migration policy of, 143–44. *See also* War on Terror

U.S. empire: coercive actions by, 164–66; informal colonies of, 103–4; Orientalism of, 41–42, 63–65; strategies of, 76–78, 178

U.S. foreign policy strategy, 55–56

U.S. immigration policy, 43, 64–65, 158; Immigration Act (1917), 189–90n11; Immigration and Naturalization Act (1965), 191n3

U.S. military, Muslim Americans in, 190n20

USA PATRIOT Act, 149–50, 158

United States v. Ali (1925), 44–45

United States v. Baghat Singh Thind, 44–45

Vietnam War and Indian Country, 77

Visas, 7, 122–23, 179

Voluntary departures, 160

Wahhabi Islam, 122

War machine, 78–80, 156. *See also* Iraq war; Torture techniques; War on Terror

War on immigration, 150–51

War on Terror: civil liberties curtailment during, 156; labor regulatory systems and, 137; opposing binary of, 4; rhetoric of, 56

Waterboarding, 190n17

White supremacy: European as referent of, 183–184n1; Islamic peril in relation to, 69, 71; scientific racism and eugenicist philosophy in, 34; yellow peril in relation to, 65

Worker sponsorship system in Persian Gulf, 120–21

Working-class migrants, 110

Workplace health and safety regulations, 135

World Trade Center attack, 68. *See also* Post-9/11 events

Yee, James Joseph, 190n20

Yellow peril, 55, 64–65, 190n12

Youssef, Ramzi, 68

Youth culture, moral panic in, 188n1

JUNAID RANA is associate professor of Asian American
studies at the University of Illinois, Urbana-Champaign.

Library of Congress Cataloging-in-Publication Data
Rana, Junaid Akram
Terrifying Muslims : race and labor in the South Asian diaspora /
Junaid Rana.
p. cm.
Includes bibliographical references and index.
ISBN 978-0-8223-4888-7 (cloth : alk. paper)
ISBN 978-0-8223-4911-2 (pbk. : alk. paper)
1. Islamophobia. 2. Muslims—Public opinion. 3. Muslims—
Non-Muslim countries. 4. South Asian diaspora. I. Title.
BP52.5.R363 2011
305.6′970954—dc22   2010049741

Made in the USA
Middletown, DE
09 February 2021